8

Dear Pam,

Thank you for all your help!

May you always
have the very best!

Best wishes,
Charlene
南妹、

ISBN-13: 978-1508700791
ISBN-10: 1508700796

Author: Charlene Lin Ung
Designer: Diana Ung

First Edition, March 19, 2015

NAM MOI
A Young Girl's Story
of Her Family's Escape from Vietnam

By

Charlene Lin Ung

In memory of
my father, Ly Sang
for providing me
the strength and
wisdom throughout
my life.

In dedication to
my mother, Kieu
and my daughters,
Natalie and Madison.

CONTENTS

PART I

Chapter 1

Who is Nam Moi?

On a warm and humid Sunday morning three children, skin browned by their daily exposure to the Vietnamese sun, barefoot, and shirtless, were playing together amidst the raw materials of a rubber band factory in a residential area of Saigon. If it were today they might be playing at the Dam Sen Water Park, one of the city's amusement parks for children. In 1971, however, these children were creating their own entertainment out of what they had at hand, using their imagination and experiencing the joy of doing things together. At first glance the children seemed all alike, as they wore only shorts and a layer of the factory's dust-like residue. A keener observer, though, would have discovered that the oldest boy rarely took the lead but mostly responded to the other two, indicating his autism. Plus, one of the boys had slightly longer hair—and might not even be a boy.

As the kids played, not caring about such differences, a woman shouted at them in her Chinese *Hakka* dialect from the house next door: "Nam Moi, come home right now. We have to get ready for the picture!"

Nam Moi (南妹) was me, the "little girl from the south." I wasn't all that clear about what was involved in getting ready for a picture, but I still submitted to the urgency of my mother's command. She scrubbed the dirt away from my four-year-old body, and I was quickly slipped into a dress that clarified my gender to any skeptics who had seen me playing with the neighbor boys earlier. Even at such a young age I was aware that the air was filled with excitement and tension as my parents hurried to prepare their seven children for the portrait session. In a rush everyone was dressed in their good clothes. Yet they had to wait impatiently for little Nam Moi—because she needed her dress sandals. At long last the sandals were found, and after a struggle getting into them, the girl who didn't normally have much use for shoes was ready.

Our home was located in one of the outlying districts of Saigon, where land was available for building homes or factories, or for keeping livestock. During our early years in the city our family had lived in one of my paternal grandparents' slipper factories. The front of the house included both a living area and a slipper assembly and packaging area. As part of the *Hakka* tradition, we referred to our relatives by numbers to signify their position in the family. Since we had so many relatives, I couldn't keep them straight as a child and often needed to be reminded by my parents.

In Phu Thanh, the slipper business meant the Ung family, and the Ung family meant the slipper business. Grandfather, Great Uncle #7, Great Uncle #9, and Great Uncle #11 were all engaged in the mass production of slippers. Our neighbors, the Diep family, were in the business of making rubber bands. Other nearby families specialized in printing fabric, making tofu, making rice wine, distributing gasoline, and so on.

Dad soon made enough money that he was able to build his own house. Like his father, he intermixed the factory area with the living quarters. Dad and Mom, seven children, and a housekeeper shared one small bedroom with no window and a loft area. The loft construction was primitive, with plywood and 4x4 support beams. Although our living area was small, it was like a castle to my parents. They no longer had to live under the same roof as my grandparents and Dad's siblings. My little brother, Buu, slept with my parents in their small bedroom. My three brothers, my

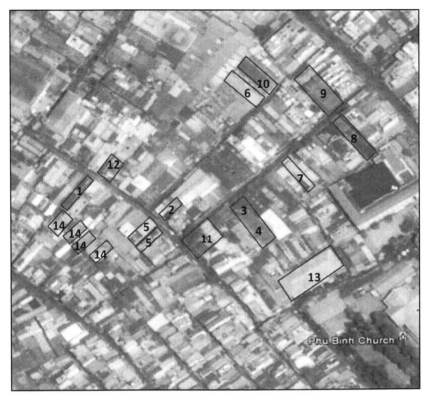

Figure 1-1: Phu Thanh neighborhood (Image: Digital Globe and Google Earth).

1. Grandparent's house
2. Grandfather's slipper factory #1
3. Our first home
4. Grandfather's slipper factory #2
5. Our new house and warehouse next door
6. Dad's slipper factory
7. Aunty Lee Guu's house
8. Great Uncle #6's house
9. Great Uncle #7's slipper factory
10. Great Uncle #9's slipper factory
11. Government office
12. Comrade Crazy 7's residence
13. Outdoor market
14. Neighbors' fish ponds

oldest sister, Zenh, and I slept together in a queen-size bed in the loft area. My sister Kien slept with our nanny, who was also the housekeeper, in a twin-size bed next to our bed.

Like most Saigonese, my family did not have an automobile. For our family photo session, we made our way to the photographer's studio by more traditional modes of transportation. My father rode a motorcycle, wearing his dress suit and carrying one child behind him and one in front. The other five kids and my mother split up on Vietnamese-style tricycles. Each had a driver in back who sat over the single steering wheel, and the passengers rode over the two front wheels on a seat or in a basket. This was the first time I remember going out as a family.

At the photography studio, Dad and Mom sat formally and unsmiling on simple straight-back chairs, with their seven offspring all standing about them with equally serious expressions. To get our attention, the photographer rang a bell that sounded like an ice cream truck's. In the end he managed to get us all arranged, looking in one direction. In the photo, I am leaning against my father's leg, subtle yet unmistakable evidence of a daddy's girl from early on.

This photo session brings back my earliest and strongest memory of my siblings. In the photo, Kien is standing on the end, next to Mom.

Figure 1-2: Family photo, 1971.

Kien had the misfortune of being born in the first month of the lunar calendar—a bad month for a girl to be born, according to Chinese tradition—and my paternal grandmother had advised giving her away. But the times were changing, and Dad's more progressive attitudes, acquired through his French military schooling and training, prevailed. Having the temerity to be born in the first month of the lunar calendar was just the beginning of Kien's troublemaking ways. Growing up, she was a tomboy. She was the instigator of many unsanctioned adventures.

Standing to Mom's left, Zenh was the eldest child. She was the best student in our neighborhood, smart, proper, humble, and introverted, especially around boys. Standing between Mom and me, Buu was the baby of the family. As the youngest, Buu would receive the most attention, care, and time from Mom. When he was not with her, he was often with me.

Standing to Dad's right was my eldest brother, Hong. He loved school and books, especially his comic books. Because he was usually unable to buy them, he used to rent comic books, reading them while squatting in the corner of a shop. To Dad's left stood Xi. As the second son, Xi had to fight harder for Dad's attention and approval. Usually, he ended up following Kien's lead on her adventures. He also protected me against older and bigger boys in our neighborhood, especially since I always wanted to be involved in whatever was going on. I never held back because I was a girl or because I was younger, even when I was not invited.

Num, standing on the far right, always seemed to be the odd man out with both his older and younger siblings. He was called "Ong Nam" in Vietnamese, meaning Mr. Fifth. My parents would have two more children, Tam and Kau, but another two years would pass after this photo session before Tam took over as "baby of the family" from Buu, and she was only be able to enjoy that position for a year.

This remarkable occasion made a lasting impression on me. With all the excitement and everyone dressing up and rushing around, it was like Chinese New Year. We could not know then how far and wide our family unit would be splintered by the tides of war.

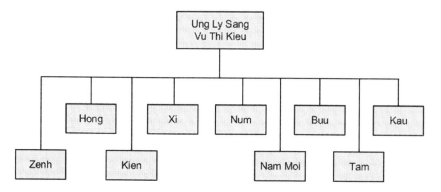

Figure 1-3 Family tree of Ung Ly Sang.

Chapter 2

The Ung Family

Traditions and Duty/Responsibilities

The Ung (吳) family was originally part of an ethnic group called the *Hakka* (客家). The *Hakka* people are a distinct sub-group of the *Han* Chinese. They are believed to come from north central China, and their path of migration wound along the basin of the Yangtze River. They moved to Guang Dong and Guang Xi due to overpopulation on the Yangtze, and they settled primarily in southern China. The name *Hakka*, meaning "guest people" or "visitors coming from afar", was given to them by the local people.

My more immediate Ung ancestors migrated from Fang Cheng (防城), in the Guang Xi province of China, across the border to North Vietnam in the late 19th century. They would continue their journey of migration from North to South Vietnam in 1954. To better understand the Ung family, I will turn first to this earlier generation that lived in North Vietnam.

My grandparents' fathers, Tai Hong and Man Cam, were very good friends, as close as blood brothers. According to the custom of the time, they agreed to strengthen the bond between their families by committing their firstborn to marry each other, thus proving the importance and sincerity of their friendship.

My paternal grandmother's name was Sao Lin, and she was also the eldest child in her family, which included two sisters and two brothers. The Sens (冼) belonged to a Chinese ethnic minority group called *San Diu* (山由). Beginning in the sixteenth century, they had migrated like the *Hakka* from Guang Dong and Guang Xi in China, moving to the mountainous areas in north and northeast Vietnam. I remember my grandmother was very tall for a Chinese woman. We were told that her family belonged to a mountain people similar to the Hmongs, who also lived in a remote mountainous area of Vietnam.

In Ha Coi, my grandmother's family conducted business with the Hmong people. The Hmong traveled by foot more than a day's journey to bring plants that people used to color fabrics. My grandmother's family bought these plants and resold them. The Hmong visitors would stay at the Sens' house overnight, and the next day they would return to their remote mountain homes. The reason the Hmong needed a local agent is that most people in Ha Coi believed the Hmong were witches with evil powers. This prejudice, based on a misunderstanding of the Hmong lifestyle and their general appearance, caused Ha Coi residents to limit their dealings with them. However, the Sen family, with their *San Diu* lineage, was able to communicate with the Hmong, and even welcomed the Hmong visitors into their home.

My grandparents became engaged at a very young age: Grandfather was eight and Grandmother was seven. To commemorate this special day, my grandfather's family came to my grandmother's house with food and gift offerings which symbolized their commitment to the future marriage. They agreed that the two would wed when my grandfather turned eighteen and grandmother seventeen.

At age seven, Sao Lin (Dad's mother) remembered dressing up to celebrate this special occasion, but her heart sank when her aunt told her that her parents had promised that when she turned seventeen she would marry Ung, Chenh Tac. She could not show her feelings outwardly, though. She could not dishonor her family, misbehave, and step out of line. She had to avoid becoming a subject of gossip so that she would not develop a bad reputation and bring shame to the Sen family.

From that day forward she was no longer permitted to be a child, not even to play like other kids. This was done to avoid any perception of inappropriate behavior. She was often told that soon she would be wed. These constant reminders were very upsetting, and she often cried about her feeling of helplessness. She started resenting my grandfather, years before their actual wedding. She knew she had to honor her father's wish to marry, but she allowed a seed of resentment to bloom and grow inside her heart. My grandmother was taught well by her family about the importance of honoring her family name and about her role and responsibilities as a daughter, sister, and wife. She was taught that marriage had less to do with love or happiness. It was supposed to be a partnership in life, designed to create and build a strong family to honor her parents and ancestors.

She passed along those values to her children and grandchildren. I felt a strong sense of duty and responsibility even at a young age. I could not do anything bad that would dishonor my parents or my family name. My responsibilities as a young girl were to be an obedient daughter, to honor my parents' wishes for me, to be a good student, to conduct myself with kindness toward friends and neighbors, to respect the elderly and to love my family.

My grandparents' marriage took place in 1935. She moved into my grandfather's house after the wedding. Because she was the eldest daughter-in-law in a family of mostly males, a lot of the household chores fell on her. Once the other sons were married, their wives would share the daily chores with my grandmother.

She had plenty of company. My great-grandfather Tai Hong, who was well known in Ha Coi, lived in a large, long house three stories tall with three sections, with all of his sons and their wives and their children. In the front of the house was an herb store, which functioned as the equivalent of a modern-day clinic and pharmacy combined. Great-grandfather hired assistants to see patients, practicing dim mac, a traditional Chinese medical method for evaluating a patient's health based on their pulse, and then they would dispense herbs for medicinal use.

The first section of the house proper was the main hall, where the people living in the house gathered, and it was also the place where they welcomed guests. Within the common area of the main hall was an altar for ancestor worship, facing the front door. In front of the altar was a table where an incense pot was placed along with lamps and other objects. Offerings and flowers, as well as incense and candles, were placed on this table during special occasions.

The second section of the house was used for storing grain and other harvested crops collected from the tenants. The last section contained the outhouse, a washing room, and an area for raising livestock such as pigs, chicken, or ducks. In addition, the first and second floors contained many bedrooms for the sons and their families. The third floor was rarely used since the house was so big.

When I was growing up, the practice of ancestor worship was central to our *Hakka* identity and customs in Vietnam and in the United States.

Hakka Culture for Women

Each of the sons in Tai Hong's household had one or more rooms to share with his wife and children. All the daughters-in-law worked together every day, cooking, cleaning, and doing other chores around the house, as well as taking care of the children. The *Hakka* (客家) people are renowned for being industrious, hardworking, honest, thrifty, straightforward, cooperative, diligent, and practical.* *Hakka* women in particular have been historically characterized as extremely hardworking. In the light of their "better halves" *Hakka* men vigorously denied and resented

---

* *Guest People: Hakka Identity in China and Abroad*, Nicole Constable, ed.

the stereotype that they were lazy compared to their women. A *Hakka* wife of an official was expected to be good and proper, as well as being able to cook and clean, since *Hakka* women in general were expected to talk intelligently to important guests. But even though *Hakka* women did most of the day-to-day work, they were still subservient to men. The Ung family followed tradition, and the men and boys ate in the main hall with the best quality food, while the women and girls ate leftovers in the kitchen area. Such were the traditions handed down from generation to generation to *Hakka* daughters.

Figure 2-1: Ung family ancestor worship altar in California.

My great-grandmother, prepared by her *Hakka* upbringing, ran both the family business and the household, and she was responsible for all the finances. She managed all the interactions and negotiations with the tenants who leased the farmland. She also coordinated and assigned chores to the daughters-in-laws.

The Little Prince

Born prematurely in the fall of 1936, Dad was named Ly Sang by the monk that blessed his birth. Growing up, he was considered small for his age, but he never let that hold him back. He had the great advantage of being the firstborn grandson of my great-grandfather Tai Hong, a wealthy rice plantation owner who lived in a large, long three-story house in Ha Coi, in the far north province Quang Ninh. As was the custom amongst the *Hakka*, all of my great-grandfather's sons and their wives and children lived together in his house. Dad's father, Chenh Tac, was the eldest of six sons living in the household. When Dad arrived, the first son of the latest generation of Ungs, he was treated like a little prince.

Dad's firstborn status meant his grandfather paid him special attention. Among other things they did together, Tai Hong took his young grandson with him when he collected rents from his tenant farmers. The experience of walking back home afterward with his grandfather carrying a bag full of money on his back made a deep and lasting impression on Dad. Because of this modeling, he would grow up thinking he too could achieve success and wealth. Even when Dad was young, his grandfather expected him to be the leader for his siblings and cousins.

Dad's father, Chenh Tac, was the first son to move out of the family house in Hai Coi. At the time he had five children of his own: Ly Sang, followed by Uncle Quan Sang, Aunty Lee Guu, Uncle Chin, and Uncle Bao. Each child was separated from his or her elder sibling by two to three years. In all, my grandparents had six boys and two girls. The three younger children were born after the family migrated to Song Mao in South Vietnam.

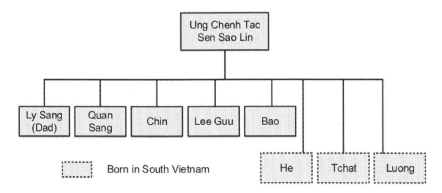

Figure 2-2: Family tree of Ung Chenh Tac.

In my grandfather's generation, he and Great Uncle #7 were the only ones who didn't serve in the military. Instead, they went into business trading goods between Ha Coi and other big cities, including Hai Phong and Mong Cai. Great Uncle #3 joined the Chinese military to fight the Japanese during World War II, and the family never heard from him again. After years of waiting for him to return, his wife finally left the family home and remarried. Great Uncle #4 worked for the French military, then later in the South worked for the American military and became a policeman. Great Uncle #9 and Great Uncle #11 also served in the French military. As a result, by the time my father came of age, the path of serving in the French military was already well established.

Migrating to the South

The French, who ruled North Vietnam during the time of Dad's youth, saw the wisdom in winning the hearts and minds of the people of far northwestern Quang Ninh Province. Accordingly, they allowed the local government a great deal of autonomy, even in creating laws. The appointed regional leader, Captain Vong A Sang, sought to educate and train his people to secure positions in the French administration and military. More than sixty tuition-free primary schools were built for this purpose, teaching administrative skills and French to native Vietnamese and Chinese speakers. In Mong Cai, the capital city of the Nung Autonomous Territory, special training centers were developed for the most elite and talented, including the Military Cadres School, the Teachers' School, the Public Administration School and the Junior Military School.

In 1949, at the age of thirteen, Dad enrolled in the Franco Junior Military Academy in Mong Cai. At first he was judged unfit for enrollment because he didn't know the French language. His school had taught him in Chinese since kindergarten. However, his mother's brother, Uncle Khau, was married to a niece of the recently promoted Colonel Vong A Sang. Because of that relationship, his uncle was able to pull some strings and Dad got into the school.

Dad learned French and Vietnamese at the same time he trained to serve in the French military. He paid his tuition off with a promise to serve for at least four years. Throughout his secondary education he lived mostly at school. He was allowed to go home only on holidays and for a few hours on weekends. Dad took his course work very seriously and studied hard to master the French language. He spent most nights and weekends catching up and later became one of the best students in the Junior Military School. He also became one of the fastest typists in his class. Those skills later opened the door for him to work in the administration and logistics department for the French military, a much safer career path than becoming a soldier and facing enemy fire on a battlefield. Dad's youngest uncle, San, joined the Junior Military Academy a year later. Because the two had similar facial features, they often were mistaken as brothers.

In June 1954, Dad graduated from the Academy and started his service with the French military. Only a few weeks later, on July 20, the historic Geneva Accords were signed, partitioning Vietnam at the 17th parallel into the Communist North and the Nationalist South. A transition period of three hundred days was allotted for population groups to migrate from the North to the South, or vice versa, depending on political or economic interests. Because the accord was signed so shortly after Dad became a soldier, he had to support the French military pullout from North Vietnam, and he was unable to travel with his family to the South. Instead, he made plans to meet them at the new settlement location where the rest of the Ung family who made the decision to flee North Vietnam would be going.

For many of the Ungs this was not an easy decision; it meant leaving their land and personal property behind, becoming refugees, and starting over in the South. Yet, like many people in the North, especially those of Chinese descent, the decision to flee was motivated by all the terrible things they had heard about living under communism and the brutality of the Viet Minh toward the people in general, especially toward the land owners.

Figure 2-3: Journey from Ha Long to the Song Mao resettlement area (Image: Google Map).

In response to the partitioning of Vietnam, the French prepared to move to the South, along with their allies amongst the Vietnamese people.

On August 20, 1954, Vong, A Sang was promoted to a full colonel and appointed commanding officer of the Maritime Zone from Quang Ninh to Quang Yen provinces. People from the Quang Ninh area were referred to as Nung people, which means farmers. The Nung people were made up of various Chinese minority groups such as *Ngai, San Diu, Hakka*, and so on. The colonel led a reconnaissance team scouting for a resettlement region for his people with the permission of the nationalist regime in the South. The selected region was a location between Phan Ri and Phan Thiet within the Binh Thuan Province. The towns consisted of Song Mao, Chau Hanh, Song Luy, Suoi Nhum, and Long Thanh.[†] Geographically, the Binh Thuan Province straddled the southern part of Central Vietnam and the northern part of the South. Although this settlement region seemed poor and arid, there were many good reasons for moving the ethnic Nung to this new home:

- The area included a large wilderness that had the potential for domestication and the creation of plantations and support of other agriculture, assuming the shortage of available water could be overcome.
- It was next to the South China Sea, promising access to fishing and shipping.
- Ground transportation was available via Route 1, a national highway, and via the transnational railroad which stopped at many stations in the region, including Song Mao, Chenh Hanh, Song Luy, and Long Thanh.
- The current local population was relatively sparse and able to absorb new immigrants.

Colonel Vong personally led the migration of the Quang Ninh refugees to South Vietnam in 1954. The transportation costs were funded by the French government and coordinated by the United Nations High Commission for Refugees (UNHCR).

Although the French government and the UNHCR planned for the massive immigration, many challenges arose in the execution of the plan. Military and administrative support personnel and their families departed relatively quickly, but the majority of the population faced larger difficulties. Communicating the offer of evacuation and transportation was often accomplished by word of mouth, especially in more inaccessible areas. Quang Ninh Province was located in the most northeastern region of Vietnam, and the people closest to the Chinese border had only days to move down to the neighboring ports of Hon Gai or Bai Chay, near

---

† Nung Ethnic & Autonomous Territory of Hai Ninh, Vietnam.

Hai Phong, on Ha Long Bay to catch one of the ships departing to South Vietnam. Even under those trying circumstances, however, most of the residents decided to evacuate, a convincing rejection of the imminent Communist rule. These people abandoned their precious ancestors' tombs, houses, lands, rice fields, fruit arbors, and personal property to start over in a potentially inhospitable land, for the sake of their families, their freedom and their future. Most believers in Catholicism left for South Vietnam as well. Although the Communists tried to win over Vietnamese Catholics to their cause, the Communist doctrine rejected religion. So they feared that their religious beliefs would single them out for discrimination.

When Dad received his orders from the military, he told his family that they needed to be prepared to leave immediately to meet the evacuation deadline. For the Ung family to live under communism would have been unthinkable because of the ties of sons and grandsons to the French military, which was still the enemy of the Communists. Not all of the Ung family was able to travel together, and they eventually reunited in Song Mao, their resettlement destination in South Vietnam. (My grandfather's cousin, Great Uncle #2, and his family were the only ones who stayed behind in North Vietnam.) My grandparents tried to sell what they could in their general store to raise money before leaving, but the circumstances were chaotic and time was short. In the end, they left everything they owned behind except the things they could carry with them. When they got to Ha Long Bay in time to meet the deadline, however, their promised transit ship was not available yet. They rented a house in Ha Long while they waited instead of living in the school gym along with other refugees. In the end, they had to wait a couple of months before they could travel toward their new beginning.

The journey by sea to South Vietnam took a couple of weeks. The Ungs and other refugees departed Ha Long Bay aboard a French military ship and disembarked at Binh Hoa harbor, close to Saigon. In Binh Hoa they boarded a train that took them to

Song Mao. When they arrived, they were greeted by the sight of a sea of white tents, pitched in preparation for the arrival of the new refugees. My grandparents and their family spent only one night sleeping in their assigned refugee tent. The next day, they started the next chapter of their lives by going to the closest town and renting a house. My grandfather's parents and grandmother joined them.

Colonel Vong had directed his men to arrive at Song Mao before the refugees to make preparations. However, they underestimated the number of refugees streaming in from the North. As a result, there were shortages of supplies and insufficient housing accommodations. In addition, hygiene and sanitation conditions were poor. Medical supplies were short and there were no medical personnel, leaving them unprepared for outbreaks of smallpox and other diseases. Many older refugees and children were stricken, and within a few weeks dozens of refugees had died. Fortunately, an international Red Cross team came to the rescue with medicine and nurses to alleviate the crisis. As a result of their prompt intervention, all the epidemics were contained relatively quickly.

Starting Over in Song Mao

Over time, the refugees moved out of their tents, and built huts to protect their families from the sun and rain that marked Song Mao's two seasons. The monsoon or rainy season lasted from May to October. Then it was hot and dry from November through April, averaging ninety degrees. Two rivers flowed through the area, Ma O at the heart of the district and Ca Giay northwest of it, but both were dry. As a consequence, residents had to walk a quarter mile away to get water for their daily use. Even though Song Mao had been selected in part for its agricultural potential, its prolonged dry season meant it was not a good place for farming. The lack of water and inability to farm led to a further migration among the populace of Song Mao. Many of those unhappy with the conditions of Song Mao moved to Xuan Loc in the Long Khanh province, Tung Nghia and Don Duong in the

Tuyen Duc province, or Di Linh in the Lam Dong province, all places with better farming prospects.

Despite the departures, bulldozers operated day and night to transform the rural area of Song Mao into a city with a road system, residences, businesses, market halls, schools, a medical dispensary and facilities for other public agencies. In the residential sector, the government created a subdivision of streets and lots, and assigned plots for each family to build a home. Gradually, Song Mao was transformed from a collection of thatched and muddy huts into a development of brick and tiled housing units. Although the city could not rely on agriculture to sustain its economy, there were many military personnel amongst the refugees who were paid regular salaries. There were also many entrepreneurs and small businesses in Song Mao, and that helped keep the refugee families afloat financially, at least in the short term. Great Uncle #7 and Great Uncle #9's families were among those who were not happy with the opportunities in Song Mao, and they ended up moving to the Cho Lon area of Saigon.

Great uncles #7 and #9 started the slipper business in the late 1950s in Phu Thanh, about fifteen minutes by vehicle to the heart of Saigon City. By 1961, Great Uncle #7 was doing well enough to build a four-story house overlooking the city of Lo Sieu. It was the biggest house in the neighborhood. His workers made slippers on the bottom floor, and the family lived on the upper floors. He was the linchpin of the business, making important connections between his factory and suppliers and buyers in the city. Business was booming, and the next year Uncle Quan Sang moved in to help with the factory work and with selling the slippers. He was able to learn the slipper trade as an apprentice.

My grandparents' family remained in Song Mao. Since they didn't live in the refugee area, they were not assigned a lot for building a house. Instead, they had to purchase a home from people who were moving out. By the time they were able to move into their own home in Song Mao, they had already lived in the rental house for a year. In 1955, my grandparents reestablished the household goods business they had run in Mong Cai. For the next eight years, until 1963, Grandfather traveled to Saigon to buy goods and then back to Song Mao to sell them to his new neighbors.

One more move would be made before my family settled down. The *Hakka* tradition of migrating would soon bring us to the suburb of Saigon where our uncles lived. Little did our family know, as I was growing up, that we would be migrating once again—farther away than any *Hakka* had gone before.

Chapter 3

The Union of My Parents

The Vu Family

Mom's father, Chun Liam, and mother, Qui, were introduced to each other in the late 1930s by a *Hakka* matchmaker. Their families agreed to an arranged marriage, according to the custom of the time.

Young men and women really had no other acceptable way to marry. Dating or getting to know one's future partner before committing to a marriage was not permitted. Any unmarried girl who associated with a man was considered a prostitute. Typically, the boy's parents would consult a matchmaker to find a suitable girl, and they would then initiate marriage arrangements with the parents of the girl. The most desirable qualities in a prospective bride were someone from a good family, hardworking, polite, with no physical defects and most important, capable of bearing children. In each case, the boy's parents considered the reputation of the girl's family, her work ethic, and the compatibility of the prospective spouses' birthdays and hours of birth.

My maternal grandfather was the youngest son in a family with four sons and two daughters. His parents were farmers who grew food crops and raised silk worms for clothing. My grandfather's father, Quoc Choi, had a reputation as the meanest and most fearless person in the neighborhood. He even looked the part, with his eyebrows sticking out like the Buddhist gatekeeper god, the protector. In a classic example of opposites, my maternal grandfather's mother was gentle, kind, and loving.

Figure 3-1: Mom's paternal grandfather, Vu Quoc Choi.

Figure 3-2: Mom's paternal grandmother, Kuan Sy.

My mother, Kieu, the eldest daughter of her *Hakka* family, was born a year after her parents' marriage in Ha Coi. At the tender age of five, she was introduced to adult responsibilities, working alongside her mother planting yams, rice, and vegetables.

Mom's father and his older brother Chun Chern, son #3, worked at the shipyard in Ha Coi, loading and unloading cargo. Following *Hakka* tradition, all the Vu (巫) sons, daughters-in-laws and grandchildren lived together in the same house. Mom's male cousin Chiming, two years her senior, was like a brother to her growing up. She was closer to him than to her own brother. My mother was two years older than her sister, Duc, and ten years older than her brother, Phong.

When Mom was six years old, her father, who was gentle and caring, like his mother, moved to Sin Chai in order to train to work as a doctor's assistant. This position was similar to a nurse, but did not require formal schooling, only on-the-job training.

Sin Chai was hours away from Ha Coi by boat, and he had to leave his wife and two daughters at home to live with their grandparents and his siblings. He returned home only once each year for the seven to ten days of the New Year celebration. Each year Mom looked forward to seeing her father during his visits, and would cry for days when he left. For those short days she was allowed to be a kid again, without having to do her daily chores or work in the field. Having her parents together in the same house was special beyond words.

After the Geneva Accords were signed in 1954, Mom's parents decided to leave North Vietnam for the South. However, her grandparents and the oldest uncle's family decided to stay behind in Ha Coi. Mom's grandmother requested that her daughter-in-law leave Mom and Aunty Duc behind to take care of them in their old age. By this time Mom was old enough to realize that she didn't want to be left behind.

One day her grandmother told her to buy a kilogram of pork and to kill a duck to pay respect to the ancestors. Mom later found out that the real reason was to pray for a safe journey to the South. Yet her trip to the market proved something else was afoot. As she was returning home, holding the pork in her hands, she saw a woman carrying a child on her back and a pole yoke across her shoulders with a basket hanging from each end. As she came closer, she realized it was her Mom carrying her brother. She asked, "Where are you going?"

"We're going out to Ha Long Bay to catch the French ship heading to the South."

Without hesitating, Mom grabbed the stick yoke with the two baskets from her Mom's shoulders, transferred it to her own shoulders, and ran back home. When she arrived, she yelled to her sister. "A Duc, A Duc, you watch these baskets and don't let Mom take them with her. She was going to leave us behind and head south with Phong and not us." Then, never forgetting her place, Mom added, "I have to get the fire started to cook dinner for everyone."

That night Mom slept on the outside of her mother's bed, hanging onto her mother's legs and not letting go. Mom was determined she would not be left behind. They waited a few days, hoping to hear news from her father. A letter finally came from the hospital in Sin Chai, saying that he was stuck packaging all the medicines for the trip to the South and would be leaving in a couple of weeks. Shortly after receiving the letter, my grandmother, Mom, Aunty Duc and Uncle Phong left home and traveled to Ha Long Bay. Mom never saw her grandparents or the eldest uncle's family again.

At Ha Long Bay, they waited several weeks, living as refugees in a school gym, before boarding a ship to South Vietnam. My grandmother got very sick with diarrhea and vomited for several days during the journey. Mom pointed out that Grandmother was lucky that her two daughters were with her, in spite of the plan to leave them behind. Mom and Aunty Duc waited in line for food and water, and they took care of Grandmother and their little brother, Phong. My grandfather traveled to South Vietnam a few weeks later. In Song Mao, they lived in a tent for almost a year before they were assigned a lot, on which they built a hut. My grandfather continued to work in the medical field, helping other refugees in Song Mao. Once they had a place of their own, Grandmother and Mom sold vegetables at the market every day. They would arrive at the train station at 2:30 a.m. in the morning to get vegetables and then sell them at the market until noon. In the afternoons and evenings they made incense to sell. On the side, my grandmother helped deliver babies in people's homes.

When my mother was growing up, girls attending school were rare. However, Song Mao offered free public schooling for both boys and girls. My grandmother was very traditional and believed that any education for a daughter would only benefit her future husband's family but not her immediate family. Therefore, Mom was not allowed to go to school. It was a moot point because Grandmother set so many tasks for Mom to complete every day that even going to night school would have been impossible. In contrast, the son, Phong, not only went to school, but was sent abroad to medical school in Taiwan.

Soldier and a *Hakka* Cinderella

In South Vietnam, Dad continued to serve as a military officer in one of the many divisions supporting the French that were led by Colonel Vong. In 1956, he was 20 years old and many girls were interested in him. His grandmother, however, did not consider any of them to be worthy as marriage material. She was naturally concerned for Dad's future and the legacy he was expected to pass on as the Ungs' firstborn grandson. Therefore, his grandmother told his mother to find a wife for him. His mother replied, "Where can I find a potential wife? It's not like I can buy one at the market."

His grandmother answered knowingly, "In fact, I have already met a very suitable girl at the market. She is very hardworking, with a nice personality. She helped me the other day carrying vegetables at the train station."

A few days later Dad's mother asked relatives and neighbors about the girl and her family. Then she proposed the idea to Dad and he agreed. My grandmother on Dad's side approached my grandmother on Mom's side with the proposed arrangement. Dad was considered a good catch. The Ung family was associated with wealth and education in Ha Coi and now also in Song Mao. Also, Mom's mother was eager for Mom to marry. She feared

Figure 3-3: Mom, Kieu at age 16.

her daughter would become an old maid, and in the afterlife she would haunt the family as a homeless ghost. Such a belief sounds like superstition to modern ears, but it was considered a very real threat within the *Hakka* culture. Therefore, when she was approached by Dad's mother, she agreed readily to the proposal.

A date was set for Dad to meet Mom at her house. Auspiciously, Dad liked her from their first formal meeting. The next date set by their parents was the wedding. In the meantime, they did not date or get to know each other. They had to take a leap of faith in committing to share their lives, not knowing if they would be compatible. Common wisdom predicted that as they spent time together and built a family, they would learn to love each other, perhaps even deeply. That ended up being the case with Dad and Mom, but if they had not been a good match it could have gone poorly. As I was growing up, my mother would lecture my sisters and me about picking a husband wisely and making a lifetime commitment to the marriage, no matter how things might turn out, even if the husband took two or three wives. As a member of my generation, I thought that viewpoint was unfair. I also thought that it was unfair that women had no power in finances and that society regarded us as subservient to males.

As the date of my parents' wedding drew near, Dad's grandmother became very sick. She passed away just a few days before the wedding. Out of respect, my parents didn't celebrate formally with friends and relatives. They only invited the immediate family for dinner to acknowledge their special day.

After the wedding, my mother moved in with Dad's parents and all of his siblings, according to *Hakka* tradition. As the first daughter-in-law she assumed the main responsibility of running the household. One of Mom's daily chores was to help carry water for the whole family for drinking, cooking, cleaning, and bathing. That meant a quarter-mile walk each way. She carried the water in two buckets strung to opposite ends of a bamboo pole that she balanced across her shoulders. Mom also had many other daily chores helping around the house and in my grandparents' general store business. Fulfilling these duties was expected; just as my great-grandmother had expected compliance from my grandmother, my grandmother expected it from Mom.

Deployment of the Soldiers

For the next four years Dad and Mom lived in my grandparents' house in Song Mao, with Dad stationed a few hours away. Three of my siblings were born there: Zenh, Hong, and Kien. In a sign of the times, Mom and my Dad's mother were once pregnant at the same time. Mom gave birth to Hong a month before the birth of Uncle Luong while they lived under the same roof. Hong was the eldest son for my parents while Uncle Luong was my grandparents' youngest son, the eighth child in the family.

In 1961, the military deployed most of the soldiers in Song Mao to various places throughout the countryside to fight the Viet Cong. The Diem government did not trust the loyalty of these soldiers to the new government, mostly tied to the Americans. That's because the soldiers in Song Mao were originally from the North. They not only had ties to the French, they spoke in the French language and not English. The motivation behind this mass redeployment was to weaken Vong A Sang's power and leadership, and soon his soldiers were incorporated in other divisions.

When Kien was only a few months old, my mother and my siblings left Song Mao to move closer to Dad in his new assignment. Before they left, Dad and the rest of the family, including Aunty Tchat, Dad's youngest sister, took a family picture at a studio. Aunty Tchat was the oldest child in the picture next to Mom. She and Zenh grew up like sisters, and she was often mistaken as Mom's daughter.

Figure 3-4: Aunty Tchat, Mom, Kien, Dad, Hong, and Zenh.

When the French redeployed their soldiers from Song Mao to other locations in the South Vietnamese countryside, many of the soldiers' wives and children also left in order to stay close to their husbands and fathers. As a result, the population of Song Mao decreased dramatically. In addition, some of the other local inhabitants also began to migrate to other cities. In 1963, Uncle Chin, who was about 18 at the time, moved to Saigon to work alongside Uncle Quan Sang in Great Uncle #7's factory. He worked early mornings at the factory and attended school in the afternoons to learn Vietnamese.

In the meantime, in Song Mao, Grandfather's business began to suffer as the population dwindled. My grandparents finally decided to move to Saigon too, and they sold their business in Song Mao. Grandfather then partnered with Ung Choi, a businessman he met through Great Uncle #7, to build and equip his own slipper factory. Their partnership was a cooperative effort in which they shared the cost of the factory, but each partner was responsible for his own raw materials and workers.

With the guidance from his brothers and the support of his two sons, Chin and Quan Sang, Grandfather established his slipper business in Saigon.

Figure 3-5: Uncle Chin and a worker in front of Grandfather's factory, 1963.

For the next five years, Mom and my older siblings lived in various small towns in the countryside, including Soui Nhum, Tay Ninh, and Ben Keo, close to Dad's assignments. Xi was born in Tay Ninh and Num was born in Ben Keo. Since my parents were away from their families, Mom had to rely on other soldiers' wives to help her with the young children while she gave birth to Xi and Num. As the war between North and South escalated, the Viet Cong insurgents began occasionally attacking civilian populations. The countryside was no longer a safe place to live. Mom recalled grenade attacks against the military housing, and several of her neighbors' houses were bombed.

In 1966 my parents decided that my mother and five children should move in with Dad's parents in Phu Thanh, Saigon. Dad took a few days off to travel with his family aboard a cargo train bound for Saigon. In those days the trains that transported people were the same as those that carried freight. There were no seats, and people just sat or laid down where space was available. Hong was frightened when he saw all the people lying down. They were only sleeping, but he thought they were dead.

My parents by now had moved around quite a lot, being displaced from their lives in the North, then moving to Song Mao. Since their marriage, they had moved from Song Mao to Soui Nhum, Tay Ninh, Ben Keo, and now they were moving again to Saigon. Luckily, they would be able to settle down and truly establish themselves in the South's capital city. Soon Dad would be discharged from the military and start a factory of his own. That's where I would grow up.

Chapter 4

Life and War

Dad's Humble Beginning

During his years of military service working for the French, Dad was more fortunate than most. He didn't have to fight on the front lines, since he was fluent in Vietnamese and French. He was able to perform administrative and logistical duties in an office, working closely with high-ranking military brass. His responsibilities included handling the paperwork needed for transfers of military personnel, as well as inventory and distribution of weapons and uniforms.

In 1966, the French military announced that any person who had fulfilled their term of service could apply for retirement. As part of his agreement after his graduation from the Military Academy School, Dad was required to serve four years. However, the French military had ignored the fact that he had already completed his four-year term because the war had intensified and the military had to have soldiers and support personnel to fight the Viet Cong. By 1966, when the French made their retirement offer, he had served twelve years. When Dad told Mom about the possibility, she insisted that he retire as soon as possible, since the fighting with the Viet Cong was escalating more and more each year. Dad informed his Uncle San of his decision, since they had started in the same military academy around the same time. They both applied for retirement and both were accepted. As part of their retirement settlement, military personnel obtained a lump sum for their years of service. With limited options, Uncle San took the money, moved to Da Lat and took up farming with his family. Unlike his uncle, Dad had his parents and another uncle living in Phu Thanh. Dad moved to Saigon and reunited with Mom and my older siblings as they started living in his parents' house.

My grandparents' house in Phu Thanh was a long house with two stories. It was so long because two houses had been combined into one with a single entrance and the kitchen placed in between the two sections. The outhouse and washroom were located in the back of the house. The house had four formal bedrooms upstairs, and other areas on the first level of the second house could be used for recreation and sleeping. At the time, fifteen people were living in my grandparents' house including my grandparents, Uncle Quan Sang, his wife, Uncle Chin, Uncle Bao, Aunty Tchat, Uncle Luong, my parents, and my five siblings.

After Dad left the military, Grandfather offered him a job working at his slipper factory, along with a monthly salary. Yet earning a

Figure 4-1: Paternal grandfather, Chenh Tac.

Figure 4-2: Paternal grandmother, Sao Lin.

salary meant Dad would not be able to afford a place of his own and would struggle to pay for private school tuition for five children. Dad also enjoyed having a big family and planned to have more children. Therefore, he insisted on starting his own business, using the 50,000 Vietnamese dongs that he had saved up from his years of military service.

Figure 4-3: Uncles Bao, Chin, and Quan Sang, and Aunty Tchat in front of grandparents' house in Phu Thanh.

The problem with that plan was that he had already given his money to Grandfather, and Grandfather refused to give it back because he didn't want Dad to risk losing all the money he had saved from the twelve years of service. Working for a monthly salary would entail no risk as opposed to competing for the same business with Grandfather and other great uncles.

Left with no choice, Dad took the opportunity to expand Grandfather's slipper business. Starting out humbly, Dad traveled to small towns to solicit orders for slippers. Then he rented a cargo truck to transport the goods to his customers. He made a good profit for each truckload he delivered. For several years after that Dad rented manufacturing equipment and paid second-shift and weekend overtime to the workers from Grandfather's factory to produce his own slipper products. The materials he used from Grandfather's factory were subtracted from the money that Grandfather owed him. Dad spent several years working within this arrangement, saving for his own factory.

By 1968 my grandparents' slipper business was booming and Grandfather expanded his business, building a second factory a block from their house. Dad took advantage of the opportunity to remodel the second factory, adding a bedroom and a loft area for our living quarters in the front part of the factory, where the slippers were assembled. The front of the building had two entries: the first led into our living quarters and the final assembly area for the slippers. The second entry accommodated the flow of workers coming and going, as well as the receiving of raw materials and machinery. Along the side of the factory entry was an open makeshift area for cooking. The main house had open ventilation at the eaves, which was consistent with typical Vietnamese architecture, allowing for passive ventilation. This design allowed for a cooling airflow during the hot, humid summer months, and did not require closing off for the mild winters.

Birth of Child #6

As Mom tells the story, in March 1967 she was very far along in one of her nine pregnancies. She could have taken time off to prepare for giving birth, but she was *Hakka* Chinese, reared by her mother in the virtues of working hard and putting duty ahead of everything else. She would not use having a baby as an excuse to slack off. True to her nature, she continued working in our family's slipper factory right up to the moment when her water broke. Her sixth child—i.e., me—was almost born in the factory. I was officially born in the Chinese year of the sheep, but the circumstances of that tumultuous period have influenced my life much more strongly than any Buddhist religious beliefs.

A month after I was born, I gained a name. *Hakka* religious beliefs have been described as a combination of Buddhism, Taoism, and Confucianism, with special deference to the spirits of ancestors. One of the Buddhist traditions my family observed was the naming ceremony. As with my brothers and sisters, a Buddhist monk prayed over me and pronounced me Nam Moi, which means little girl from the South. My formal birth name was Chong Lin. My middle name represented the Chong generation, just as my grandfather's generation name was Chenh and Dad's generation name was Menh. All of my siblings, including my cousins, share the Chong middle name. In contrast, my Buddhist name was chosen to reflect important personal or spiritual characteristics about me, divined through the monk's spiritual awareness. It was not just symbolic; I was known as Nam Moi by all of my family and neighbors. Many years later, after leaving Vietnam, I would choose my own Western name, Charlene.

That year the Vietnam War was ravaging our family's adopted country. American troops fought alongside the South Vietnamese against the Viet Cong and Viet Minh soldiers from the North. The countryside was very unstable and the exposed citizens lived in constant fear. We were comparatively fortunate to be living in Saigon. Kids growing up in our neighborhood were aware of the war, but for the most part it was fought in other parts of the country. Typically we would hear of someone's father or relative losing their life in the fighting. But soon enough, we would find out that we were vulnerable also.

In early 1968, my parents, my five siblings and I moved into our new home in the factory, a block away from my grandparents' house. This was a very important step for my family, especially for Dad, because moving out meant he was no longer under Grandfather's authority. Dad could make his own decisions regarding his family's welfare.

Dad directed the business and Mom worked alongside him in addition to being a housewife. As an entrepreneur, Dad wore many hats. He was the factory production manager, overseeing the procurement of raw materials and the processing of those materials into the sheet stock for the slippers. Another hat was for distribution and sales management, negotiating with vendors and handling order fulfillment. Mom was responsible for cutting the slipper patterns and for the assembly and packaging of the slippers.

Tet Offensive 1968

The Lunar New Year Holiday, known as Tet, was the most important holiday of the Vietnamese calendar. Both Vietnamese and Chinese people celebrate Tet.

In January 1968 the Vietnam War was raging, but North Vietnam agreed to a seven-day cease-fire to celebrate Tet. In previous years, the holiday had been the occasion for an informal truce between South Vietnam and the Viet Cong Communists. In 1968, however, the North Vietnamese military commander, General Vo Nguyen Giap, used the cover of the cease-fire to set up a coordinated offensive of surprise attacks, starting on January 30, with the intent of causing the Army of the Republic of Vietnam (ARVN) forces to collapse, and to foment discontent and rebellion within the South Vietnamese population. It was hoped that would lead to the overthrow of the regime in Saigon. Giap also believed the United States was not strongly committed to the Vietnam War; he hoped the Tet offensive would convince the American leaders to give up.

Early on the morning of January 30, Viet Cong forces attacked 13 cities in central South Vietnam, just as many families had begun their observance of the Lunar New Year. Twenty-four hours later, People's Army of Vietnam (PAVN) and Viet Cong forces struck a number of other targets throughout South Vietnam, including cities, towns, government buildings, and U.S. and ARVN bases. In total they launched more than a hundred attacks. In a particularly bold assault on the U.S. embassy in Saigon, a Viet Cong platoon penetrated inside the complex's courtyard before U.S. forces destroyed it.

The 1968 Tet was my family's first New Year celebration since moving into the factory. My sister Kien was so excited that she woke up early. She remained lying in bed, unable to decide which new outfit she would wear for each of the days of celebration. The traditional thinking was to wear your most beautiful outfit on the first day of the New Year, the second best on the second day and so on. As she was lying in bed, waiting for the rest of the family to be awakened, she looked through the openings of our house and saw artillery rounds flying by like fireworks. At first she thought they really were fireworks, set off for the New Year celebration, but as she continued to listen, it sounded more and more like bombs and artillery fire. She screamed for my parents' attention and woke up all the siblings. We heard later that the main fighting was at the Phu Binh Catholic Church (Nha Tho), only a few blocks from our house. Fighting also erupted in surrounding towns.

All of that day and through the night we continued to hear gunshots, loudly and clearly, a constant reminder of how close to home the fighting was. The situation was so threatening that all of the Ung family households living in Phu Thanh felt they had to leave and find a safer place. They traveled by motorcycle, bicycle, or on foot, and headed toward Great Uncle #7's four-story house in Lo Sieu, a few kilometers away. Dad took Kien, Num, and Xi first on his moped. That journey left vivid horrifying memories imprinted on the mind of my sister, Kien. She told me years later, "I will never forget the images of dead bodies along with the smoke and sounds of gunfire and bombs going off." It was like a scene from a horrible war movie that kids were not supposed to see. Dad had to navigate the street with dead people lying everywhere, bombs going off right and left, and soldiers trying to fight back against the Viet Cong. Kien believed it was a miracle that they survived the journey without harm. Dad made several trips back and forth to bring our other family members to what he hoped was a safer place, away from the fighting that was raging all around us, day and night.

Figure 4-4: Great Uncle #7's house in Lo Sieu.

Several hundred people, including many entire families, took refuge in Great Uncle #7's house, filling every quarter of it. Besides the Ungs were many other people from the neighborhood who received shelter on the bottom floor, taking advantage of the home's steel-reinforced concrete structure. The Ungs mostly stayed on the upper floors. There were not enough bedrooms and beds for everyone, so people slept on mats on the floor. Each family brought with them portable cookware and enough food to cook meals for themselves for several days. After the fighting subsided, the families walked back home, an hour away. As they did, they found soldiers everywhere on high alert, with weapons ready for firing. Even that journey, with its looming threat of more violence, was a terrifying experience. Our family carried their belongings on their backs and their fear on their faces. I was only nine months old, and Mom carried me on her back.

In some towns and cities the Communists were repelled quickly, within hours. In others, weeks of fighting were needed to dislodge them. In Saigon, the Communists succeeded in occupying the U.S. embassy, once thought impregnable, for eight hours before it was retaken by U.S. soldiers. All in all, U.S. troops and South Vietnamese forces did not regain control of Saigon for two weeks.

Figure 4-5: Vietnam War, 1968 by USIA. Likely taken in the aftermath of the Tet Offensive. Terrified women and children flee under the direction of South Vietnamese troops. In the foreground, one of the dead still holds an RPG launcher. National Archives.

The fighting flared up again after we came back home. This time, even Lo Sieu was not deemed safe, so my family decided to camp out at the hospital along with many other people. The reasoning was that if anyone was injured, we would already be where we could get urgent care and maybe even save our lives. My family camped out there briefly before the renewed fighting ended and they were finally able to return home. The terrible Tet offensive of 1968 was an experience that Ung children and adults alike never forgot. As my siblings and I were growing up, we would hear further tales from our parents, relatives, and neighbors about how horrifying the Tet offensive was for the citizens of Saigon.

So many traumatic things happened during my first year of life, it makes me wonder about the subconscious impact on my psyche. I know that I was too young to understand what was going on, but I remember being terrified and crying at the sounds of bombs exploding. I was also aware of how nervous people were around me, the lack of peace and calm. I grew up a very jumpy child, and I often panicked when I heard unexpected loud noises.

Uncle Bao

Our family lived every day with the constant dangers of the war swirling all around us, both in Saigon and in the countryside, but the impact on our lives was limited to routine wartime hardships. Dad had served in the French military, but was now retired. Besides him, no one in the extended Ung family participated in the Vietnam War in a combat role until my Uncle Bao enlisted with the Army of the South. He was in his late teens and his parents wanted him to hide from the government during the military draft. During a year of hiding at Grandfather's slipper factory he lived in constant fear of being discovered. Finally, at age nineteen, he volunteered for service in supporting the American military. He refused to be a victim any longer.

Uncle Bao was stationed near Da Lat. Today it is a famous tourist destination in the beautiful central highlands of southern

Vietnam, very popular with honeymooners. However, during the Tet Offensive it became one of many takeover targets for the Communist forces. Even though North Vietnam had agreed to a cease-fire during the holiday season, U.S. and ARVN military commanders were on alert. They warned their soldiers not to travel during Tet, but not knowing the barrage that was coming, they stopped short of making it an order.

As with many of their target cities, before attacking Da Lat the Communists infiltrated the area with scouts and snipers. Roads leading to the city were filled with curves, and the countryside was heavily treed and mountainous, making defense against an ambush difficult. The Viet Cong snipers just waited in hiding for any military targets moving along the roads.

Just as Uncle Bao had not listened to his parents about staying out of the military, he disregarded his commanders' warnings against traveling during Tet. He wanted to visit his uncle in Da Lat for the Tet celebration, and he hitched a ride off the military base with a two-star general. They must have enjoyed the drive, with morning mists giving way to clear skies and the beautiful landscape, especially the bright yellow and orange tree-marigolds in full bloom. Uncle Bao must have been anticipating getting away from the war for a few days. It's likely he never saw the ambush until the attack was already taking place, coming in the form of rocket-propelled grenades, command detonated mines and automatic rifle fire. Death must have come quickly for the three travelers.

In the end, the Communists could not hold Da Lat, or any of their major targets, including the ones in Saigon. Nevertheless, they dealt a damaging blow to the morale of ARVN and U.S. forces, and many young men lost their lives. After the fighting in Saigon had subsided and the Ungs thought they were returning to their normal lives, a government official brought my grandparents the news of Uncle Bao's death. The news devastated my family.

This was the second time my grandparents had suffered the loss of a son. Son #5 had died from illness at age two, and now son #4 had lost his life as a soldier. Afterward, Dad made the long, sad journey to Da Lat to claim Uncle Bao's body, and he returned with it for burial in Saigon.

Uncle Bao was here one day, vibrant and beloved by his family. The next day he was no longer with us. In the face of this tragedy, we took the only comfort we could in family traditions. Buddhist monks conducted a one-day and one-night wake ceremony to send Uncle Bao's spirit into the afterlife. Since my uncle did not have a wife or child, my siblings, Zenh, Hong, Kien, and Xi, took on the somber duties of performing family-related tasks during the wake ceremony. After the burial, for seven weeks, on the same day of the week that he passed, the family gathered for prayers and rituals to help send Uncle Bao into the afterlife. The final closing rite occurred a hundred days after his passing. The family invited the same Buddhist monks back to perform the concluding ceremony. For those hundred days my grandparents had been continually reminded of their son's passing, but this was understood to be a necessary part of the mourning process and of letting go.

The war had truly touched our family now. Yet his death was only the first blow the Communists would mete out to our loved ones. As they grew ever more victorious, they would make our position increasingly perilous. Slowly but surely, all of the rewards that we had worked so hard for would be stripped away from us.

Chapter 5

Growing-Up Years

Moving Up the Social Ladder

Dad's success at selling slippers enabled him to build a large, tall house in Phu Thanh. Dad spent 600 ounces of gold to build a four-level cement dwelling with reinforced steel bars, laid with marble and ceramic floors. In 1971, the construction cost was $30,000 in cash, given the price of gold calibrated at $50 per ounce. To provide some perspective, the salary of a worker in 1971 was a few U.S. dollars per month.

Before he had the house built, the site was a big fish pond. The land was split into two equal lots and was shared with an ethnic Chao Zhau family who originally came from China. Separate houses were constructed on each of the two lots over the course of the same year. Before construction started, Mom engaged the services of a Buddhist monk to bless the site and to invite the god of Protection, one of many Buddhist gods. The monk set up an offering table, complete with an umbrella to protect the offerings from any rainfall throughout the duration of the construction period. The purpose of the blessing ritual was to pray for the safety of the site and to prevent people working on it from harm or accident. Each day during the construction Mom or Dad prayed and burned incense. On the new moon or full moon days they brought offerings of fruit.

Dad worked a couple of hours every day alongside the construction workers. I loved going with him to the new house and seeing the progress that was being made, and I would go every chance I could. I was fascinated with the stages of building, starting with a tract of swamp and transforming into two tall buildings with steel rebar and cement foundations and walls. As the construction matured, I got more and more excited, spending many hours from afar watching the buildings being erected.

Their being built together would also have consequences later on. I and Me (which means little sister in the Chao Zhau dialect), my neighbor's daughter closest to my age, became very good friends. After our houses were built, the wall on the terrace of the top floor of my family's home was low enough that we could climb over to reach each other's house. Sometimes when I stayed too late at Me's house, I was able to sneak back home after hours by way of the third-floor terrace wall. This was only possible, however, with the help of an accomplice. My big brother Hong kindly left the terrace living area door open for me.

Figure 5-1: Our house in Phu Thanh turned into a daycare center after 1978.

Construction was finally completed in 1972, and we were ready to move into the tallest house in the neighborhood. Mom told all of us to get our stuff ready to move. It took place on Sunday because our workers worked five and half days each week, with a half day on Saturday and off Sunday. We moved our things using carts that we pushed because the new house was only five houses away. I paraded back and forth from the old to the new house, holding my pillow and blanket. We only brought our clothing with us. My parents furnished our new house with all new furniture: sofas, beds, armoires, and two big round tables. The table on the second floor was provided for all the kids to do their homework, and the other was for dining on the ground floor. The pieces of furniture were hoisted with ropes to the upper floors since they came pre-assembled and were too big to move up the indoors stairs. It was such an ordeal to maneuver all the furniture into our house, all the neighborhood kids and adults came to watch.

My parents slept on the first floor while most of the children slept in the second-floor bedrooms. There was also a large common area on the second floor, where five siblings and I, except for Hong, did our homework. One big bedroom was for the boys and another big bedroom was for the girls. Each room was big enough to fit three to four queen-size beds and several armoires. The only one toilet on the second floor was in the girls' room. Hong, the eldest son, slept in the bedroom on the third floor with his own desk, but he played his guitar on the sofa in the common area on the second floor.

Also on this floor was my sister Zenh's sewing area. In Vietnam, we ourselves made the light cotton clothing we wore every day around the house and in the neighborhood. It was common to have someone in the family who knew how to sew. For the clothing that was required for work and business settings, which consisted of more complex styles, many families would buy fabrics and had a professional seamstress make the outfits for them. The ready-made clothing sold at the market was very limited, including such items as school uniforms, children's clothing, or men's polo shirts. Some clothing was custom-made by the store owner.

As the eldest daughter in our family, Zenh took on the traditional responsibility of learning how to sew and make clothing for the family. She took lessons twice a week from a woman who lived on our street, learning to design and to fashion clothing. As with everything, of course I wanted to be involved. Kien and I used to walk with Zenh to her lesson and sometimes we were able to overhear what she learned. Even though we did not receive direct instruction, our attention to Zenh's lessons eventually paid off. When Kien and I finally had the opportunity to sew clothing ourselves, we already knew what to do.

Life in the new house was very comfortable. For the first few months we had two housekeepers taking care of us kids and cooking for the family. After that, most of the kids, including Buu and I, started school, and our old housekeeper, who had been with us many years, retired and moved away to live with her son. The new housekeeper was also in charge of the meals, but she was not a very good cook. One day in particular she made beef with onions, and the onions were undercooked. All the kids had a hard time finishing the meal, but Mom and Dad said that we had to be polite. After that meal, we learned to be more selective about what we put in our bowls for dinner. We didn't eat onions again for weeks. In fact, from that day forward my sister Kien stopped eating onions altogether.

We were leading lights in our little neighborhood, living in one of the two tallest houses with Dad's slipper business booming. Everyone who lived nearby, and even strangers outside of our neighborhood, knew us as the sons or daughters of Ung, Ly Sang. That's because every day we had so many people coming and going, doing business with my parents.

Hard to Live Under the Same Roof

Before Dad moved our family from Grandfather's house, Uncle Quan Sang and his family lived with us in Grandfather's house for over a year. Uncle Quan Sang's wife, Bac Moi, disliked my family. (Bac Moi means "the eighth girl.") Mom and Bac Moi shared the responsibility of cooking for the family and making lunches for the workers. Perhaps living and working so closely together for that year intensified the feelings of jealousy or enmity that Bac Moi felt toward Mom and our family. At the time, I was too young to understand why Bac Moi disliked us, but I did suffer the consequences of the bad blood.

One time I hid the money I had received during Chinese New Year in a brown bag under my parents' bed for safekeeping. When we were getting ready to move to the new house, I looked for it in its hiding place, but I couldn't find it. Bac Moi had found it, and she announced to everyone in the neighborhood that she had found free money. I heard about her announcement from a friend and came right away to claim my money. She wouldn't give it back, but instead threw it into the street, where all the neighborhood kids grabbed it up. As I screamed and cried in anger, she had a big grin on her face, seeing my desperation to get my money back. From that day on it seemed like she delighted in being mean to me and my family. I don't remember ever disliking anyone as much at that age.

Bac Moi wouldn't let her children play with me, or with my brothers and sisters. They were even forbidden to talk to us. When we moved and had our house-warming party with friends and family, we celebrated with food and drink. Dad's friends from the French military came to celebrate with us, wearing their uniforms. That was the first time I was aware that Dad had served as a soldier. I remember being able to drink orange soda, a special treat.

During the party, Uncle Quan Sang's kids, Nam and one of his brothers, stood in front of our house staring at us. I asked Nam, "Do you want something to eat?" He looked like a hungry dog, drooling from the side of his mouth. Mom gave them some chicken drumsticks and let them share a bottle of orange soda. We knew they would be in big trouble if their mother found out, but since we were kids, we were not too smart about hiding evidence. When Nam and his brother went home with orange lips, their mother became so furious that she beat them with a broom, chasing them out into the street. As I watched this happening, I realized how awful she was, both as a mother and as a person.

Six months later, they moved again to Dinh Quan, in the countryside. My grandparents had purchased a banana farm and built a little house for them to live in. After they moved, we never saw our cousins again.

Grandfather Vu's Visit

Grandfather Vu visited us each summer in Phu Thanh, traveling from Song Mao. After his family had moved there in 1954, they never left. He also brought my uncles and aunts to visit us during their summer school break. Mom was the eldest daughter of eight children; she had three brothers and four sisters, and the youngest five siblings were born in Song Mao. Even though I saw Grandfather Vu every summer, I didn't meet my grandmother, Qui, until I was eight years old, when she and Grandfather came to escape the Viet Cong advance at Song Mao. Grandfather Vu's visits were also memorable because he often brought us cooked seafood that he picked up on the way to our house from Phan Thiet Town, a place well known for its superb seafood. The boiled blue crabs, squid, and shrimp that he brought were special favorites.

Figure 5-2: Maternal grandfather, Vu Chun Liam family picture without Kieu and Duc, 1972.

In the summer of 1972, Grandfather Vu brought Uncle Phong, and he stayed with us for a couple days before leaving on a plane from Tan Son Nhat International airport in Saigon. He was attending college in Taiwan, and Dad agreed to support Uncle Phong's education abroad. However, Dad didn't realize then how large of a financial burden he was assuming.

A few years later, the Vietnam government cut off all forms of financial transactions to the outside world. Uncle Phong had to rely on himself financially.

Booming Slipper Business

A large part of Dad's business early on was exporting slippers to Cambodia that had the unique Cambodian dragon design with red color straps, white slipper surface and a red bottom. When Cambodia stopped importing slippers from Vietnam, Dad had to change his business model. Instead, he designed a new slipper product to attract local Vietnamese customers. The typical slipper design was white on the top surface and had a colored bottom with an oval shape around the toes. Dad's slipper design had surface tops in pink, blue, or black, with multicolored asterisk patterns all over. In addition, the height of the slipper was an inch and half to two inches compared to the typical half-inch thick slippers. The slippers in the picture below were Dad's slipper designs worn by my four siblings.

Figure 5-3: Dad's slipper designs worn by Zenh, Hong, Kien, and Xi, 1978.

With their unique slipper design my parents' business was booming by 1973. Because it offered young men and women in Saigon with different options of color and patterns, it became very popular. We soon had many employees working on the ground floor, otherwise known as the slipper assembly integration area. The workers cookie-cut sheets of processed rubber for a variety of sizes. After that the straps were attached, and then each slipper pair was packaged in a plastic bag. Twelve pairs of slippers were packaged into a big bag for wholesale. Business was so good that weeks before the New Year, people would line up for hours to order our slippers.

All of the raw materials, rollers, and pressing ovens were kept at Dad's new factory. At times powder would choke the room, a byproduct of the processing activities in the factory. It was not a healthy environment for the employees, and the children were not allowed close to the machinery. However, I was curious about the factory, and I would take advantage of any opportunity to visit it with Dad or to bring food for the workers.

One weekend when production was stopped, a machinist came to repair one of the machines. I was allowed to hang out at the factory alongside Dad. I wanted to know everything about how the machines worked. I asked Dad how throwing a switch from one position to another made the machines work. He explained to me how the switch

Figure 5-4: A worker putting raw rubber and other powders into a roller press.

turned on the electricity that drove the motor of the machine. I remember thinking how cool it was and how it worked like magic. Of course, I did not know then that one day I would become an engineer, but when I look back, I can see the seed of curiosity that has been a part of my nature from the beginning.

The Unauthorized Fisher Folk

That curiosity also extended in other directions. As a child in Phu Thanh, there weren't many things to do, and that meant we were required to use our imagination. We were lucky to live on a cul-de-sac, because the street was our playground. We played many games, such as soccer, throwing slippers at a tin can, high jump rope with a lengthy rubber band tied up as a jump rope, badminton, gyro on a string and so on. One day Dad bought a small black-and-white TV for us. We suddenly became one of only a few families in the neighborhood with a TV. Seizing full advantage of our privileged status, I charged the neighborhood kids the equivalent of five cents apiece to watch a James Bond

007 or a cowboy movie. Those were always the most popular. Our little house was always filled with slippers and bags, so the kids would sit anywhere they could find a free space to watch the movies. Sometimes they would even sit on the bags or on piles of slippers.

My Uncle Luong, who was the same age as my brother Hong, and his friends would often come over to our house to play ping pong with Hong, Kien, Xi, and Num. Dad had bought a ping pong table and stored it in the slipper factory area behind the house. I was too short to play, but I couldn't stand not participating. Hong and Xi found a box that I could stand on and play whenever the boys gave me a turn. We played ping pong almost every weekend.

That was great fun, but sometimes we craved a bigger challenge. We knew several families in our neighborhood had fish in their ponds, and we thought it would be fun to catch some. We knew that if we asked for permission, the answer would probably be no. But that suited us perfectly! Not only would the fishing be fun, there would also be an element of danger. Individually, none of us would have gone any further with this temptation, but as a group, led by mastermind Kien, we worked up our courage and goaded each other on. We made our own fishing rigs with hooks, rocks for weights, and string for the lines, rolled up onto tin cans. We also came up with the idea of digging outlet channels from the ponds that the fish would swim into after a heavy rainfall, making it easier for us to catch them.

With our bold plan we actually did catch some of the neighbors' fish. When we caught one, we would cook it in rice porridge and share it among all the kids. One day, though, Dad came home and saw what we were up to. He warned us not to do it again, because we were stealing the neighbors' fish. We were undeterred by Dad's warning; it just added one more element of risk to our adventure.

After that we waited until Dad had to drive to town. Sometimes he was only gone for an hour, but often he made longer trips. The problem was, we didn't always know how long he would be gone. Inevitably, one day Dad came home earlier than we expected and caught us again in the act. Because we had disobeyed his earlier warning, he devised an ingenious new punishment to make an impression on us.

Since I was still very young, Dad asked me if I knew what I was doing or if my sister, and baby-sitter, Kien had coerced me. Even at that age, my sense of responsibility was strong and I readily admitted my guilt. With my complicity in the crime verified, Dad ordered us all to stay next to the outhouse toilet for an hour, without any water to clean the toilet if someone used it. Imagine Hong, Kien, Xi, Num, Uncle Luong, and I, all squeezed into a tiny, warm, humid, smelly, claustrophobic outhouse, with only two concrete platforms to stand on with a hole in the middle. We thought things couldn't get any worse, but we were wrong! Five minutes into our already smelly confinement, our little brother, Buu, had to use the toilet. And he didn't just pee. I won't try to describe the excruciatingly putrid smell we had to endure for nearly an hour. It was one of my worst childhood experiences.

After that, we had no more use for our homemade fishing tackle. We gave the tackle to other neighborhood kids, who claimed they caught fish from the ponds at night.

Private School Days

When I was growing up, all the kids I knew attended a small private Chinese elementary school called Lap Chi (立志). It was only a ten-minute walk from home. The classes went from kindergarten through sixth grade, and while we could also have attended a bigger private Chinese school that went up to eighth grade, it was thirty minutes away, walking by foot. The high school was too far away to walk at all, and Zenh and Hong had to ride a bike to get there.

Kien didn't start school until she was seven years old, because she was helping Mom by baby-sitting Num and me. When she finally went, she was the oldest kindergartener at Lap Chi. She and Xi were in the same grade and mostly hung out with the same friends during their growing-up years. In the fall of 1972, I started kindergarten at Lap Chi and a year later Buu joined me.

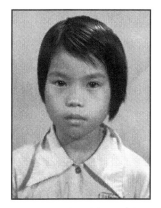

Figure 5-5: Nam Moi and Buu in Lap Chi Private School.

In those days, there were no preschools or any other formal preparation for elementary school. Parents were too busy working or running their businesses. Also, many of the mothers and some of the fathers had never gone to school themselves.

While we were young, kids would play in the streets with their friends in just their pajamas. But when we went to school, we had to wear uniforms. Girls wore white shirts with navy skirts and boys wore white shirts with navy pants. We also had to sit up properly; we had to be well-behaved and listen to instructions.

Bullying in school was common. When I first started going, though, the meanness of other kids was a shock to me. In the beginning, several students stole my pencils and erasers every week. Mom got upset with me because I kept asking for money to buy pencils and erasers every few weeks. After a while I finally told Kien that the same girl took my stuff, for the most part. Of course, telling on her didn't help; the girl who was bullying me got angry and continued to give me a hard time throughout my kindergarten year. Being pushed, shuffled, or knocked over was a common occurrence during recess. Kien and Xi had to take turns of duty as recess guards to watch over the younger students, and I learned to play only within range of their watch.

Figure 5-6: Kien and Xi as junior guards in Lap Chi School.

In second grade, I started hanging out with a few girls who were not very nice. One time we ganged up verbally on a shy girl who had no father because he had died during the war, and whose older siblings were much older. She soon was so miserable that she didn't want to come to school anymore. One day she came into the principal's office in tears with her older sister. I was terrified that she would tell on me or the other girls and I would get in trouble with my parents.

Yet I also regretted the way I had treated her. She didn't mention my name as one of the bullies causing her pain, but I realized all the same that despite the fact that I disliked bullies, I had become one myself. I apologized to her and thanked her for not telling on me. To my surprise, she told me that I was one of the nice girls in class. Starting that day, we became good friends for many years.

I also became more aware of how I interacted with other kids who were less fortunate than I. I tried to protect them if I could, as Kien and Xi did for me when they were on duty as junior guards.

As for schooling, I asked Dad to help me at first, but he was too busy and had no time for any of us. He set up the rule that the next older sibling of each child was responsible for tutoring. If the subject was too hard and the older sibling couldn't help, then we moved up the order. Each of us would sit at the round table next to the sibling who was supposed to help us. My brother, Num, was responsible for helping me, but of all the children he was the one who was least likely to follow Dad's rules, leaving Xi or Kien to help me with my homework.

The official language of the country was Vietnamese. Because the school was Chinese, we learned everything in Chinese and not in the country's native tongue. The teachers themselves spoke Mandarin in class but Cantonese during recess or after school. We also spoke Cantonese with our neighbors and friends. At home we spoke *Hakka* with our parents, siblings, and relatives. We learned enough Vietnamese to buy things, developing basic communication skills for purchasing food and snacks. In kindergarten, I had to learn both how to write basic Chinese characters and the Vietnamese alphabet.

The distance from our home country was reflected in our social relations as well. A Vietnamese family lived next door to us and a few Vietnamese families lived at the end of our cul-de-sac, but we didn't interact socially with any of them. Our next-door Vietnamese neighbor was a poor Catholic family. The husband was serving in the military and seldom came home. I remember seeing him one time for a week or so. In 1973 he died in the fighting. His body was delivered to the family's house for the funeral service. It was displayed in an open coffin for a couple days, and many relatives, close families, and friends came to pay respect to the deceased.

This was a recurring scene in our neighborhood. As a child, I didn't understand how these fathers were killed and who killed them and why. One day they came home to visit, and the next their bodies came back in coffins. My siblings and I grew up with the fear of losing our dad like so many of kids we knew without fathers.

As Christmas approached, our Vietnamese neighbor displayed nativity scenes, with figurines of baby Jesus, mother Mary, and the three wise men. We watched them celebrate Christmas, but in a community of mostly Chinese families the occasion seemed very foreign. Even so, the relationships between Chinese and Vietnamese families were peaceful. Most Chinese families had a business producing goods of some kind, and a few rich Vietnamese families lived in our neighborhood. One had a fabric-printing factory and another family sold gasoline. Two of the Vietnamese families later left the country before the fall of Saigon. Their houses would be taken over by the Communist government and occupied by government officials we would learn to call "comrades."

Three generations of the Ung family had been born in Vietnam since our ancestors' immigration from China in 1898. But our identity was still strongly *Hakka*. In my neighborhood the Chinese didn't even talk much with our Vietnamese neighbors. I used to ask Mom why we didn't have any interaction with them. Her response was that it would be like chickens talking to ducks. They acknowledged each other's existence, but they lived separate lives. In three generations or a hundred, she told me, chickens don't become ducks.

Because of their businesses and wealth, most Chinese in our neighborhood were better off than the Vietnamese. Like them, my family was Chinese and wealthy living in a big three-story house. These distinctions soon would be a severe liability for all of us.

Chapter 6

Holiday Celebrations

New Year Celebration

As a child, I loved the Lunar New Year Celebration. The whole country, Chinese and Vietnamese alike, celebrated the holiday season. Every year it seemed to take forever to come. As we counted the days leading up to the New Year, the kids got so excited that we often couldn't sleep. The whole country stopped work during the first seven days of the New Year, and most factories stopped work for fifteen days. Young and old alike enjoyed the celebration.

Each family got their houses ready for the New Year by doing an annual top-to-bottom cleaning. All our neighbors would sweep and clean and throw out unwanted things. Some used the occasion to furnish their houses with new things.

For the final two weeks before Lunar New Year, Dad also cleaned his financial house, collecting debts from people who owed him money for the slipper products. He came home flush with money stacked inside his undershirt. He would ask me to close the metal front door, and then he would pull his undershirt out and let all the money fall on the floor. I

Figure 6-1: Tam standing in front of the metal door in Phu Thanh,1976.

remember money raining out of his body! My task, along with my brother Buu, was to count all the money he collected and write down the quantity of each bill type, then total them up. That was my first lesson in accounting, when I was only six years old. The process took two to three hours to complete. Buu helped me for a short while, but he got bored and left me to complete the counting and to record the total amount of money. Then I put all the money in a metal container and locked it up in a metal cabinet, hiding the key.

Through Dad's military education and career he had learned to value the benefits of processes and rules. This administrative training would later contribute to his business success. With the growing number of children in his family he also relied on processes and rules to help him bring up his kids. One example was having each one take responsibility for helping the next younger sibling with their school lessons. Another was buying sets of new clothes for each child at the beginning of the New Year. This became an Ung family tradition: new clothes to wear on New Year's Eve, New Year's Day, and New Year's 2nd, 3th, 4th, and 5th days. The clothing was usually colorful, often including red to invite wealth and health. Wearing of white or black clothing was discouraged and sometimes forbidden during the New Year. For Chinese, white clothing was worn for funerals and the color black symbolized bad luck, neither of which belonged in a joyful celebration.

Tet is the Vietnamese word for New Year, but the timing for the celebration was the same for both Chinese and Vietnamese. It fell between late January and mid-February. The Lunar New Year celebration lasted for fifteen days, but New Year's Eve and the first seven days of the New Year were the most special. That's when we would celebrate, eat, drink, gamble, and get lucky money from married relatives. We could stay up late at night, even close to midnight. Normally, people would close their doors for bed at eight or eight-thirty, so staying up so late made the celebration even more special. It was a time of revelry for our immediate and extended families, friends, and neighbors. Best of all, the Lunar New Year celebration had the biggest fireworks of any celebration.

New Year's Eve was the first major event, since it was both the end of the past year and the start of the New Year. In the afternoon we started getting ready for the celebration with a bath, washing our hair and putting on new clothes. That's because on the first day of the New Year, the tradition was to abstain from washing. The idea behind that timing was simple. Taking a bath or washing our hair so soon after the end of the old year would symbolically wash away the wealth that we had carried over from the year. One year my brother Num took our Chinese tradition too far, though: he didn't bathe for five days straight!

Another important part of our New Year's celebration was the prayer ceremony. The Buddhist religion calls for a food offering and burning of the *yi chi*, a kind of paper we burned for our ancestors in the afterlife and firecrackers, as part of the offering to our deceased ancestors. Mom prepared food for the prayer ceremony, which was performed in front of our house to pay respect to Heaven and Earth. The food was placed on a table that faced the street. She always included a boiled whole chicken with head and feet still intact, a slab of pork, a roasted whole duck, and roasted pig, purchased from a restaurant. Other offerings included fish, fruit, rice, wine, tea, two red candles, and different types of incense. When we prayed at the offering table, we would ask our ancestors to make our wishes come true. My parents would ask each of us to "*yagya* to our ancestor." For all my childhood years, I thought *yagya* was a *Hakka* word. I later learned that the word *yagya* comes from the ancient Vedic tradition of India. Traditionally, it is the process of making offerings in an act of worship with the desire to gain the favor of the divine or to gain support of the laws of nature.

Our usual wishes were for good grades for the kids, lots of profits from business for the parents, and good health for the elderly and babies. Dad would end the ceremony by burning lots of *yi chi* and firing off a big roll of firecrackers chained together. The wealthiest family would burn the longest chain of firecrackers, often lasting fifteen minutes or more. We usually had to hang the firecrackers from a big pole to keep their explosions a safe distance away. One New Year's Day, we had such a long string of firecrackers we had to hang them from the second-floor balcony.

At the New Year's Eve dinner, we ate all the food we had offered to our ancestors, along with other vegetable and noodle dishes. It was not unusual to have a ten-course meal. During the New Year celebration, my parents allowed the kids to mix a bowl of cocktail drinks with champagne and fruit for everyone to share. Every time I drank it, I had to take a nap. I didn't like falling asleep for a small cup of cocktail drink, but all the same, I never missed this once a year treat.

The tradition of offering food followed by a grand dinner was repeated on New Year's Day and on the second day of the New Year, minus the roasted pig. On New Year's Day, we would have lunch at my grandparents' house from Dad's side. Grandmother often cooked everyone's favorite, duck stew, for lunch. After lunch at my grandparents' house we would visit our extended family, including great uncles and aunts; we would wish them good health and offer well wishes, which earned us kids lucky money. Since we had so many relatives and only a few days to make all the rounds, we had to strategize about which relative to visit first to maximize the money set aside for the holiday. Because we had to keep moving, the visits at each house usually lasted no more than an hour.

After the New Year's Eve dinner, my parents passed out lucky money to us kids. By tradition we slept with the lucky money underneath our pillows to signify the money coming to us in the New Year. We could also be given lucky money from extended family and even adults who were not part of our family, as long as we greeted them with well wishes. Kids were trained by their parents to be polite and sweet, and to know the right things to say in order to coax money out of the adults.

In a unique tradition for our family, Dad initiated a game in which we earned money for our knowledge. It was a new way for us to earn more lucky money. In truth, Dad was teaching us in a practical way that we really could make our own luck. The game started with the youngest child and finished with the oldest. Dad would pay one dong for each four-word Chinese poem we could recite without notes, and without repeating any of the poems. Typically this included "Kung Hey Fat Choi" (prosperity blessing), "Son Ning Fi Loc" (Happy New Year), and so on. My brother Kau and sister Tam were too young at that time to participate. Since I was the second youngest child to participate in the game, I had lots of incentive, and I spent days memorizing those poems. The best I ever did was twenty poems for twenty dongs, which was a lot of money at the time. We could buy a small bowl of noodle soup for quarter dong at the street vendor and for three-quarter dong we could buy a big bowl of noodle soup at a restaurant.

We all had to pay attention during the contest, so we wouldn't repeat any of the poems. As the oldest child, my sister Zenh had the toughest challenge because she had to follow my brother, Hong. He was very good at these types of games.

The New Year celebration also included time off from work to spend with family, relatives, friends, and neighbors. Our neighbor's house was like a mini casino, where all ages could play card games with real money everywhere. The adults usually played Pai Gow poker. Kids and teenagers played other card games.

Figure 6-2: Xi, Buu, Tam, and Mom (Kieu) at the Saigon Zoo, 1975.

Families also visited attractions like the zoo or visited Saigon harbor and other city landmarks. During the 1974 New Year celebration, Dad took Buu, Mom, and Tam to the Saigon Zoo. Xi followed with his bike to join them.

Figure 6-3: Family picture on the third floor terrace, 1975.

Figure 6-4: Mom (Kieu) and Kau on the first floor patio, 1975.

Chin Ming Holiday—Honoring Ancestors

Besides the Lunar New Year, Chin Ming (青明) is the holiday that stands out most in my mind. Chin Ming is a traditional Chinese holiday for paying respect to one's ancestors, a very important component of the Chinese culture, especially the *Hakka*. Chin Ming lasted about two weeks, falling in the second month of the lunar calendar, which corresponds to late March to early April. In Vietnam we had a few days off from school for Chin Ming observances. Parents and grandparents would tell stories of their ancestors and deceased relatives, because transferring this knowledge from one generation to another is an important way to pay respect.

My parents and elder relatives told us that the Ungs' ancestors were *Hakka* Chinese people. The year 1898, which was marked by mass famine and many deaths, led to the first generation of Ungs from Fang Cheng (防城), China, migrating to Vietnam. Fang Cheng is located in Quang Xi Province, close to the border, not far from Mong Cai in Vietnam. My grandfather's grandparents were part of that migration and made their way to Ha Coi, Quang Ninh province, along with their two little sons. Tai Hong, three years old at that time, would later become my grandfather's father. His brother Ung Tai Nan was two years old. My great-great-grandmother carried her sons into Vietnam in two baskets held aloft at either end of a rough-hewn pole balanced across her

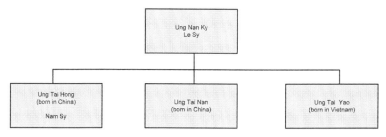

Figure 6-5: Great Great Grandfather (Ung Nan Ky) family tree.

Figure 6-6: Great Grandfather (Ung Tai Hong), Great Grandmother (Nam Sy), and Great Great Grandmother (Le Sy).

shoulders. The family carried the rest of their valuables with them as they walked across the border.

The Ungs brought nothing with them to their new country, and that meant the start of the Vietnamese chapter of their history began in severe poverty. On more than one occasion, Tai Hong would tell his children and grandchildren about how he grew up wearing clothes with holes in them, and that he didn't have even one nice set of clothing. In his youth he was responsible for watching ducks. By his late teens he had replaced duck watching with a sugarcane business—and a love for gambling. Inevitably there came a time when he gambled away all the money from his sugarcane earnings. He got into so much trouble that he promised never to gamble again.

He passed along the experience that gambling is bad. The lessons he learned from his failure were passed down and imprinted on his children, grandchildren, and great grandchildren. In his early twenties Tai Hong built a business buying and selling goods between Vietnam and China. He started investing in farmland early on and became a landlord at a young age, leasing the farmland in exchange for a portion of the grain harvested. He continued to invest in a great deal of farmlands with his gains as a landlord over the years.

Given our strong *Hakka* identity and traditions, the Ung family created a family couplet many years ago and passed it down from generation to generation.

Relatives told us that the Ung clan was associated with wealth and political power a long time ago. In Chinese history, feudal states/territories were awarded to nobles by the emperor, who had the right to take them right back. The name of the territories would use the last name of the noble man. Dating back a few thousand years, there was an Ung (吳) State in China. Ung (吳) as a last name sounds and spells like "Wu" in Mandarin, "Ng" in Cantonese, "Ung" in *Hakka* from Vietnam, or "Ngo" in Vietnamese.

The Ung family couplet on the left read: 吳 宗邦源遠。萬世其昌. On the right it was: 門 祖德澤香。蓋大正明. Together they were usually displayed on the entrance door to the main hall. The phrase claims to be brilliantly insightful with clarity, righteousness, and impartiality.

Figure 6-7: Ung family couplet.

The left side of the couplet had two phrases of four characters. The first four characters, 宗邦源遠, means "The Ung family lineage/feudal state were established long time ago."

64

The second four characters, 萬世其昌, means "The Ung clan has been prosperous over thousands of generation."

The right side of the couplet also had two phrases of four characters. The first four characters, 祖德澤香, means "The virtues of our ancestors, like water and fragrance, spread and continue." The second four characters, 蓋大正明, means "The Ung clan looms large with righteousness and integrity, clear and bright."

The Ung families inherited from our forefathers a couplet, and the words in the couplet were used in naming each generation of the family members. The generation name was presented by their middle name and connected with all the other members of the same generation.

Great-great-grandfather from China had the middle name of Nan (蓋). Great-grandfather had the middle name Tai (大), Grandfather had the middle name Chenh (正), Dad had the middle name Menh (明), and I had the middle name Chong (宗). The next generation is Pong (邦).

This tradition applies to naming the sons but not necessarily the daughters. Chinese traditions, especially the *Hakka*, contain many differences between sons and daughters. However, Dad tried to treat both females and males in the family equally to the best of his ability. Dad named all his children, boys and girls, with the same middle name. My Chinese name is 吳宗蓮 Ung, Chong Lin.

The *Hakka* are more deeply attached to the series of generation names than other *Han* people. This connection with our origin is what gives us collective confidence and internal peace of mind and equilibrium.

My great grandfather Tai Hong had six sons and a daughter. By *Hakka* tradition, sons were numbered and known by their birth order, along with any male first cousins who shared the same surname. Each generation was represented by their middle name,

Chenh (正). My grandfather was the eldest grandson; therefore, he was named "eldest uncle." His uncle Tai Nan's eldest son was referred to as "Uncle #2." My grandfather's brothers were Great Uncle #3, Great Uncle #4, Great Uncle #7, Great Uncle #9, and Great Uncle #11.

My grandfather's cousins from the Ung Tai Nan family were Great Uncle #2, Great Uncle #5, and Great Uncle #6.

My grandfather's grandmother, Le Sy, passed away in 1955, a few months after they emigrated from Ha Coi. Life in Song Mao was very hard for the elderly, and it was especially traumatic for Le Sy to lose all her wealth and her lands and to have to start all over again. My grandfather's mother, Nam Sy, passed away in Song Mao in 1956, days before my parents' marriage. In 1970, Tai Hong passed away in Saigon.

Although only a few Ungs initially migrated to Vietnam, over the course of seventy plus years and three generations, the numbers grew to over 100 Ungs. It was a big event for all the Ungs to go and pay respect to my great-grandfather, Tai Hong. My grandfather's mother and grandmother had passed away in Song Mao and their remains were buried there, at least for a while before they were moved to Saigon. To pay respect to our deceased relatives in Chin Ming, we hired several passenger vehicles to take all of the family members to the grave sites, except for the elderly or kids not old enough for school. I remember the first time I was able to join the big kids for the day trip to the cemetery. Each family brought lots of food to the gravesite. We brought several kinds of meats, including chicken, duck, whole roasted pigs, and fried fish. We brought homemade *Hakka* food like *mo chi*, rice cakes, sweet rice with red beans, and so on. The journey to the gravesite in Saigon, "La Tieu," was slowed by all the traffic of other families going to the cemetery, and took over two and half hours. It was not unusual to have to sit through an hour and a half of bumper-to-bumper traffic heading into the cemetery. Once we arrived, our first task was to clean away any overgrown grass or weeds. In front of Great-grandfather's grave we would place all the food from the families of the five sons and the families of the grandsons. The five sons were my four great-uncles and my grandfather. The grandsons were Dad and his cousins.

Visiting Great-grandfather's grave and bringing food offerings left a lasting impression on us kids, and helped to teach us the importance of paying respect to our ancestors. We were participating in a tradition that has been passed down from generation to generation for many centuries. The best part of the Chin Ming celebration was eating and sharing all the special homemade *Hakka* food and

Figure 6-8: Left: Great Uncles #11, #9, and Uncle Chin at Great Grandfather's (Tai Hong) gravesite in La Tieu, early 1970s.

desserts after the prayer ceremony. Since the food was on display as part of the offering, all the kids would wait patiently and talk about what they wanted to try or their favorite desserts. Once we heard that we could start eating, all of the children would jump for joy. We all had lunch eating the different food we brought. Tai Hong's gravesite was large compared to a typical gravesite. It signified the deceased person was associated with wealth. The property was nicely constructed with walls, tile floor, benches, a garden box in the center with plants, and a tombstone as part of the wall, inscribed with Tai Hong's picture, name, and beloved phrases. It felt like a private picnic party at the gravesite after the praying ceremony where everyone started eating, drinking, and catching up with each other. The experiences reaffirmed our connection to the past and strengthened the bond with our extended families.

Hakka people are known as "guest family or visitors from afar." They have the reputation of traveling and migrating to a new land together as a clan. Wherever they went, they would take their ancestors' tombs with them. One important *Hakka* tradition called for digging up the graves of family members ten to fifteen years after the burial, then pulling out the bones, putting them in a ceramic jar, and reburying them. A *Hakka* family would dig up the graves of their deceased relatives' bodies and rebury the bones close to their new land. The ancestors' tombs could not be abandoned, which meant the gravesite must be visited at least once a year during Chin Ming. Otherwise, it was believed, unfortunate things would happen to the deceased person's relatives.

My grandfather's mother and grandmother were buried in a rural area of Song Mao, so each year during Chin Ming, my grandfather or his brothers would make a trip to Song Mao and pay respect at their graves with food offerings. They worried, however, that the next generation would not be able to perform this duty once the older generation passed away, and they decided to move the two deceased relatives' bones to Saigon along with Great-grandfather Tai Hong.

My grandfather told us the story of how they struggled to carry the smelly bones of his mother and grandmother to Saigon for reburial. He and his cousin Great Uncle #5 took a train to Song Mao to dig up the graves. They hired two gravediggers for the first part of the job. The collected bones were put into two separate luggage bags. The two of them and the two bags of bones spent the first night at a motel. The next day they traveled in a truck converted for carrying passengers from Song Mao to Saigon. The task was made more difficult because of the smell coming from the luggage bags and because of the importance of keeping those bags from any harm until the task of reburial could be completed. Grandfather and Great Uncle #5 rode with their precious cargo from Song Mao to Saigon, guarding them as if they were the most valuable treasures in life. If they had failed to treat the bones with respect or to deliver them safely to their new burial site, *Hakka* tradition teaches that unfortunate events would have happened to all the people related to the deceased. Fortunately, Grandfather and Great Uncle #5 successfully completed the reburial of the two deceased relatives' bones. They were relieved and so were all their siblings and relatives.

The New Year and Chin Ming celebrations brought a sense of awareness and reinforced our *Hakka* identity and culture. Growing up in Saigon, I always enjoyed these two yearly celebrations, the twin highlights of my youth. It was a special time to celebrate not only with our immediate family but also with our extended family. However, these happy days were coming to an end very soon.

PART II

Chapter 7

Fall of Saigon

The Beginning of the End

We knew the People's Army of Vietnam (PAVN) as the Viet Cong. They had started conducting operations in South Vietnam before I was born. I never lived in a country that was at peace during all of my years of growing up. Saigon had not seen much action since the Ung family had moved there to escape the Communists, and the people of Saigon had endured relatively little suffering. In the spring of 1975, however, when I was eight years old, all of that changed. As the last U.S. troops were being withdrawn, the Viet Cong launched a massive assault on the South, advancing rapidly toward Saigon. The South Vietnamese Army (the ARVN, or Army Republic of Vietnam), backpedaled in disorderly retreat before the Communist onslaught, and the prospects for turning the tide did not look good. Major South Vietnamese cities were lost to the Viet Cong. Hue was taken over on March 25, and Da Nang fell just three days later.

In Song Mao, my maternal grandparents' family was desperate to escape the countryside before the Viet Cong reached them. They fled their home to stay with us. My grandparents, along with Auntie Anh, Auntie Lan, Auntie Ngoc, Uncle Sanh, and Uncle Han, all moved in with us. That was when I and my three younger siblings, Buu, Tam, and Kau, first met our grandmother Qui. She was a very tall and physically strong woman, honest and direct, with little use for tact. The joke was that she was really of Mongolian descent and was not a *Hakka* at all. Grandmother Qui helped with baby-sitting my brother Kau, who was only nine months old at the time, and fed him rice porridge.

The Viet Cong victories and their advance on Saigon created intense stress and worry for Dad. With a Communist victory, he realized that his money would soon have no value. In anticipation, he stockpiled the ground floor of our house with hundreds of fifty-pound bags of rice and soybeans, firewood, and other supplies. He also bought a tractor and a chainsaw for cutting wood in case we were forced to relocate to the country. Entire truckloads of raw materials were stacked on the ground floor and in the warehouse next door.

An even more urgent matter was my parents' fear that Dad's history as a French soldier would lead to his arrest once the Viet Cong took over. My parents didn't want to take any chances that my dad's past would be discovered. They burned all evidence of his military past, including pictures, awards, and certificates from his years in French Military Academy. They also burned all the pictures of Dad and his friends during his military service or in uniform. My parents only kept a family picture taken at a photo studio in Song Mao with Dad wearing civilian clothing.

After Dad had retired from his military career and settled in Saigon, he was careful never to talk about his earlier days in the French military. He held onto a small hope that the people in Phu Thanh wouldn't know about his past.

Then, late in March, Dad was hospitalized with a lung infection. He was coughing up blood, a sure sign of internal bleeding. However, his life was saved because there were still American doctors and medicine at the hospital. He finally came home from the hospital after a month, just days before the fall of Saigon.

Mom's cousin worked at the United States Embassy. He found out about the U.S. helicopter operation that was evacuating the

Americans and Vietnamese to the fleet offshore, and he told our family about it. Mom and the rest of the family decided that even though Dad's medical condition had stabilized, he had not recovered enough strength to travel safely as a refugee. Mom's cousin and his family left Vietnam days before the fall of Saigon and immigrated to Los Angeles in 1975.

The older Ung generation had run away once from communism in 1954, but this time we would not be able to. The stark realization set in that our family would have to embrace the new, fanatical regime.

While Dad was in the hospital, the South Vietnamese Army made its last stand against the Viet Cong Army at Xuan Loc, only thirty-eight miles from Saigon. They were outnumbered seven to one, but still held out against the Communists for nearly two weeks, until at last they were forced to retreat. As the fighting intensified in Xuan Loc, Great Uncle #6 was worried that his general purpose store in Dinh Quan would be looted. He convinced his eldest son, Long, and brother-in-law to travel to Dinh Quan with him and retrieve the goods from his store. But on the journey back to Saigon, their truck struck a roadside bomb. Long and brother-in-law died at the scene. Great Uncle #6 suffered minor injuries to his legs.

Dad took Buu and me to the wake ceremony for Uncle Long. We had to greet all of the relatives one by one as part of respecting our elders. However, we couldn't do it without Dad's help, reminding us of each person's name. Uncle Long's funeral was very sad. He was only twenty-two years old and left behind his young wife and three daughters, age four, two, and three months. His brother-in-law left behind three wives and many children.

Uncle Long's wife, Say Van, stayed as a widow since her husband passed away in 1975 and raised her three daughters by herself as a single mom. Culturally, a *Hakka* woman is married for life to one person only, and Aunty Say Van stayed true to her *Hakka* duty and responsibilities. This custom, however, does not apply to *Hakka* men.

In the final days before the fall of Saigon, the North Vietnamese army began shelling the outlying areas heavily. We could hear helicopters flying overhead from the American evacuations and the explosions from the Communists' heavy artillery barrage, both near and far. I watched and heard the earth-shaking explosions in all directions from the top floor of our house. Boom, boom, boom. Like a fireworks show, only much more awful and deadly.

At night, some of our neighbors sought shelter from the nonstop bombing in the ground floor of our house. In my ignorance as a kid, I remember thinking at first that it was fun having my friends sleeping over in our house. It was frightening, however, to see so many men, women, and children running for their lives, with fear and desperation on their faces. They were trying to escape from Phu Thanh with whatever they could carry. I asked my parents if we were going to leave our home like those people passing by our street during the day. They told me that we had no place to run. But Mom told my siblings and me to be ready to flee anyway, in case a bomb hit our house.

My parents devised a plan in which each of my siblings would carry some form of jewelry or money on their bodies. My brother Buu and I would carry the most valuables. Mom said we were old enough to understand my parents' instructions, and that the government officials wouldn't expect young children to carry valuables. Buu and I would wear homemade money belts stuffed with hundreds of U.S. $100 bills, along with special pants with hiding places for gold chains in the elastic waist linings. By now fear had me fully in its grip. I got jumpier every time an artillery shell exploded, especially the ones closest to home. Huddling together was not fun anymore.

The Viet Cong was knocking at our door, and life as we knew it was coming to an end. The Americans and other foreigners were fleeing Saigon. The whole city was in chaos. We stopped going to school, or doing anything else, as the Viet Cong invasion approached Saigon. The government enforced a day and night curfew for the citizens. We stayed home all day, never going outside our house, and watched the activities nearby from our third-floor bedroom. On the afternoon of April 30, 1975, the news came that the Viet Cong had raised their flag over the Presidential Palace.

As a little kid, I didn't know what Communists or Viet Cong were. I had this image of them as deformed humans, resembling rats, and embodying darkness and evil. I heard they were ruthless people who killed men, women, and children, especially those with ties to the Americans or the French. When I finally saw some PAVN soldiers in a tank waving their flags on television, I said out loud, with relief in my voice, "They look just like any other Vietnamese!" Looking back, that was a strange comfort.

We continued to stay inside our house for a week after the fall of Saigon. General Tran Van Tra, the administrative deputy of the PAVN commanding general, was placed in charge of the city. The new authorities held a victory rally on May 7.[*] The people of Saigon soon realized that order was being maintained, that the new authorities looked physically the same as other Vietnamese, and the bombing had stopped. They started to calm down a bit. Life slowly went back to normal, but people were cautious about what the future held for them under the Communists.

A few months later, Great Uncle Khau and Uncle San were arrested because of their ties to the French and Americans during their years of service in the military. Although Great Uncle San had retired in the late 1960s, his brother Khau had continued serving in the military till the fall of Saigon. Uncle San's arrest was

---

[*] Information from Wikipedia: "Fall of Saigon"

a shock to our family. From that point on, Dad lived in constant fear of being arrested like his uncle, since the two men had served together. Both Sen great uncles were taken away to re-education camps. For a few years their locations were unknown. During the time they were in jail, their wives and children suffered financially and emotionally, not knowing if they were alive or had been executed.

Following their story further, in 1979 the United Nations High Commission for Refugees (UNHCR) reached an agreement with the Vietnamese government that allowed Vietnamese citizens to immigrate to United States. To do this, the UNHCR set up the Orderly Departure Program (ODP). In 1988, the United States government arranged with the Vietnamese government to take 100,000 political prisoners—people arrested for disagreeing with the government—to be released through the Orderly Departure Program. Uncle San and Uncle Khau's families were part of those who emigrated to the United States.

Living Under Communism

After the Communists captured Saigon, one of their first orders of business was to take advantage of the wealth of the South. The South Vietnamese first dong was replaced by a new currency known as the "Liberation Dong," at a rate of 1 liberation dong for 500 first dongs. This appropriation was a shock to the citizens of what had been South Vietnam. Yet the news that the dong had been devalued was only the first blow.

The new regime would also reduce how much each family could have. The government asked the citizens to come exchange all their money, but each family could only get a small amount of money back regardless how much was turned in. The amount of the remaining money was written in a small notebook provided by the government, showing the name of the head of the household and the amount available in the account. Money could only be taken out in situations of extreme hardship.

No one we knew ever got back any of the money that the government seized. Dad had anticipated that his money would be devalued under the new government. That's why he had converted most of his money into raw materials, as well as gold and US dollars. However, most Saigonese had not anticipated the Communists' confiscations and lost all their wealth after the new currency was established. Many wealthy people suffered massive losses and some ended up committing suicide or went insane and never recovered.

One of the other main objectives for the Communist government was to reduce the population of Saigon. It had become overcrowded from the influx of people during the war, and now had many unemployed people. One way they achieved this objective was by forcing former soldiers of the South Vietnamese Army to relocate to the countryside and take up farming. This was mandated under the guise of "reeducation classes" that were required if former enemy soldiers ever wanted to regain full standing in society. Widespread rumors whispered that government hoodlums would visit someone's house at night and force the family to move to a rural area and take up farming.

Most people in Saigon lived in fear of the new government and its ideology of what was good for the country. The official line of the socialist republic of Vietnam, conveyed to all its citizens, was that all people were equal. But what did that mean? Government propaganda said that all businesses belonged to the government and there could be no privately owned businesses. Officials came to each factory and took inventory of all the raw materials, machinery, and finished products owned by private citizens. They inventoried our house and appropriated all of the raw materials Dad had stockpiled, which included hundreds of fifty-pound bags of rice and soybeans, our tractor and chainsaw. Dad and other business owners worried that if they produced and sold goods, the government might accuse them of not paying taxes or of starting production without government oversight. Any perceived wrongdoing, especially by a citizen against the government, could lead to an arrest and imprisonment for life. As a result, after the war Dad's factory rarely produced anything.

Our family's lifestyle changed by necessity after the fall of Saigon. We let our housekeeper go because we had to live like everyone else. Mom went to the market daily for groceries, like everyone else. The oldest daughter, Zenh, had to take on the responsibility of cooking lunch and dinner every day. With her added responsibilities, she accepted the fact that she wouldn't be able to continue with her education. However, she was able to learn acupuncture at a trade school, attending the school in the afternoons after she finished cooking lunch and before making dinner. As a young adult, Zenh was also required by the government to do field work on one weekend each month. When Zenh's turn came, she found out the work was hard labor, and it had to be performed in extreme heat. It was so hard that my parents paid someone else to go in her place after that.

Kien had to help out with doing the laundry and taking care of Tam, who was only three years old. Tam slept with Kien at night, since Mom had to take care of Kau, sixteen months younger than Tam. At age eight, my daily responsibility was to feed the livestock kept behind the storage building next to our house. My chores also included chopping *ong choi*, or water spinach, a popular and plentiful vegetable in Vietnam, and mixing it with leftover rice porridge or rice with water. As for our livestock, we had four geese and a couple of ducks and chickens. The geese were our watchdogs with feathers. Their territorial nature and loud honking prevented the next-door Vietnamese family from stealing our goods in the storage warehouse.

Another one of my chores was to hand-wash the dishes each night after dinner, even on weekends. I only got off when I was really sick. I tried to come up with excuses to avoid washing the dishes, but my sister Zenh would just rinse them and the dishes would be waiting for me to scrub the next day. After a while I stopped making excuses, since they didn't work with Zenh. I finally learned to just accept my responsibilities.

Some of the Vietnamese families who lived on our street had been very poor before the fall of Saigon. As a result, when the government declared that all people were supposed to be equal, these families and their kids started speaking out more. The Vietnamese kids often called us names, like "*ba tao*," which means boat people. They told us, "You should go back to your country, China." I told them that this is my country. I was born here. But since we lived in one of the tallest houses in our little neighborhood, the tensions between us and the poor Vietnamese families increased, especially between the kids.

A new proclamation went out, requiring school age children to attend "reeducation classes" to learn about communism and Ho Chi Minh, the founding father of our new Vietnam. The classes, divided by age group, were held within walking distance of our homes at the neighborhood center. We called it the government's attempt to brainwash us. They taught us that Ho Chi Minh was our true grandfather. He was more important than our own blood parents or grandparents. We were all supposed to give up our wealth and comfort for the greater good of the country, and to help others who were not as fortunate. Of course, we disagreed with this concept, but our parents said just to follow along and accept what they told us unconditionally. Any refusal or disagreement could have singled out our families for arrest.

After one of those classes, a group of us girls were walking home. A gang of Vietnamese kids in the neighborhood, including a set of twin boys, began taunting us with cries of "*Ba tao*, go back home." They kept chanting as we walked past. As we approached our houses, they started shoving and pushing us. The twin boys were slapping me and pushing me lightly. I asked them to stop harassing me, but they slapped and pushed me harder.

At last I lost my temper and hit them back. I got into a fistfight with the twin boys, taking on both of them. They were about my size or a bit smaller. We exchanged a lot of punches before the fight finally ended. I took a hard punch to my mouth that gave me a split lower lip, and blood started coming out of my mouth. Yet I managed to land punches as well, hitting the boys in the eyes and around their faces.

I got into big trouble with my parents. They were disappointed in me for getting into a fight. Mom said that she couldn't believe her daughter had been fighting. She would have expected that from one of her sons, but not a daughter.

I tried to explain that the boys had been harassing me for several blocks, and kept hitting me even after I asked them to stop. My parents didn't accept any of my explanations. They said that life under the new Communist rule was not like before. Our family was now a target for those people who were jealous of our wealth and our big house.

I felt the pain from my swollen lower lip for a few days. The next day after the fight, I rode my sister's bike to the local outdoor market to get something for Mom. One of the women in the neighborhood said out loud to Mom, "What happened to Nam Moi's lip?" Mom explained to her that I stupidly got into a fight with the Vietnamese twin boys the night before. She said, "You should see the twin boys' faces. They looked worse than Nam Moi." I quickly took off with my sister's bike to avoid being yelled at by Mom again.

Attending Public School

After the end of the war there was some expectation that life would return at least in part to its normal routines. Yet life was not normal. For months we didn't go to school because of the widespread instability. The Chinese private elementary school was closed down altogether. The owner's adult children had been the teachers at the school, but they had gone back to Taiwan even before the fall of Saigon. One couple in their sixties had stayed behind, but they were later found dead from hanging. The rumor was that they were burglarized by young people. When they refused to hand over their gold, money, or jewelry, they were hanged. The school was so big that the neighbors did not hear any screams or other sounds of foul play. The only way the murders were found out was through their absence. In Vietnam, people go to the market daily for food and groceries, but this couple was noticed missing. After a while someone looked for them and their bodies were discovered.

When we finally started going back to school in the fall of 1975, we had to attend a Vietnamese public school called Loc Suong, a thirty-minute walk from home. In those days a student's class grade was based on his or her rank in the class, not by a letter grade. The students were ranked from number one through the number of students in the classroom. This ranking was very important to the parents and the neighbors as a comparative measure of their child's success in school, how smart their child was, and even the likelihood of his or her future success. Yet in the new school everything was taught in Vietnamese, by Vietnamese teachers. Since we had been attending a Chinese private school before the war ended, with most of the teaching done in Chinese, our relative lack of fluency in Vietnamese put us at a disadvantage. I couldn't understand the class lectures or even the instructions for homework assignments. In the first semester of my third-grade class, I was ranked in the lower fiftieth percentile. In those days anything less than the top tenth percentile was considered unsatisfactory to my parents. As a result, I was lectured by my parents on my unacceptable performance in the class and the need to move up in the classroom rankings.

My parents, especially my mother, emphasized the importance of an education. She had not been able to attend school due to her family circumstances and her own mother's objections to schooling for daughters. My mother was offended that I was not taking full advantage of an opportunity she never had, saying to me, "I didn't get to go to school at all. Being illiterate is like being blind. You must not be like me. Simple daily life tasks are a challenge for me."

I knew she was right, and I sought help from Thuy, one of the Vietnamese girls in the class. She was ranked first among all the kids, most of whom were Chinese. Her family was in the business of making glass jars and collecting recycled glass. She and I became very good friends. Because of her help, my academic performance in the second semester improved dramatically and my rank rose from the bottom half to the top tenth percentile. For the first time I realized that with hard work and tutoring I could learn a new language.

Learning better social skills was also a necessity. Although teachers were highly respected in our society and especially by the students, they were not paid very well. My siblings and I lived in a nice big house, and I had gradually forgotten about my parents' humble beginning, living in the front of my grandparents' factory. I had become a snobby rich kid. One day as my teacher walked by during recess, I made a giggling remark about my teacher's clothes to my friends: his blue pants were faded and had a small hole in the rear. He heard my remark and looked angrily toward me. After recess, he continued to be really unhappy. He told the class that we were going to have a surprise quiz that day. He would call on each student to provide answers to his questions.

After the second question, he called my name. Of course, I was not able to answer his question. Then he summoned me to the front of the class and asked me to bend over for three hard spanks with a bamboo stick. This method was sometimes used, but only for a very disobedient student. Most of the time a teacher would just rap our palm with a stick. My friends and I were surprised, but I knew he was taking his revenge.

I learned from that experience about the mistake I had made. I realized that my parents' attitudes had not changed since their humble beginning. And I learned to be more sympathetic toward others, not only with other students but with adults too. I understood that my teacher had had to forgo buying new clothing to use the money he earned for his family's essential needs.

Harassment of the Rich

Under the new regime, Communist party members, or "comrades," took over the houses of families who had left Saigon. In many neighborhoods these comrades lived among the local residents, acting as the government's representatives to watch over the citizens. The comrades had the authority to arrest anyone for any perceived wrongdoing. Some of them were reasonable, but others were little despots. On our street a few comrades moved into a house which had been owned by one of our Vietnamese neighbors. One comrade was nicknamed "Crazy 7," because he was so irrational. He targeted our family right from the beginning, and harassed us almost daily because of our big house and our possessions, including the things Dad had stockpiled in the months prior to the fall of Saigon.

Crazy 7 had a particular fixation on my family's motorcycles. Dad had an old model, but Zenh and Hong had newer ones with more horsepower. Crazy 7 would greet us in the traditional Vietnamese manner, asking us, "Are you well?" After that he would seat himself on one of the new motorcycles. One weekend Hong was playing a record on the first floor of our house, which overlooked the ground floor and the front door. Comrade Crazy 7 was walking by our house and heard the stereo playing Chinese songs by Teresa Tan, a famous singer from Taiwan. Dad had taken Hong and Xi to see her concert when she came to perform before the fall of Saigon.

Crazy 7 kicked open the metal gate, ran into the house, and charged up the stairs angrily. He grabbed Hong by the front of his shirt and accused him of trying to overthrow the government by playing unapproved music. He broke Hong' record into pieces and confiscated our stereo system and other records. He said the government did not allow citizens to have a radio, because we would use it to get information on how to overthrow the government.

That was all a lie, of course. The next day, as I was playing with other kids in the neighborhood, we heard him blasting my family's stereo system, playing one of our Santana records.

I was very upset and resentful about these "comrades," especially since they were just poor farmers from the countryside. Communist propaganda told us that all citizens were equal and all were loved by the founding father of our country, Ho Chi Minh. In reality, the methods used by the Communist government to control the citizens in the South put power in the hands of poor government officials, without effective checks or balances. Corruption was widespread, and many officials took advantage of their power to take revenge on wealthy people, including many of Chinese descent, because of their longstanding resentment and envy.

The Mentor

In early 1977, Great Uncle #7 made arrangements for his two younger sons, Tac and Kan, to escape Vietnam by pretending to work on a fishing crew based on Phu Quoc Island. He paid an undisclosed amount of gold for this arrangement, with the intent that his sons would leave the country at the first opportunity. Tac and Kan were 16 and 13 years old at the time. After many unsuccessful escape attempts, finally in October 1977, they managed to board a fishing boat heading toward Thailand. As they got close to that country's shores, though, they were accosted by Thai pirates. The thieves boarded their boat, and took all the gold and diamond jewelry that the refugees were wearing. However, they were reluctant to rape the young girls and women, as they often did, because in this case the refugee boat contained mostly men. The refugees outnumbered the pirates. Instead, they proceeded to slowly tow the boat for hours as they discussed the next steps amongst themselves. Eventually, the two boats reached Song Ka Island in Thailand, which housed many Vietnamese refugees. As the two boats approached the island, the refugees on the island noticed the Vietnamese refugees on the boat and flagged them down. In response, the Thai pirates released the refugee boat and took off.

Tac and Kan spent six months living in the refugee camp on Song Ka Island. Since they were both minors, a church in San Francisco sponsored them and arranged for them to live with a family from the church. On April 6, 1978, they immigrated to San Francisco. After living with the sponsored family for several months, they asked for permission to move in with a family friend from Vietnam who was living in Los Angeles. Their sponsor family agreed and bought them the bus tickets they needed. Tac and Kan were the first Ungs to arrive in the United States. In time, they would become sponsors for more Ung refugees.

Figure 7-1: Great Uncle #7's family with Uncle Hai's wife, Binh, 1974.

According to the new Vietnamese government, within two years of the capture of Saigon, a million people had left the city. To them, though, that was only partial progress. The state wanted another 500,000 to leave.

In 1978, the government began to restructure Vietnamese society. It nationalized private businesses, and announced that citizens living in the city would be relocated to rural areas to work in agricultural communes. Since the Communists had taken over, we had heard a lot of propaganda, but not seen much action in forcing citizens to relocate. This time, however, the government really did take action, and forced some families to leave their homes. We were nervous about this policy because, at that time, most of the wealthy people in Vietnam were of Chinese descent. We lived frugally, so as not to show off our wealth. But still, we would make ideal examples for the socialist government.

The Communist had tried various approaches in controlling the citizens in the South. They unsuccessfully attempted to enforce a policy that required all the citizens to buy government-produced goods. Their trucks brought certain types of vegetables, fruit, and meat to our neighborhood. Each family was supposed to buy set amounts based on the size of the household. However, we bought our daily groceries from an outdoor market that was a ten-minute walk from our house. When the government closed the outdoor market, people bought goods from makeshift markets which operated only a few hours each day to avoid government action. A Vietnamese woman came to our house and asked my parents what they needed, and then she delivered the order discreetly, either the same day or the next day. That was how Dad bought his beer and premium beef.

To further complicate our position, Vietnam and China had very poor relations and became enemies. In fact, China would attempt to invade Vietnam in February 1979. The Communists feared that the Chinese living in Vietnam would side with China and attempt to overturn the government. For this reason, the Vietnamese government wanted all people of Chinese descent to leave the country.

In response, many families in Saigon sought to find berths on boats leaving for Malaysia, the Philippines, Hong Kong, Singapore, or Thailand. Prior to 1978, many refugees found asylum by crossing by land into Thailand, after which they were either sent to Malaysia or stayed in Thailand for processing and resettlement. Others were ferried in small boats to the territorial waters of other countries in Southeast Asia. Many of these boats were not seaworthy and had to be rescued by larger vessels while in international waters.

Life as we knew it was over after the fall of Saigon. Ever since the communists had taken over Saigon, my family's position in Vietnam had steadily deteriorated. Being Chinese with a successful slipper business made us the target. Our family endured daily harassment by the local comrades in the neighborhood. After Great Uncle #7's two sons successfully escaped from Vietnam, my parents were determined to find ways so that we could all leave and find freedom.

Chapter 8

The First Wave

After more than a year of living under the Communist regime, many families with the means tried to find ways to flee the country. On most days Dad would wake up from his afternoon nap, get cleaned up, put on business clothes, and then head to town. He would meet with his friends or acquaintances at a coffee shop or restaurant to find out the latest news.

In 1977, Dad started to take the entire family out to dinner at different restaurants, mostly on Thursday nights, but sometimes he mixed up the routine. He had a specific objective in mind. The first time we all went out to dinner, he locked the front door of our house. In Vietnam, people opened their front doors in the morning and left them open until they were ready to head to bed at night. Seeing our front door closed in the evening alarmed our neighbors. When we came home from our outing, some of them were surprised to see us again. They thought we had abandoned our home and left the country. The next day, the whole neighborhood got the word that we just went out for dinner.

Dad had expected this reaction. As part of his escape strategy, he wanted people in the neighborhood to become used to our coming and going as a family. When the day came when we would actually attempt to leave the country, we would not be detained by local comrades or blocked by our poor neighbors.

On these restaurant nights, Dad came home around 5:30 p.m.

As we heard the roar from Dad's moped, I would make the announcement to everyone, "Dad is home." We all gathered on the ground floor to hear Dad's plan for the evening, which restaurant we were going to and the type of food they served. Then the whole family headed out to dinner. Since we had eleven family members and no car, we had to split up on several bikes and one motorcycle. Dad took Mom, Buu, and Kau on his moped. Kien took Tam on her bike, with Xi on another bike, Hong and Num on a third bike, and Zenh and I on the fourth bike. If the restaurant was far away, Hong and Zenh would take the motorcycles, even though this was rare. The people with bikes would leave the house a bit earlier to get a head start on the motorcycle riders.

Dad introduced us to all the different kinds of food Saigon had to offer. As we enjoyed the meals, we would talk about how the food was prepared, a topic which engaged the whole family. If the food was new to us and we had no idea how it was being prepared, Dad would give the restaurant owner or the waiter some money so we could talk with the head chef.

On one special Thursday, Mom asked us to get ready earlier than normal. This time and several other times my parents invited Phuong, granddaughter of the neighboring Gip family, to join us for dinner. She was the same age as Tam, with their birthdays less than a month apart. Her grandfather, Mr. Gip, was very close to us when we were kids. My brothers Num, Xi, Buu, and I spent many summer nights at her grandparents' house listening to her grandfather telling us stories about the olden days. We spent more time with Mr. Gip than our own grandfather, since Phuong was the Gip family's first grandchild.

On this special day, my parents had arranged to have a family picture taken before my four older siblings left home—for good. To avoid attracting attention from government officials or people who might know us, Dad arranged for the photo session at a private home and not a studio. We all lined up on the terrace, with all ten of us children, including Phuong, from the shortest to the tallest.

Figure 8-1: Nine Ung siblings and Phuong, April 1978.

Figure 8-2: Family picture with Phuong, April 1978.

For one of our last meals eating out as a family, Dad took us to a boat restaurant called My Canh, which means "beautiful scenes" in Vietnamese. I remember asking for our usual favorite, Hai Nan

chicken on rice. But Dad said
that because this was a fancy
restaurant in the busy section
of Saigon harbor, we should try
lobster or crab. That was the
first time we tried the popular
dish of steamed lobsters dipped
in melted butter sauce. My
younger siblings and I were not
used to eating lobsters or butter,
so we didn't enjoy our meals.
However, we knew that we
were more fortunate than most
people. They had never been to
a fancy restaurant like My Canh
in their entire lives.

Figure 8-3: Mom (Kieu), Dad (Ly Sang), Buu, and Kau at My Canh restaurant, April 1978.

After dinner, everyone rushed to get home, since it took a
while by bike to ride to Phu Thanh from the harbor. When a
photographer asked Dad if he wanted to take a picture with the
children he was taking, he decided it would be a good idea. That's
why the picture included just the four people who were traveling
on Dad's moped: Dad, Mom, Buu, and Kau.

In April 1978, my parents decided the time had come to find
passage for my four oldest siblings. Desperate to find a way out,
they entrusted this task to a Chinese businessman who had a
toothpick factory in the neighborhood. His brother Wan was a
close friend of Zenh's. For twenty-four ounces of gold, equaling
six ounces per person, he arranged for Zenh, Hong, Kien, and Xi
to leave Vietnam on a private fishing boat, similar to the plan used
earlier for Tac and Kan. Dad paid half the payment of gold up
front and the second half after my siblings successfully escaped.

In the weeks prior to leaving home, Zenh made a set of traditional
Vietnamese clothing, with a cotton shirt whose buttons started
from the center of the neck toward the armpit and along the side

and pajama-like pants for her and Kien. They washed and hung the clothing in the sun several times to make them look used. That way they would fit in with the locals as they traveled by public transportation from Saigon to Binh Tuy.

The journey took over eight hours by bus. Kien and Hong went first, and Zenh and Xi followed the next day. Many desperate families from the city chose this option since it was a proven route. Government officials set up checkpoints entering Binh Tuy, and only residents were allowed to enter the area. If they were questioned by the police at the check point, they were told to pretend that they lived in Binh Tuy. All four siblings arrived at the staging house safely from Saigon. Then they waited for the opportunity to leave.

Dad's Arrest

Soon, the word spread that my four older siblings were no longer at home. The Communist government office in Phu Thanh sent a group of officials to check our house and to inventory everything to make sure that my parents were not trying to overthrow the government. The fact that my older brothers and sisters were suddenly gone was just an excuse for the government officials launch an investigation. In a follow-up visit, four officials came to our house early in the morning.

This time the inventory was focused on personal items in our house, including money, jewelry, the number of bicycles, motorcycles, stereos, yards of fabric, and pots and pans. They also counted the number of bags of rice, the square footage of wood, and so on. Mom asked me to follow two comrades who were inventorying the items on the second and third floors of our house. Zenh kept a cabinet full of fabric and sewing materials and her personal jewelry in our second-floor girls' bedroom. I saw one of the officials put a necklace with a heart pendant in his pocket. I thought it was not right, and when they all met up on the ground floor, I asked Dad why this comrade had put my sister's necklace in his pocket. He told the head inspector what I had said, and the comrade with the necklace said, "Oh, I forgot to put it back since we had so many things to account for." They left the house taking things they deemed excessive and unnecessary for us, especially now that my four oldest siblings were gone.

The next night after dinner, comrades from the local Phu Thanh office came to arrest Dad. They read him a statement about why he was being taken. They put him in handcuffs and immediately led him to a car, in his undershirt and shorts. My siblings and I stood there in shock at seeing my father taken away. We began crying and grabbing his feet, refusing to let him leave. He calmly told us that he would come back home soon. He was not a criminal and he hadn't done anything wrong. It was all a misunderstanding, and it would be resolved. He told me to help Mom take care of my younger brothers and sister. I nodded obediently even as tears streamed down my face.

Since our older siblings had left, Tam and I had slept in the girls' room alone. Buu and Num had to sleep in the room next door by themselves. The second floor felt strange with so few of us. It had been filled with people and activities. Sister Zenh would make clothing in her sewing area. Hong would practice his classical guitar. Kien would study her English out loud. Yet now the second floor living area was too empty and scary quiet. Even our own shadows made us jumpy.

My life changed dramatically after my older brothers and sisters left home. I became the oldest daughter. There were no maids to help, and I had to take on some of the tasks that my two older sisters had done. Each evening after arriving home from school, my chores were to cook rice, build a wood fire to boil hot water for baths, and chop *ong choi* with leftover rice to feed the chickens, ducks, and geese. I also had to help take care of my younger sister Tam. On weekends I had to wash all the clothing by hand and hang them on the clotheslines on the first-floor terrace. When the government truck arrived in our neighborhood, I had to get in line for food, representing my family.

My older brother Num, thirteen years old and two years my
senior, didn't feel any need to contribute to the family, and my
parents didn't ask him for help. After all, in the *Hakka* tradition
household tasks were supposed to be done by females only. My
younger brother Buu was only nine years old. He and I were
close as kids because for a long time we were the two youngest
children, before Tam and Kau came along. I was also responsible
for tutoring Buu in his schoolwork. During my parents' absence
he was glued to my side most of the time.

The day after Dad's arrest, Mom went crazy like a chicken with
its head cut off. She tried to find out where they took Dad. Being
illiterate and speaking Vietnamese poorly had made this task
especially hard. She went around to all the temples, praying for
Dad's return.

For the next few weeks she often left Kau and Tam with me. My
mother was and still is a very religious person. Actually, I believe
she is more superstitious than religious. In keeping with her
beliefs, she started a ritual of lighting incense in a chain so as not
to let it burn out, from 7:00 a.m. to 10:00 p.m. each day during
Dad's absence. This ritual supported her prayers for Dad's safe
return.

I had the responsibility of keeping the incense going on the days
I had no school and each day after school. Every twenty minutes
or so, I had to light a new incense stick. Since I often played with
girls in the neighborhood in front of our house and the incense
offering was on the second-floor balcony facing the street, I
sometimes had to race upstairs get to it in time. I was only four
feet tall, and it took me a few minutes since we had a big house.

One time I forgot to keep track of the time and the incense
burned out. Mom got very mad at me and said, "If you want your
dad to come home, then you have to do your part in keeping
the incense going." She laid the guilt on me, which I felt was too
harsh. Like her own mother, Mom treated her daughters unfairly

compared to her sons. She put so many expectations on me since I was now the oldest daughter in the family, but I was only a kid.

One day Mom said she would be away from the house for hours to visit temples and seek answers regarding Dad's prospects for a safe return. This was Mom's way of trying to make sense of the new world under Communist rule. Before she left, she instructed me to cook lunch for everyone, along with baby-sitting four-year-old Tam and three-year-old Kau.

Buu tried to be helpful, but he was a kid himself at age nine, with no prior responsibilities of any kind. I had to cut and chop pork into fine pieces like ground meat, chop dry vegetables, then cook them all together in a clay pot. In those days I also had to build a fire with coals before we could cook. We didn't have any modern conveniences for cooking food, except for a rice cooker. This simple meal required a lot of preparation, especially while taking care of my two youngest siblings. Everyone got hungry, complaining about when the food would be served. I was overwhelmed with taking on the role of an adult. When I finally got this simple meal ready, I decided it would be easier to eat it picnic style since we were all kids. I put a big mat on the floor and we all sat around the rice cooker and steamed pork with vegetables in a big bowl in the center.

As we were starting to eat the food I had prepared, my older brother Num came home from playing with his friends and demanded to eat. I asked him to help feed Tam and Kau because they were very hungry. But Num only served himself, putting half the food in his bowl, and ignored my request. I asked him again and he said, "I don't care about anyone else except for me." I got very angry with his attitude after my ordeal of cooking and watching my younger siblings. I said to him, "You are so selfish. Our dad is in jail and Mom is out trying to find help to get Dad home. Our older siblings are not here to help out any longer. How can you be so selfish?"

He ignored me and continued eating, like a hungry dog gulping down food before anyone else could get to it. I was so outraged that I ordered him to not eat any more. I told him, "You selfish jerk. You can't eat all that food."

He said "If I can't eat it, you guys can't eat it either."

I defended the food as though my life depended on it. I had never been so angry. I knew that I couldn't win fighting him. He was much bigger and stronger. But I didn't care and was determined to not let him eat any more. I grabbed his bowl and we started yelling at each other. The younger kids started crying and asked us to stop fighting.

Then Num knocked the food over: rice, meat, and vegetables spilled all over the floor. Enraged, I jumped on him and wrestled with him. After several minutes Num finally managed to push me off and left us. He had eaten half of the food, gotten in a fight with me, and then just walked off.

Mom had always treated him like he was special, overcompensating for the way our neighbors teased him like an adopted child, with the nickname "Ong Nam." That means "mister number 5" in Vietnamese. She made excuses for his misbehavior and irresponsibility throughout all of his childhood.

As I was cleaning up the mess we had made, with most of the food on the floor, Mom came home. Tam, Kau, and Buu ran to greet her with joy. Then she walked into the dining area and saw the mess we had made. She was shocked to see food everywhere. She yelled at me, "I left you alone one day with these kids, and look at what a mess this is!"

My younger siblings told her how hungry they were and how they were scared because Num and I were fighting. Mom helped to feed Kau and Tam as I cleaned up the mess. I grew up really fast that day, feeling the full weight of an adult's responsibilities.

My brother Num never apologized to me, nor I to him. We both felt we were right. I remember thinking, why couldn't he be the one who had emigrated? None of my other older siblings would have done that.

In May 1978, one week after Dad's arrest, the government required all citizens to replace the Liberated Dong with the new Vietnamese Dong. No one had any warning beforehand. We had to change our money for a second time since the Communist government took over. The Liberation Dong was replaced by the new Vietnamese Dong, at a promised exchange rate of one new Dong for each 0.8 Liberation Dong. I had no way of knowing how to avoid this government thievery, because Dad was in jail and Mom was out praying at various temples, leaving me home to watch over Tam and Kau.

A government "comrade" came to our house and told me that we needed to go exchange our money, because we were one of the last families who had not done so yet. I knew where the metal container was that my parents kept their cash in. It was too big and heavy for me to carry, so I dragged the box to the nearby house that the government had commandeered for their local office. The officials counted all the money in the container, but only handed me a couple hundred new dongs back, plus a small book in which they recorded the total amount they had kept. I was shocked, and asked them why they had given me back so little. The comrade's explanation was that every family got the same amount, regardless of the amount we turned in. I was outraged and told the comrades how unfair this system was, and how they were trying to cheat me out of my money because I was only a child. There was no logical explanation of how this could be fair. I felt helpless, and got so angry that I demanded that they give me the old money back. I'd rather use it as toilet paper than give it to the government. That was my parents' hard-earned money.

The comrades threatened that if I were older, I would be arrested and sent to jail or even executed. Some of my neighbors saw that I was yelling at the comrades, refusing to accept their treatment of me. They hurried to fetch my grandmother, and when she arrived, she ordered me to go home. I said I would not go until I had gotten my money back.

She pleaded with me, and said because of my behavior the government could execute my family, including my grandparents and our extended family. I knew I had to give in when she said, "You don't want your family to be executed, do you?" I shook my head and agreed to go with her. I cried all the way home, holding her hand with one hand and the bank book with the paltry amount of money in the other.

A makeshift meeting was finally called to judge Dad's crime. Government officials held a so-called judgment by the people of Phu Thanh regarding the crimes Dad committed. He had to kneel in public in front of everyone with his hands tied behind his back. He was labeled as a "bad man" for being a businessman. The officials asked the people whether Dad should go to jail for the crime of not knowing the location of his four older children after they left home, since they were minors, and for profiting from the labor of the people by being a businessman. The government officials said, "Should Ung Ly Sang be put in jail for his crimes? Or should the government let him go free?"

Dad had a reputation of being generous to our neighbors and poor people in our town. He helped pay for families who couldn't afford medications. For several months before he sold his van, he used it as an ambulance to take people to the hospital for free, sometimes in the middle of the night. He gave money to his sister to build a two-story house since her husband was poor. On many special occasions, he would buy an entire roasted pig and share it with all the neighbors. The citizens had the opportunity to punish Dad, but instead they said he had always been a generous man with a good heart.

After the so-called judgment by the people, Dad was released, but the meeting was actually just for show. Dad came home only after several weeks in jail, suffering the public humiliation that goes with being behind bars. The story Dad told us was that he paid off a series of government officials with small or large amounts of money, depending on their individual ranks. He realized, as he lay in his jail cell, that he had made a mistake in not bribing Comrade Crazy 7, which led to his being jailed in the first place.

The people working for the government had a very low salary, barely enough to support their families. Therefore, Dad insisted on paying for lunch and dinner for everyone who worked at the jail. He also offered to pay two months of lunches and dinners for each government worker in the office if he were set free, and he honored his agreement after being set free. He was more honest than the government that had arrested him.

Escape Plan Fails

While all of this was going on, my older four siblings still were waiting in limbo. After Zenh, Hong, Xi, and Kien arrived at the safe house in Binh Tuy, they had to wait for the right opportunity to escape on a fishing boat. Most of the time they were left alone in the house with the windows closed and covered. While they were hidden, the man responsible for their escape, Mr. Wong, was taking three- and four-day trips with his wife to visit friends and family. They were living it up with the gold Dad paid him. After six weeks my siblings were taken out twice on a small fishing boat, but each time they ended up turning back for one reason or another.

Dad got word of what was happening and had a change of heart. He heard about possibly chartering a Panamanian ship that would carry asylum seekers out of Vietnam, with the government's blessing. Many people had lost their lives on small boats, like the fishing boat in the original plan, because they were not sufficiently seaworthy in the ocean, far from the safety of shore. The Panamanian ship would provide a far safer passage.

In those days people did not have telephones in their homes, and telegraphs were not safe from government spying. Dad paid a woman he trusted who had relatives living in the same town to send word to my siblings to return to Saigon because we were abandoning the plan. Since it would not be safe for them to return home, Dad arranged for the four of them to live in three separate locations. Kien would live with Uncle Ho, who owned a restaurant where we had eaten regularly and become good friends of the family. Hong and Xi stayed at Great Uncle #7's house on the top floor in Lo Sieu, and Zenh stayed with a friend's family.

For several months they hid in their rooms most of the time. They could not let anyone see them or know of their presence in the house. Zenh and Hong loved to read, so they spent their time reading books, newspapers, and old magazines. Xi was the youngest and he had the hardest time, just doing nothing and being bored. The situation for Kien was different. She worked alongside the Ho family in their home, preparing food for the restaurant's business at night. Having a daily working routine made her days go by quickly. Every few weeks Mom and Dad visited each of my siblings, but did not bring the younger kids, to prevent the possibility of our accidently telling our friends about my siblings.

Amid all the secrecy and rumors swirling about possible escape routes, the strain of waiting reached a peak. Luckily, a way out finally opened up. My four oldest siblings would find a safe passage abroad. And the rest of the family was not far behind them.

Chapter 9

A Safe Passage

With the rise of anti-Chinese sentiment in Vietnam, many ethnic Chinese like my family became increasingly desperate to leave and were willing to pay smugglers to guarantee a successful departure. This created a lucrative opportunity for people who had boats, government contacts, and who were willing to traffic in asylum seekers. This created a demand for more boats, peaking in mid-1978. The problem was, Vietnam lacked shipyards for building large vessels, and many of the small boats built for smuggling were unsafe in the open sea.

Would-be Chinese refugees with sufficient means looked for something larger and safer. The Panamanian ship *Southern Cross* was just such a vessel. An ethnic Chinese businessman negotiated an arrangement with the Vietnamese government to buy the ship to transport asylum seekers. It was a good deal for the government, which was able to get rid of unwanted ethnic Chinese. At the same time, it could appropriate a significant part of their wealth. Still, for ethnic Chinese it presented a relatively safe and cost-effective way to escape the increasingly repressive conditions in Vietnam.

Word got around in the Chinese business community about this opportunity for anyone with the ability to pay in gold. The fee, which was shared between the Vietnamese government and the boat promoters, was eleven ounces for each child and fourteen ounces for each adult. The government looked the other way to allow the refugees to escape, but no one was fooled by this quasi-official pretense. In order to convince the asylum seekers that there really was a ship waiting for them close by, grapes and apples were provided as tangible proof, since grapes and apples were not commonly available after the war ended.

Great Uncle #7 told Dad and other Ungs the news, and gave Dad some grapes to take home with him. When Dad showed the grapes to Mom and the kids, he gave me two of them. I ate one, and the second one I sucked in my mouth for hours. I only took it out now and then to show my friends. When Mom asked me why I was still sucking on the grape, I told her that I wanted to save it. I finally ate it just before I fell asleep, because I didn't want to choke on it as I fell asleep.

Boarding the *Southern Cross*

Passage on the *Southern Cross* was a second chance for my older siblings to leave the country. Fortunately, my parents still had enough gold to pay for their passage. In late July 1978, Zenh, Hong, Kien, and Xi were ready to board the ship. My parents took me to say goodbye at a secret gathering place, an abandoned chicken farm outside Saigon.

The thought of them actually leaving us was hard on me emotionally, especially because I was so close to my elder sisters. Each was more like a second mother to me, since Mom had always been busy with running the business or caring for my younger siblings.

After we arrived at the chicken farm, I saw the four of them, along with many of other relatives who were also leaving. Altogether there were more than twenty people, including Great Aunty #7 with two of her daughters, Aunty Mui, Aunty My, Great Aunty #7's mother, Great Aunty #7's younger brother's family of eleven people, and Great Uncle #9's family of nine people. Uncle Luong, Dad's youngest brother, was also leaving, along with Aunty Tchat with her husband, Ho Minh, and two young sons Tuong and Quy. Great Uncle #11's son, Uncle Gieng was also leaving on the *Southern Cross*.

At that time, I had not seen my siblings for months. I was very excited and sad at the same time. Seeing them again brought me joy. Yet it was hard to say goodbye, especially because of the unknown risks ahead of them. We did not know if we would ever be able to reunite with them. Many people had already died at sea. At least they were taking the safest boat we could find.

The time to end our visit came too soon; my parents and I had to head home. I started crying loudly, nonstop, clinging to my sisters Zenh and Kien. My parents had to peel me off them. After the visit, the worst thing was that I couldn't even tell anyone about it because that could have put Dad at risk of being arrested again. I was sad and on edge for days, hoping that we would hear news that they had made the journey safely. For weeks Dad and many Ung relatives were glued to the AM radio, listening for any news related to "*Southern Cross*." We even avoided flipping over the fish we cooked while they were at sea. My family and most Chinese people held the superstitious belief that flipping over a cooked fish would cause a boat to capsize.

After we left that afternoon, I later learned, Zenh, Hong, Kien, Xi, and our relatives waited at the chicken farm until after dark. They were then transported by bus to Cat Lai harbor, and transferred to four large fishing boats. They spent the rest of the night trying to sleep in the cramped boats. The next morning, the *Southern Cross* collected hundreds of asylum seekers waiting at the mouth of the Saigon River. The ship forged into international waters, where it radioed for assistance, claiming that it had been swamped by hundreds of asylum seekers from four large fishing junks.

The strategy was to convince Singapore or Malaysia that this was a legitimate rescue of desperate refugees, in hopes that they would be taken into the refugee camps of one of those countries. Neither Singapore nor Malaysia bought the story, however, for they were aware of the Vietnamese government's complicity in receiving money from the passengers. They were concerned that if they received these boat people, they would be encouraging human trafficking by the Vietnamese government.

Unaware of these issues, my brothers and sisters and relatives just tried to survive the journey. The refugees were given coal and food supplies for individual families to cook for themselves on the upper deck of the ship, but most of our female relatives were too seasick to care about food. Fortunately, in July and August the sea was relatively calm; otherwise, their suffering from seasickness would have been worse. Great Uncle #9 led the Ung young men to the upper deck to cook food for their families, using a large cracker tin can as a pot. They cooked rice gruel for everyone.

When the *Southern Cross* attempted to land in Malaysia, the passengers were not allowed to disembark, but the Malaysian authorities did take the critically ill off the ship. After the Malaysian navy escorted the ship back into international waters, the *Southern Cross* tried to land in Singapore but was rejected there also. Finally, after two weeks at sea without a safe port available, the *Southern Cross* sailed into Indonesian waters and deliberately drifted onto a rocky outcrop called Pengibu Island. The Indonesian authorities were suspicious about the ship grounding, but didn't suspect that the ship was trafficking refugees. The United Nations High Commission for Refugees (UNHCR) requested that the Indonesian authorities grant the Vietnamese passengers temporary asylum while third-country resettlement places were found.

For two weeks they stayed on Pengibu Island. Each day they trekked up a mountain to a spring to get water for cooking and drinking. Only one family lived on the island, and the refugees were so hungry that they looted all the livestock and the house itself. When the family arrived home at the end of the day, they were greeted by more than a thousand Vietnamese refugees.

After those two weeks the Indonesian government transported the refugees to a refugee camp. A collection of plywood houses were constructed, but with so many people, the amount of space allotted for each person was merely a foot and half by six feet on a plywood panel.

Because Dad was liable to be arrested again, he had devised a plan for my brothers and sisters to send a coded telegraph message to a neighbor's house to let us know when they arrived safely. The coded message was "Phung Xi Moi," which are the nicknames of my siblings. Zenh was Phung, Xi was Xi, and Kien was Moi. When put together, the three nicknames sounded like the real name of one person. After my siblings reached the Indonesian refugee camp, four weeks after departing Vietnam, a telegraph arrived at our neighbor's house with a message saying "Phung Xi Moi from Indonesia."

Figure 9-1: *Southern Cross* Panamanian Ship grounded in Indonesia, August 1978.

Seeking Asylum

The refugees on the *Southern Cross* were affluent Chinese people from Vietnam. They carried with them United States dollars and gold. Great Uncle #9 personally carried $1,000 with him on this journey, kept hidden, of course. He and Great Aunty #9 carried the money on their bodies in a money belt. Many local businesses saw an opportunity to supply the demands of these refugees and set up businesses close to the camp. Since the refugees were free to come and go, those with money could buy food and products for

Figure 9-2: *Southern Cross* refugees camp out on Pengibu Island, Indonesia, August 1978.

Figure 9-3: Great Uncle #9 (fifth man from the left) with his fellow refugees.

Figure 9-4: Great Uncle #9 with his fellow refugees study English in the Indonesia refugee camp, 1978.

their daily needs. On one occasion, all the Ung relatives were able to dress up and visit towns and temples in Indonesia. Although my brothers and sisters and my Ung relatives were refugees, they took the best advantage of their opportunities.

The slippers my siblings wore on their journey were specially made for them by my parents. Twenty-four-karat gold necklaces and rings were embedded in each of the slippers. Since the Communist government didn't allow the refugees to leave the

Figure 9-5: Indonesian boating excursion. Far right boat: Xi, Aunties My and Mui in the front; Kien, Hong, and Zenh standing.

Figure 9-6: Four siblings, relatives, and friends' excursion to town in Indonesia, 1978.

Figure 9-7: Zenh, Hong, Kien, and Xi in Indonesia, 1978.

Figure 9-8: Ho Minh's family with Luong in Winnipeg, Canada, 1981.

country with U.S. dollars or gold, Dad thought of this ingenious way around the prohibition. For weeks my parents had experimented with how to insert the right amount of gold weight without impacting the functionality of the slippers.

Since my four siblings were minors, Dad had told them to register for refugee processing as members of Great Aunty #7's family. This would guarantee my siblings' asylum in the United States, since Uncle Tac and Uncle Kan already lived in California and could act as sponsors.

Uncle Tac also sponsored Great Uncle #9's family and Uncle Gieng to immigrate to Los Angeles. Great Aunty #7's brother's family of eleven people immigrated to Australia.

Aunty Tchat, her husband, Ho Minh, and two little kids, Tuong and Quy, along with Uncle Luong, immigrated to Winnipeg, Canada.

Aunty Tchat, her husband Minh, their two small children, along with Uncle Luong arrived in Winnipeg, Canada, just a few days before Christmas in 1978. I'm sure the frigid weather, typically 10 degree F., in December was unexpected. However, their decision to immigrate to Canada was influenced by wanting to end the difficult journey for Tuong and Quy, their two small children. Aunty Tchat and her husband Minh chose one of the first countries willing to accept them. Soon after they arrived, the entire family settled into a small apartment and Minh found work at a textile factory. Over the next few years, the family would adjust well to life in Canada, and Aunty Tchat gave birth to their third child, Sam, in 1980.

In February 1979, my siblings, along with Great Aunty #7's family of four (Grandma, Great Aunty #7, Aunty Mui, and Aunty My) immigrated to Los Angeles. For the first year the eight of them, plus Uncle Tac and Uncle Kan, all shared a two-bedroom apartment in Chinatown. It was a far cry from our spacious house, but they were home free at last. Now all we had to do—the seven of us who were left behind—was to join them. That would prove far harder, and longer, than anyone had ever imagined.

Chapter 10

Risking It All

Escape by Night on the *Tung An*

Including the *Southern Cross*, a total of four Panamanian ships were carrying human cargo and paying off the Vietnamese government. The other three with similar size were the *Hai Hong* to Malaysia, the *Tung An* to the Philippines, and the *Huey Fong* to Hong Kong. Each was forced to carry close to 2,500 refugees to maximize profit for the officials, twice as many as the *Southern Cross*. Since the *Southern Cross* refugees were the first wave of a massive exodus from Vietnam, there was a push to get them resettled to Western countries as soon as possible, because thousands more refugees were following behind them. The refugee crisis peaked during July 1979.

After my four siblings arrived safely in Indonesia, Dad decided that the time had come to risk it all. He began to make plans for the rest of my immediate family to leave Vietnam. As for the grandparents from Dad's side, the plan was to leave on a later ship with their other children's families, Uncle Quan Sang or Aunty Lee Guu. Dad also made arrangements for Mom's parents and the three unmarried siblings (Sanh, Han, and Ngoc) to leave together with the hope that they would repay Dad in the future. Overall, Dad spent a total of over two hundred ounces of twenty-four-karat gold for our family of eleven and grandparents' family of five. The cost of gold in 1978 was $200 per ounce, which equates to nearly $45,000. The remainder of Dad's gold was given to his sister Aunty Lee Guu so her family could leave on a later ship.

However, she and her husband decided to stay in Vietnam.

In early October 1978, my grandparents' family of five traveled from Song Mao to Saigon and waited for the day they would depart. During that time my grandparents lived at Grandfather's sister house while Uncle Han and Aunty Ngoc came to live with us. We were told that they came for schooling in Saigon. A few days before our departure in early November 1978, Mom gave one brown nylon carrying bag apiece to Uncle Han, Aunty Ngoc, Num, Buu, and me. My parents told us not to mention anything to our friends or neighbors; otherwise, the local comrades might stop us from leaving home.

We packed our bags with four sets of our newest clothing, toothpaste, toothbrush, toilet paper, a light blanket, and some dry goods. In addition, I carefully packed a few of the smaller family photos in three or four layers of plastic bags to protect them from water damage. These photos were the most valuable memories of our lives in Vietnam.

On November 17, 1978, the night before we had to report to the gathering center, my parents hired a truck to drive Num, Buu, Uncle Han, Aunty Ngoc, and me to a relative's house ten minutes away so that we could sleep there. Dad handed me a new Orient watch like the ones he had given Kien and Zenh, except my face plate color was purple. Mom gave me a gold necklace with a heart pendant to wear. I left home without saying goodbye to any of my friends or relatives. Each of us left carrying our brown nylon bag and my parents' luggage along with a bag of dry goods, two tin cans of powdered baby milk, a red bucket, scissors, a small knife, a blue tarp, and ropes. My parents were more prepared than other refugees. Dad thought of bringing a bucket for carrying water, a tarp along with ropes to block the sun, and tin powdered milk cans that could be used as cookware or to store food. Handles were soldered onto the tin cans for carrying hot food or water. As for Dad, Mom, Tam, and Kau, they would leave home in the morning on his moped, like any normal day heading out to town, without any telltale luggage.

We spent a long night filled with anxiety. We had so many questions with no answers. What would this journey be like? I had never been on a ship before. At age eleven and a half, I knew this was not a vacation. Everyone we came in contact with were sad and fearful, like this was the last time they would ever see us. We had heard of people who had died at sea because they fled the country in small boats. In our minds dying at sea was a real possibility. To ensure against such a fate, my parents had paid a higher amount of gold to get us on a Panamanian ship that they believed would be safer. But no amount of insurance can cover all risks, and we didn't know what this voyage held in store for us.

The next morning, my parents, Tam, and Kau joined us, as planned. A small passenger truck came to pick us up at dusk and drove all of us to a chicken farm where everyone assembled. Several of our relatives were accompanying us on this journey. Grandfather had his family of five (Grandfather, Grandmother, Uncle Sanh, Uncle Han, and Aunty Ngoc). Great Uncle #11 had a family of six people—Great Uncle #11, his mother-in-law, his wife, daughter Cun Kieu, daughter-in-law Aunty Cong, and a one-year-old grandson, Ken. Great Uncle #11 had three sons, but the eldest son, Giao, remained in Vietnam. His second and third sons were twins. The eldest twin, Cong, had died in 1976 while his wife was pregnant. His wife and little son, Ken, came on this journey with us. Great Uncle #11's youngest son, Gieng, had left on the *Southern Cross* earlier.

Uncle Chin's family of five included Uncle Chin, his wife Gin, and three young children Phung, Thu, and Lan ages under six. The two younger children were not born yet. Aunty Gin was seven months pregnant carrying Filipina Moi.

Uncle Hai's family of three (Uncle Hai, Aunty Binh, and three-year-old daughter Lac) and a brother in-law, Lu Hai, were on the same boat.

A family friend from the neighborhood, with his wife, two-year-old daughter, and grandmother, also came with us. We waited all day until after sunset, and then our names were called to board the bus leaving for the harbor. Unfortunately, there was a mix-up with the name list. The names of my grandparents' family, Uncle Hai's family, and Great Uncle 11's family were not called. They had to find a place to spend the night and then return to the chicken farm the next day.

Those of us on the bus were taken to Cat Lai harbor. Small boats were waiting to take us out to the sea. We spent that night sleeping in a boat, squatting on the floor, packed in like sardines. My siblings and I obeyed my parents' instructions without complaint, no matter how uncomfortable we were. They told us the journey would take us to our older brothers and sisters and we would live in the United States someday. We shouldn't be complaining about a little bit of inconvenience. We were luckier than most people in Vietnam because we had the means to pay for a passage on a large ship. The next morning, we sailed farther out to the sea and got our first glimpse of our new home, a rusty Panamanian freighter called the *Tung An*.

Boarding the *Tung An*

As we—Uncle Chin's family of five and our family of seven—took turns boarding the *Tung An*, it was obvious to us that it was a freighter built to carry commercial cargo, not fitted or prepared for carrying people. We climbed a ladder up the side of the ship to get on deck. The ship was already overcrowded. It was immediately apparent to Dad that staying on the main deck would be too dangerous for us, since we had so many young children and a seven-month pregnant woman, Aunty Gin. How could we survive the ocean waves splashing across the deck or the hot sun constantly beating on us? Dad took us down one level below the deck.

The cargo area of the ship was covered with layers of nylon bags filled with white flour. For the duration of our stay aboard the

Tung An, those nylon bags became the ground under our feet, our sofas, our beds, and our tables. They weren't ours alone, however. As we entered the cargo area, we were met by survivors from a smaller wooden boat, the *Gi Mai*, which had recently capsized. They were the first ones to board the *Tung An*, and had claimed enough space to let them lie down flat when they slept at night. Each of the more than two hundred survivors from the *Gi Mai* had just had one or more family members or friends die only days before. It sank shortly after its passengers had boarded, even before it had a chance to leave Vietnam waters. The owner of the boat had reserved the spaces in the body of the *Gi Mai* for his family and relatives. The boat had tipped over as the passengers were jockeying for the best spots, with too many people on the deck. More than two-thirds of the passengers perished, including children, husbands, wives, fathers, and mothers. In Vietnam, most people, young or old, did not know how to swim. The survivors were not paying passengers on the *Tung An*, as we were, but going back home was not an option for them. They demanded to board the *Tung An*. There were no dry eyes amongst the broken-hearted *Gi Mai* survivors. For weeks we heard sobbing and loud cries as they mourned the loss of their loved ones. We became all too aware of the reality of life and death early on in our journey.

Unluckily for us, the *Gi Mai* survivors defended their territory they had claimed in the cargo area of the *Tung An* ferociously, as if their lives depended on it. All the living areas had already been claimed. We ended up living in the passageway between the two compartments of the ship body, an area about five feet by five feet in size.

A fire broke out the first night we spent on the ship, when a family put a shirt over a lamp to block the light. It caught on fire in the middle of the night, and people began screaming as the family sleeping under the lamp tried to put out the fire.

The next day, my grandparents' family, Great Uncle #11 family, and Uncle Hai's family came aboard the *Tung An*. They ended up finding a spot on the upper deck with seating room only. Some of the women and elderly squeezed in with us on the lower deck. Before the voyage had even started, we were sorely missing the comforts of home.

Life as Refugees

The living conditions aboard the *Tung An* were unsanitary and barely tolerable. There were just too many people. We were packed like human sardines, living on top of those nylon bags filled with flour. A number of people got violently seasick when the ship was in rough water, so sick they couldn't move, even when they soiled the flour bags with diarrhea. We also sweated on those bags and spilled water on them, and they became infested with insects. At first we were frightened when we saw a bug, but after many days of living in those terrible conditions, we no longer noticed when the insects bit us. Worms would cling to our arms, legs, faces, and bodies. We just killed them or brushed them away. Many of the refugees developed boils and open sores on their arms and legs, all resulting from a lack of personal hygiene.

Conditions were not so bad for the captain and crew, as they had private quarters separate from us. Only one public toilet was available for the 2,318 refugees. It was located at the end of the boat, but it wouldn't have mattered where it was since it could not begin to handle the needs of thousands of people. Without a bathroom or shower area, we took care of ourselves in pairs, with one person holding a vinyl tablecloth or blanket as a makeshift washhouse and outhouse, with the other person inside it. People used the side of the ship as their toilet, urinating over the side or using paper or plastic bags to catch their solid waste, then throwing it into the sea. We would get water from the sea by lowering a rope attached to a tin can to clean up after ourselves as best as we could. We used the ocean water to rinse the urine or solid waste. However, not everyone brought along ropes or tin cans or had any means to catch the solid waste to throw overboard. As a result the people who lived close to the side of the ships had to endure the constant smell and sight of human solid waste.

We didn't have any means of bathing for weeks. The last time we washed up was the night before we left home. Every three or four days, women used salt water to wash their privates, attempting to avoid itchiness and infection. Although many females on the ship brought tampons along with them, it was still hard to have their menstrual period while living on the *Tung An*. They had no way to properly clean themselves. I was lucky I was still too young.

The ship's galley was not nearly big enough to prepare normal meals for all the people on board. Many families had brought along their own food and various provisions, but there was not enough and they ran out quickly. Twice a day, the refugees were fed half a cup of rice gruel, which was made by cooking rice in vats of water and then letting it sit until it reached a pasty consistency. Families were assigned to groups of fifteen to twenty-five people each, and then food was passed out for each group. Group leaders were chosen for bringing the food rations to the people in their group each day. As our group leader, Dad used a red bucket we had brought with us to collect the rice gruel for our group.

Encountering a Stormy Sea

The *Tung An* set sail on November 22, 1978, a few days after we boarded. Most countries in Southeast Asia did not welcome Vietnamese refugees. These countries were already overwhelmed by their own problems, and they didn't want the burden of caring for thousands of refugees, especially because they might bring disease and other health problems with them. It was always going to be a major challenge to find a port where we would be allowed to land. Many people onboard spoke Cantonese, and so the captain pointed the *Tung An* toward the British-held, Cantonese-speaking port of Hong Kong, where camps for refugees had been set up with the aid of the International Red Cross and the United

Nations High Commission for Refugees (UNHCR). We could only hope that we would be taken in.

Before we made much headway, nature intervened. Our journey by sea quickly turned into a nightmare of giant waves and rough waters.

Our relatives living on the upper deck soon had to come down to join us in our area to get away from the large waves splashing over them. In this tiny area, stretching the limits of occupancy, twenty-four people settled in for our voyage, with only about one square foot per person. Packed in were thirteen kids (Phung, Thu, Lan, Tam, Kau, Lac, Moi, Ken, Buu, me, Num, Ngoc, Cun Kieu), eight women (Gin, Mom, Binh, Aunty Cong, Man Sim, Grandma, Great-Grandma, and neighbor's Grandma), and three men (Dad, Uncle Chin, and Yoo Qui).

At night, we slept leaning against each other's bodies. It was not uncommon to have children sleeping on top of their parents or people taking turns to sleep during the day. If we accidentally crossed into our neighbors' spaces, they would yell at us and demanded that we stay clear of their space. At first I told Dad that it was unfair to live in such a small living space compared to the *Gi Mai* survivors next to us. They were able to sleep lying flat and even had room to stretch out.

Dad said, "It is not true, Nam Moi. We are better off than them. We may suffer physically, but our family members are here, alive. Since their loved ones drowned in an instant in the open sea, they were not able to claim the bodies of their family for burial. They are suffering emotionally in ways that you cannot see."

It was hard for me to imagine the pain they must have felt losing their loved ones, not to mention the trauma they went through witnessing the catastrophe. Dad was right. We were better off. I stopped complaining and just accepted my fate. I had more sympathy for them after Dad's explanation. From time to time, I accidentally crossed into their space and got yelled at. I politely apologized and tried to squeeze back into our overwhelmed space.

The massive storm lasted for close to a week. The large waves splashed into the cargo compartments as well and got everyone below decks wet. The waves caused the ship to roll, surging up really high as the waves crested, and then dropping low into the troughs, cycle after cycle. Everyone was praying, chanting for the gods and goddesses to protect us. Children and females were screaming with fear as the ship rocked up and down. Our new world was churning, and nearly all of us got painfully seasick. Mostly we stayed put, just cuddling each other for whatever comfort we could give.

While the ship was traveling in the stormy waters, we were paralyzed with motion sickness. We couldn't go up on deck to use the makeshift toilet. People were throwing up in buckets, and some vomited on their own clothing. Others had diarrhea from the food they had eaten over the previous days. Since Dad was the only one not affected by the conditions, he took care of us. He helped us throw up into the red bucket. Mom was the most severely seasick of all the people in our group. She was so sick she had to lean against the wall. Sometimes she threw up in her clothing and sometimes Dad was able to set the red bucket next to her in time.

Several times, we had to relieve ourselves into the bucket too, the only one available. When it came time to collect the rice gruel in the red bucket, Dad washed it out with salt water as it splashed in from the sea. He told us that he washed the bucket as best as he could under the circumstances. Then he would eat the first bowl of rice gruel from it, saying, "What is cleaner? When you can't see it or when you wash with water?" We were very hungry, and we didn't have any options. We had to eat to survive.

After a few days of endless vomiting and diarrhea, everyone was very weak and had no energy to scream, cry, or be scared. I remember Tam said in a soft voice, "Mom, I want to go home and not stay on this ship anymore. I am so hungry that I would rather eat the leftover rice with water that we fed the geese back home."

Mom responded, "Tam, home is far from here and turning back is not an option for us. Dad is coming with food soon. Go to sleep and I will wake you up when the food arrives."

We were hallucinating and lethargic. Dying at sea seemed to be a real possibility, especially knowing about the tragic incident on *Gi Mai*. With the little energy we had left, we told our family members and relatives how much we loved them. We even wondered aloud if we would be related again in the next life. Some of us spoke of what they wanted to be in their next life. Others just lay there, suffering quietly.

If we had taken a small wooden boat, our lives would have vanished along with the boat, swallowed up by the magnitude of the giant storms. The fact that we survived was a miracle. The value of the extra gold that it had cost my parents to escape Vietnam on the *Tung An* instead of a small wooden fishing boat was more than validated.

Seeking a Safe Harbor

After close to a week of traveling in stormy waters, the vessel had been driven off its intended course to Hong Kong. For the next several weeks the ship sailed a southerly course in the calmer waters close to the Vietnamese coastline. Along the way, we encountered several fishing boats in distress, also filled with refugees. In their attempts to escape, those refugees had brought food and various provisions, but there was never enough. The people on the fishing boats inevitably ran out of water and food. They were very happy to be rescued by the *Tung An*. It might have been an unsanitary, miserable place, but the ship was far more capable of withstanding the stormy weather, and it carried tons of flour and rice in its holds. We had hot water and enough rice gruel to at least survive.

While we lived on the *Tung An*, our daily lives revolved around the kitchen schedule. The kitchen opened between 5:30 a.m. and 6:00 a.m. and distributed hot water until 9:00 a.m., then sometimes reopened in the afternoon from around 2:00 p.m. until 3:00 p.m. The rice and water gruel was distributed in the morning between 10:00 a.m. and 12 noon, then again for dinner after 4:00 p.m. Besides the twice a day rice gruel, children and old people were given one cup of powdered milk every day, and we were allowed a tin can filled with hot water.

We were terribly hungry all the time. Since we were lying on top of bags of white powder flour, my parents tried mixing it with hot water. We quickly discovered, however, that the white flour was starch. It didn't have any nutritional value and it turned into a tasteless jelly paste when mixed with hot water, like glue, that was not edible. We were very disappointed since the ship was filled with nylon bags of flour.

Before dawn, Mom would wake up Num, Buu, and me to line up at the galley for the morning ration of hot water. We used the empty baby milk powder tin cans. Each person in line was allowed a quart of hot water. We stood in line for one to two hours just to get that tin can filled. However, the first people in line each morning were able to get one extra can. So, each morning Mom would rush me to get in line early. I would squat on the floor of the galley each morning, sleeping sitting up, in order to be one of the first people in line. If I got the first tin can of hot water, I would bring it back to my family with a sense of accomplishment and happiness. Yet Mom never once praised me or my brothers for our contributions, or showed any affection toward us, even after we had waited in line for hours. That was how she was raised by her parents, to sacrifice for the greater good. Her natural response was to say, "Rush back to get in line. Don't waste a moment."

I would tell her, "Mom, I am tired. I want to rest for a few minutes." That was not an acceptable request in her mind. I had to get back in line and stand for hours all over again. I wasn't even able to squat down in line until we reached the galley way. When the line was long, we could only stand, because the deck was wet from people brushing their teeth or cleaning their clothes.

After nearly three long, miserable weeks at sea, we came to a small Indonesian island where we hoped to land. The captain of the *Tung An* tried to negotiate a deal with the local Indonesian officials to unload the refugees. The negotiation went on for days. Finally, we thought an agreement was reached. A half dozen small boatloads of people were ferried to the island. Uncle Hai's group, with his family, was on one of the boats. While they were waiting for the others to arrive, Aunty Binh and several other refugee women got to wash their hair in a stream. But after an hour we learned that the captain was unable to make a deal, even after offering gold to the Indonesian authorities, and the refugees were recalled to the *Tung An*. Even so, the ship was allowed to anchor close to the island for a few more days, to replenish water and oil before sailing out again. Although we were not towed out into the international waters, the coast guard remained standing by to make sure *Tung An* departed. In all, we stayed over a week before heading back out to sea.

Next, the *Tung An* headed to the British protectorate of Brunei. The authorities there, however, refused to take in any refugees. They said there were too many people on board, and the risk of them carrying disease was too high. The Brunei government provided canned food, water, and engine oil for humanitarian relief. The six- to eight-ounce cans of food consisted mostly of pinto beans and some tangerines and green beans. For more than a week we ate canned pinto beans for breakfast, lunch, and dinner. The beans were not seasoned and had no taste. After a few days I was sick of eating them. If I had a choice, I never would have touched a pinto bean again, but I had no choice. Since that time of utter desperation, I can say that I have never again eaten pinto beans, and will not unless my life again depends on it.

With no better alternative in sight, the *Tung An* sat at anchor in the Brunei port for several days, refusing to leave. Eventually, the Brunei authorities towed the vessel out to sea along with a helicopter escort to make sure we left. Dozens of young men jumped overboard and refused to leave, but the Brunei coast guard picked them up and returned them to the ship. Finally, the *Tung An* was towed out into international waters.

Not Allowed to Land

We left Brunei, discouraged and still looking for a port of refuge. A few days later, on December 26, 1978, more than a month after boarding the *Tung An*, we entered Manila Bay in the Philippines. We were very excited to see the lights of a big city. The next morning, a customs patrol boat circled close to our ship.

Figure 10-1: *Philippine Daily Express* photo of the *Tung An* in Manila Bay.

A news story by reporter Manny Silva appeared in the *Philippine Daily Express* on December 28, describing our plight from the eyes of our potential host country:

> *More than 2,000 Vietnamese boat people lined up by the railings atop the bridge of the "Tung An," a freighter of Panamanian registry anchored on the explosive area of Manila bay opposite Isla Putting Bato. This is about 8 kilometers from the shore.*
>
> *As we approached on customs patrol craft P58 at 7 p.m., we were met by the foul smell from the jampacked freighter. Men stripped to the waist could be seen on the bridge together with some women and children who stared at us.*

At the forecastle railing is a large streamer saying, "We Wish to Get On Land" in big, red letters . . . The refugees looked weary, malnourished and exhausted. They showed eagerness to communicate with us but we were prevented by the Coast guard authorities from talking to them.

Coast guard men in barring us explained that "we have no orders to allow you." In spite of the size of the freighter—about 4,000 tons—the refugees are packed like sardines. Clothes lines crisscross along the deck. Some of the women refugees were observed lowering tin cans tied to a string to fetch water from the sea.

The next day a helicopter flew overhead. My brothers Num and Buu went with me topside to see the helicopter. A picture was taken of the *Tung An* with us on it. The blue tarp in the picture was where my grandparents lived. Mom had brought along the tarp, but since we lived in the lower deck, she gave it to my grandparents for protection from the sun and rain. On the left of the blue tarp, close the edge of the ship, was where Uncle Hai and his brother in-law were camped out on a metal bench. They had seating room only and their luggage was stowed underneath the metal bench.

The first order of business for the Philippine government was to provide food and water to the thousands of starving refugees. With a Philippine coast guard boat anchored alongside the *Tung An*, the sailors passed out water and bread rolls. Many hungry refugees were so excited that they practically spilled over the rail trying to get to the water and food. So many people crowded on that side of the ship that the *Tung An* started to list. The captain screamed over his loudspeaker, asking people to return to their respective side of the ship or they would capsize the boat. The refugees responded with alacrity, since the memory of the *Gi Mai* was fresh in everyone's mind.

Figure 10-2: *Tung An* freighter with Vietnamese refugees in Manila Bay.

Figure 10-3: Nam Moi, Buu, and Num on *Tung An.*

The girl in the circle is me, Nam Moi. Next to me is my brother Buu and next to him is Num. We were leaning against the railing, watching the helicopter fly by.

Several Philippine officials came on board the following day to assess the living conditions. One of the people on board took a picture of us with a Polaroid camera. We had eighteen people packed in our little area at the time, with seven out of ten kids under the age of six, an elderly, and a pregnant woman, eight months along. One of the seven children required special needs.

This picture, shown below, was later given to my Uncle Chin in Manila.

Figure 10-4: Ung family living area on the *Tung An*, December 1978.

The Philippine government, however, would not allow the *Tung An* refugees to go ashore. According to the foreign ministry, they had already accepted more than 3,000 Vietnamese, and any more refugees would severely overcrowd their Fabella refugee center. However, for humanitarian reasons, the government agreed to provide us with food, water, and medical supplies.

Deputy Foreign Minister Jose D. Ingles defended the decision, saying, "The Philippine government has done all it could within its limited means to help refugees, having accepted nearly 4,500 of them from 1975 to 1978, of that total 2,000 are still awaiting resettlement." Ingles also met with a representative of the Social Service Commission and the Ministries of Defense and Health to seek for ways to alleviate the deplorable conditions on the *Tung An* ship. His office also worked with the United Nations High Commission for Refugees (UNHCR) to look for permanent settlement answers for the Vietnamese refugees. An operations center was set up to coordinate Philippine government assistance, and the following measures were agreed upon:

1. Provision of food and other immediate necessities.
2. Medical treatment for the seriously ill.
3. Vessels to be stationed near the *Tung An* for 24 hours for such necessities as may be required by the refugees, especially by those with ailments not requiring hospitalization.

Five people suffering from malnutrition and other medical problems were taken to a Manila hospital for treatment. Three were in their late sixties, one was an infant a few months old and the other was a young woman who had given birth a few days before. The baby hadn't survived and had been tossed overboard.

A Philippine navy vessel visited the *Tung An* twice a day, bringing food from Manila. The morning breakfast delivery between 8:30 a.m. and 9:00 a.m. consisted of one small piece of bread for each person. The afternoon delivery between 2:00 p.m. and 2:30 p.m. brought each person a small square piece of beef or pork, a clump of rice, and a small bag of green beans or bitter melon. A few bananas were also distributed to each group, about one banana for every two to three people. Since we had boarded the *Tung An* close to six weeks ago, we hadn't had a real meal. Back home my siblings and I would have refused to even try bitter melon. However, on the *Tung An* it tasted delicious and we didn't even notice the bitterness. We ate every grain of rice even when the rice was not fully cooked.

The *Milwaukee Sentinel* reported on December 29, 1978, that Associated Press photographer Andy Hernandez had boarded the *Tung An* to get a close-up look at the more than 2,000 Vietnamese refugees waiting in Manila Bay, since they had been refused permission to land. Philippine officials had refused to allow reporters on board, but Hernandez hired a boat anyway and tried his luck. He managed to get aboard the *Tung An*, avoiding the Philippine Navy guard. He pointed at his camera and signaled to the refugees that he wanted to climb aboard. They threw him a rope to climb up.

Figure 10-5: *Tung An* refugee ship receiving help in Manila Bay.

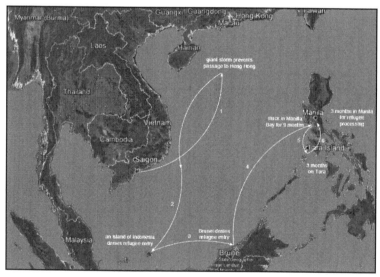

Figure 10-6: Journey from Saigon Vietnam to Manila Philippine (Image: Google Earth).

In his report he stated, "Aboard the *Tung An*—Two things hit me when I boarded this black freighter carrying unwanted refugees from Vietnam: the sight and smell of a mass of humanity. There were people everywhere. The official figure is 2,300 . . . I couldn't count them all. Many were sleeping. Some lined up at the galley for their breakfast ration of rice and water gruel, and others held tin cans filled with a tasteless looking potion. The only other food I saw was an open container of powdered milk in the hot and foul-smelling hold. Clothing were strung everywhere, topside and below. The refugees washed their garments with water scooped from the sea in tin cans at the end of long ropes . . . As I climbed back into my boat, the refugees wished me luck and told me to make sure the world knows about the *Tung An*."

The first leg of our escape from Vietnam had ended. We were still suffering from the miserable conditions, but at least the situation was stable. Now we just had to wait for someone willing to let us off that boat.

Chapter 11

Daily Hardships on the *Tung An*

For six weeks we'd had no means to wash our bodies. Rinsing with salt water was worse than not washing at all. The salt residue on our skin was more uncomfortable than the sweat itself. Over time we'd got used to our foul-smelling body odor and no longer were bothered by it.

Filipino public health officials, though, worried that hygiene aboard the ship was so bad, with the evidence of human feces everywhere, that contagious disease epidemics might break out. Within a week after we arrived in Manila Bay, we were temporarily transferred to a Navy ship, while the *Tung An* was cleaned and sprayed with disinfectant. Male and female toilet areas were constructed with wood panels to make a narrow, covered extension about fourteen feet long on one side of the ship, providing a separation between female and male areas. Each area contained enough room to accommodate six to seven people at a time. A three-foot section of the ship's railing was notched out for access to the latrines. Rolls of toilet paper and tampons were passed out to each family. Since the structure was so primitive, young children and elderly needed the assistance of another person holding onto their hands to avoid going overboard accidentally while they squatted down to relieve themselves.

Treated water was also provided for us to drink. While we were onboard the Navy ship, we were able to take showers, with men on one side and women on the other. Unfortunately, some

Filipino Navy officers pierced holes in the female shower area to provide themselves with a cheap show. We covered up the holes as best we could while showering, but they made more holes the next day. We got smarter to their peeping-tom ways and showered with our clothing on.

After a week, we moved back to the *Tung An*. The ship was so clean. We saw no trace of the dirty nylon flour bags filled with insects that we had lived on for the last two months. We had a layer of new nylon flour bags and the old ones were removed.

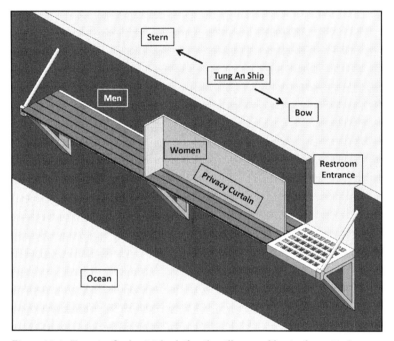

Figure 11-1: *Tung An* flank—Makeshift toilet. Illustrated by Anthony Turk.

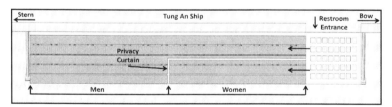

Figure 11-2: *Tung An* flank—Makeshift toilet top view. Illustrated by Anthony Turk.

After we returned, a coast guard boat was assigned to anchor next to us in case of medical emergencies. Some of the refugees saw this as an opportunity to cadge more water or food from the coast guard crew. Many young teenagers and women took to begging for water. Some of them would write notes in English and throw the notes into the coast guard boat. A typical note would say silly things like, "What is your name?" or "I like your hair, shirt, face" and so on. The coast guards responded to each note and threw it back to the *Tung An*. This was a game that went on for hours during the hot summer nights.

When Mom heard that some coast guards were passing out water and even food, she told Num, Buu, and me to join the beggars. Num and Buu refused because we already received enough water for drinking each day from standing in line for the morning rations. But Mom wanted extra fresh water for her personal hygiene. Living on the *Tung An* was hot and sweaty, especially in the below-decks cargo area. Mom gave up on the two boys, and instead applied more pressure on me, saying how she wished she could do it herself if only she were able. She said, "Since you are a girl, the coast guardsmen will be more likely to give you water than the boys." I knew those were excuses she made for the boys, and that she was being unfair to me as a daughter. I suppose that I also could have refused to obey her orders, but somehow I felt obligated. I was eager to please Mom, and wanted to make my family's life better in any small way that I could.

The little girl in me feared that I would lose Mom, since she was incapacitated from motion sickness, and my two younger siblings, at only four and five years of age, were unable to contribute. I gave up my feelings of resentment and executed her wishes without further questioning. I would do whatever it took to survive.

I was only eleven going on twelve, and I had to grow up too fast for someone of that age. The first English phrase I learned was "Sir, sir, please give me water." The second was "Thank you, sir" and the third was "Sir, I am hungry. Please give me some food."

When I was able to obtain water and bring it back to Mom, however, she again never once gave me any praise. She made me feel that it was my duty to my family. Already my brothers and I had been standing in line to collect hot water and gruel in order to spare Dad from doing those humiliating tasks. There was an unspoken awareness that all of us had sunk very low, compared to where we had come from, especially Dad. He had been a successful, wealthy businessman. Knowing this, I was willing to take on the extra task of begging for water. I told myself that I was not only a refugee but a beggar now. I was not proud of it, but I did it for my family and to spare my brothers from lowering their self-esteem even further.

President Marcos' government took a hard line with the *Tung An*, refusing to bring any of the refugees ashore except to take resettlement flights out of the country or for medical treatment. We were forced to continue living on the *Tung An* until we were selected to resettle elsewhere.

Every day we woke up to further hardship and the unending struggle to survive until the next day. The food that was provided was not enough to satisfy our hunger, only enough to keep us alive. The number of people in my grandparents' group was fifteen people, and our group was close to twenty-five, yet each group was given the same amount of bananas or a single bag of dinner rolls regardless of the number of people in the group. The first time my grandparents' family had extra dinner rolls, I asked my grandmother if she would give me half a roll since I was still hungry. She told me, "No, I am saving them for your Aunt Ngoc and two uncles in case they get hungry later on."

I pleaded with her for a piece of one of those dinner rolls, "Grandma, Aunty Ngoc, and uncles are full now, but I am not." She insisted that she could not give any of her food to me, her own granddaughter. I was shocked by her response because my mother and father had given her family so much when we were in Vietnam. Every time the aunties had visited us from Song Mao, they returned home with suitcases of material goods. Mom was a very generous person and she had given a lot to her side of the family. Dad also supported Uncle Phong financially when he attended medical school overseas. Dad had even paid for their family of five's journey on the *Tung An* with his hard-earned gold.

I felt betrayed by my grandmother. I went through various emotions of shock, anger, regret, and acceptance within the next two hours, crying nearly nonstop, seated on the edge of the deck and staring out to sea. Being hungry all the time was becoming too painful for me. Everyone, though, was just defending their own families, and my grandmother was no different. My parents and relatives asked me why I was crying, if I was hurt. I didn't know how to articulate my grievances about the situation. So, I just shook my head and continued crying until I had no more tears left.

From that day on, I didn't waste any of my energy on wishing things were different and how life shouldn't have to be so difficult and miserable each day from hunger, humidity, rain, and sun beating down on us. Instead, I consciously chose to live every day with the hope that very soon we would leave this filthy ship and reunite with my siblings in the United States. I started to play tricks with my mind to turn negative situations into positive ones. When someone left the boat to resettle to another country, I would say, "I will come visit you someday when I make lots of money. I will." I would make a mental list of all the countries that I would visit someday amongst all the people I knew on the ship. I told my brother Buu that we needed to make lots of money in order to visit our friends and relatives all over the world. Dad said that we would have to study hard and get a good education in order to realize our dreams. That was the seed my father planted in our consciousness: getting a higher education is the key to realizing our dreams.

Saving the Children

Late January 1979, Aunty Gin was rushed from the *Tung An* to a Manila hospital, where she gave birth to a girl. We called her Filipina Moi. A week after the birth, Aunty Gin came back to the *Tung An* and was relocated close to the crewmen's quarters, next to the kitchen. She got three meals a day and a better living arrangement, where she could lie down. Baby Filipina Moi stayed at the hospital in Manila.

A few weeks later, another one of my young cousins, Great Uncle #11's grandson Ken, came down with a high fever. He was rushed to a hospital in Manila with his mother, Great Uncle #11's daughter-in-law. They stayed in Manila for over two weeks. Later, we heard my cousin had passed away. His mother, Aunty Cong, came back to the *Tung An* with a broken heart. Her husband had died in Vietnam after they were married for less than a year, and now with passing of her son, she no longer had any connection with Great Uncle #11's family or the Ungs. A few months later, her name was called and she went to Canada alone.

Uncle Chin and Aunty Gin had a tough decision to make now that baby Filipina Moi was born, especially after hearing about the death of Great Uncle #11's grandson. Should they hold out hope to immigrate to the United States and remain close to their extended family? That meant they had to risk their three young children getting sick and dying. They also had to let baby Filipina Moi spend her young life with strangers who wanted to adopt her as their own.

The decision was made after the death of the baby cousin. In order to keep their family safe, they must leave the *Tung An* and resettle in any country willing to take them immediately. They could always immigrate to the United States later. As it turned out, Denmark was the first country to offer asylum. That choice did not seem too bad, since their kids, being so young, would be able to adapt to the Danish culture and learn a new language more easily than older children.

After spending four miserable months living on the *Tung An*, their names were called to head to Manila. While they were processing their documentation for Denmark, one of the Philippine officials recognized the family, especially the children, and handed them a Polaroid picture of us taken on the *Tung An*.

In a group of 35 people in total, Uncle Chin's family arrived in Denmark on March 18, 1979, not knowing what to expect. It was truly a foreign land, different in so many ways from Vietnam and even the Philippines. The family arrived at the end of winter wearing their thin cotton and polyester clothing, not suitable for the cold weather. Even before getting off the airplane, a stewardess gave them blankets to wrap around their bodies. The leader of the Danish refugees aid organization and a co-worker had accompanied the families on the long trip from Manila to Bangkok and then to Copenhagen and their final destination, Aarhus.

Figure 11-3: Arrival of Uncle Chin's family at the Copenhagen airport, taken by a reporter.

In the picture above, taken at the Copenhagen airport by a reporter, Uncle Chin is holding Lan, age two and half, and Aunty Gin is holding baby Filipina Moi, who was only six weeks old.

Thu, who was almost four, is standing with a blanket covering her and six-year-old Phung is squatting down. Filipina Moi saw the picture in one of the refugee books from the school library and made a copy to show her family.

Upon arrival, Uncle Chin's family was provided with an apartment in Aarhus as a temporary housing. Their first impression was that the place was flawless with everything taken care of; the apartment was furnished with beds for all the family members, a dining table with chairs and so on. The fridge was filled with fresh groceries, and there were even diapers and pacifiers for baby Filipina Moi. The foundation for a new beginning was handed to the family.

The next hurdle to overcome was adapting to their new land, assimilating to the local lifestyle and learning the Danish language. Social workers showed up daily to guide the family. Only one week after arriving, Uncle Chin and Aunty Gin started in language school. It was not always easy going to school by bus when bringing four children aged from a few months to seven years with them, but it was a necessity in order to succeed in their new land. After seven months of learning the language, Uncle Chin was asked about his hopes for a future career. Since he already had experience with operating machines, he was able to enter a trade school and learn how to service computer-operated machines. This prepared him to enter the Danish workforce.

Aunty Gin didn't work, but continued to spend a few hours each day attending school to learn Danish in addition to the housekeeping and taking care of four kids. By this point the family had moved to a new apartment that fit the family's needs better. It was a four-room apartment located in Holme, a suburb of Aarhus, in a good community close to kindergarten and school so later on the kids could walk home after classes.

Phung, the oldest child, couldn't start kindergarten because she couldn't speak or understand Danish. As a consequence, she was held back a year. That worried Uncle Chin and Aunty Gin, so they made it a priority for all the kids to learn Danish as early as possible. The kids adapted fast and soon spoke Danish as their mother tongue.

As a consequence, Chinese was spoken less and less at home. There were only few other Chinese families in Aarhus, and Uncle Chin's family only occasionally interacted with them. The kids were also too young to be fully rooted in Chinese culture, so they adopted the Danish culture as part of their identity. Uncle Chin and Aunty Gin spoke Chinese with each other and to the children, but eventually the kids only spoke Danish, and they lost the ability to speak Cantonese Chinese.

As an offering for students with a different background than Danish, the two older kids, Phung and Thu, studied Mandarin at Chinese school for two hours every Saturday for several years. Their teacher was from China, and she couldn't speak Danish or Cantonese. Since the kids didn't understand Mandarin, there was no common language, so it was hard for them to learn and eventually the classes stopped.

In 1984, Uncle Chin was trained as a machinist and for many years was the single provider for the family. He had a stable job at the city's biggest machine factory until 1991, when the company had rounds of layoffs and eventually had to declare bankruptcy. It was a hard blow for the family. All of the children, now five of them, were thriving in school and Aunty Gin had just started preparing to enter the labor market, taking short training courses like sewing.

Figure 11-4: Uncle Chin, Phung, and Thu in Denmark 1980.

The following period was
unstable with Uncle Chin
being alternately unemployed
or taking different temporary
jobs. It affected the whole
family with worries and
uncertainty about the future
for the next couple of years.

Figure 11-5: Aunty Gin and her daughters.
First Chinese New Year in Denmark, 1980.

The turning point came when one day Aunty Gin, like a true
Hakka woman, decided to take matters into her own hands and
showed up unannounced at Vola A/S, a well-established Danish
Company manufacturing Arne Jacobsen designer taps and other
bathroom accessories.

Her perseverance paid off, and soon both Aunty Gin and Uncle
Chin had permanent well-paid jobs at Vola A/S. This meant an
improvement of their financial situation. With only youngest
child, Sinh, still living at home, it was possible to save up money
relative quickly, and a few years later they bought a medium-sized
town house.

Uncle Chin and Aunty Gin chose not to focus on living in the past
and regretting what could have gone differently. Risking the lives
of the family and making the sacrifices that came along with it
was worth the effort as long as their children's future was secured.
Feeling lonely and missing the extended family was undoubtedly
their biggest issue all along.

During the first years living in Denmark they had hoped to
immigrate to the United States, but with time they learned
to adjust to their life in Denmark. A decade and a half later,
permission finally was granted, but Uncle Chin decided that the
kids were too old to adapt to a new country and didn't have the
heart to tear up the roots of the young tree which had been solidly
planted in the Danish way of life.

Still on *Tung An*

Uncle Chin's family was only the first to leave. On March 8, 1979, Uncle Hai's family of three, along with his brother in-law Lu Hai, left to resettle in Canada. Unfortunately, Uncle Hai, Aunty Binh, and Lac didn't pass the physical exam to resettle, since Lac required special needs—she had sustained mental impairment and physical disability in her mother's womb—and was not able to walk at age three. So the Canadian government rejected their request. Lu Hai alone left for Canada after a few months at a Manila military camp.

Uncle Hai's family stayed in the military refugee camp. While they were unable to go to Canada, they were fortunate in that they were not required to return to the *Tung An* while they were waiting for approval to emigrate to the United States.

Figure 11-6: A Filipino worker, Aunty Binh, Uncle Hai, and Lac in the Manila military camp, 1979.

Figure 11-7: Aunty Binh and Lac in the Manila military camp, 1979.

The United States was the first choice for my family, my grandparents' family, and for Great Uncle 11's family. My older siblings had settled in Los Angeles in February 1979. We had to wait for their telegraph to provide proof that we had family in

America. Finally early in March 1979, we received word from my brothers and sisters, verifying their residence.

At last we could qualify to join the list of people wanting to immigrate to the United States. Even so, long months of waiting would pass while the paperwork was processed. As part of the resettlement application, our family was asked to take a picture of the whole family with Dad holding a sign with "Ung Ly Sang, family of 7." That would allow U.S. officials to identify us with the names on our documents. The picture was taken on the deck of the Navy ship with the *Tung An* in the background.

Figure 11-8: Family picture on a Navy ship in Philippines, 1979.

By that time we had lived on the *Tung An* for close to nine months, most of the time as unwanted guests of the Philippine government. Our refugee community was like a patchwork floating town, with multicolored tarpaulins supplied by the Navy providing makeshift shelters from the tropical sun and the almost daily rains. Yet most refugees took advantage of the tropical showers by standing out in the open, cleaning their clothes and washing their bodies with the rain water.

Many refugees set aside private areas, where they stored extra food and personal items. Clothing was strung everywhere, topside and below decks. Hanging over the rails were plastic bags tied with ropes, some partially filled with rice and some only plastic bags saved from the daily meal.

After the *Tung An* was anchored in Manila Bay, the galley's role had changed to that of a supplemental kitchen. Its main function was to distribute hot water daily to the refugees. The kitchen water distribution schedule lasted longer during morning and a couple of hours in the afternoon. Rice gruel distribution after the hot water distribution was reduced to the morning only and on an as-available basis.

Every four to five days, the *Tung An* had its fresh water refilled from Manila by boat. The refugees took advantage of the event and lined up to beg for water with whatever they could use as a container to hold the water. One by one the water was filled by the marine on the boat. On that day the refugees had means to bathe, if only partly. The refugees learned to first wash their bodies with salt water from the sea and then rinse their bodies with fresh water afterward.

A typical day on the boat started with Mom waking me up before dawn, along with my brothers, Buu and Num. We would go to the galley way, holding our tin cans, and wait for over an hour for hot water. Each tin can contained about a quart. After we brought the water back to our family, we would brush our teeth before eating breakfast. We lowered a tin can with a string to haul up water from the sea to brush our teeth and clean our faces. Of course, this ocean water was less than sixty feet away from the human waste being discharged from the toilet platform, so we tried to draw water as far away from the platform as possible.

The three tin cans of hot water each morning were used to mix Ovaltine cocoa milk powder drink for the whole family of seven people. Cans of Ovaltine were distributed to each family as part of the supplement for breakfast along with a small roll.

While the food from Manila was never enough to fill us up, at least we weren't starving the way we had been before the ship reached Manila Bay. Still, after eating only bread and sometimes rice gruel in the mornings, we were always very hungry by the time the afternoon food delivery arrived. That provided the largest meal of the day, with rice, meat, vegetables, and bananas. This meal was both lunch and dinner. Seeing the Navy vessel approaching the *Tung An* always brought excitement and happiness to the refugees on board. We could hear cheers and hurrahs throughout the ship from young and old alike.

Along with the food delivery came the mail. Getting mail from family members was the highlight of each day. Hearing news about other refugees' families from distant shores gave us hope. In May 1979, we received a letter from Xi, which was an unexpected and pleasant surprise since he seemed like the most unlikely person to write to us. We had expected a letter from Zenh or Hong. Xi's letter contained a picture of him standing by a nice sports car in Los Angeles. It was what we needed to keep our hopes alive as we continued to wait in the unbearable conditions of the *Tung An*. We dreamed of eating a full meal, driving a nice car, living in an air-conditioned house and sleeping in a soft, comfortable bed someday. When we got discouraged after not being called to leave the *Tung An*, Xi's picture kept us hoping for a better tomorrow.

Figure 11-9: Xi in Los Angeles, California, 1979.

In June 1979, Kien sent us a letter while we were still onboard the ship. She had completed the ninth grade at Nightingale Middle School in Los Angeles. Starting in September, she would join

Figure 11-10: Kien's 9th grade graduation at Nightingale Middle School, 1979.

Figure 11-11: Uncle Hai's family in Manila military refugee camp, August 1979.

Hong at Belmont High School. Along with the letter, she sent a self-portrait from her ninth-grade graduation. The dress she wore had been designed and assembled by her. Since she didn't have the money to buy a nice dress after immigrating only four months earlier, making a dress was cheaper. We were so happy to see a picture of her. She looked different than the last photo from Vietnam, having gained weight, which symbolized the good life waiting ahead of us in the United States.

On August 4, 1979, we got a letter from Ung Hai from Manila, along with a picture of his family in the Military Refugee Camp. He reported that the Canadian government had disapproved Uncle Hai's family immigration request. They would remain at the camp, waiting for his brothers Uncle Tac and Uncle Kan in Los Angeles to sponsor his family.

During the time we were living on the *Tung An*, more than six hundred fellow passengers received word that they could leave for new homes in other countries. Another five hundred and seventy-five were moved to a suburban military camp, where they underwent final processing for resettlement. That left close to a thousand refugees on the freighter, stuck in a life of perpetual boredom.

Throughout this time Mom was incapacitated with motion sickness and lack of nutrition with low glucose levels. She was bedridden for as long as she was on the ship, unable to function normally. Her activities were limited to essential toilet functions and sitting up to eat food.

Most of the refugees idled away the long hours between breakfast and dinner, but others tried to stay busy. The people next to my grandparents had a radio. Several people, including Dad and my uncles, would stand listening to the news. Some people had brought playing cards; a card game was an activity that entertained both young and old. People wrote or read letters. Many people shampooed their hair, brushed their teeth, and bathed or washed clothes with salt water scooped from the sea.

One day my brother Num decided to join other boys in diving into the bay's dirty water to scrape shellfish from the freighter's hull. He dived over the side and I lowered a tin can by rope for him to put the mussels in. After an hour, he was able to almost fill the can. We cooked the mussels using the tin can as our cooking pot and plastic bags which we had saved from our daily meal distribution as cooking fuel. Each member of the family was able to eat two or three mussels apiece. That was an exciting change of pace for us.

Tung An refugees saved every single plastic bag from the food delivered each afternoon to use as cooking fuel. One of the reasons was that the delivered rice often was half cooked. The refugees would put the rice in a tin can and add water to cook rice porridge.

Some people whiled their time away simply leaning against the railing of the ship, staring out to sea. Depressingly, we often saw pieces of wood floating on the waves, spars belonging to capsized refugee boats that had been too small to survive the local typhoons. Frequently, these broken fishing boat panels floating by in the current would be followed by human corpses.

We stopped feeling anything for them because the sight was so common. I listened as my grandparents discussed the behavior of a dead body in the water. They said it took three days for a dead body to rise to the surface, and they observed that men's bodies usually floated face up and women's bodies floated face down. A friend and I made a morbid game of identifying the sex of dead bodies floating by. If I correctly identified the dead body as male or female, she would give me her half banana from the day's ration. When I won for the third time, my friend got mad at me for gloating. I was so excited about winning that I was jumping up and down with joy.

I said to her, "I am right again. Give me half of your banana."

She responded angrily, "You are a cheater. You tricked me to give you my bananas. You are not my friend, and I don't want to play with you anymore."

Playing such a game was ghoulish, and I wondered what I had become. How could I be so happy about a dead person in the water? That deceased female was someone's daughter, sister, or mother, and the deceased male was someone's son, brother, or father. The family of the deceased might never know what had happened to their kin.

To my friend I revealed what I had learned from my grandparents, and assured her that I didn't cheat. Yet that day had a larger meaning for me. I realized that we also could have been dead bodies floating in the ocean. We had risked our lives on this journey to freedom. Life on the *Tung An* was not easy, but we were luckier than most to be on board a ship large enough to be safe from storms, pirates, and starvation.

Figure 11-12: *Tung An, Times Journal,* June 23, 1979.

A Times Journal article described the *"Tung An* refugees: A Life of Boredom" after we lived on the ship for over six months.

TUNG AN REFUGEES: A LIFE OF BOREDOM
Times Journal, June 23, 1979

Six months after becoming unwanted guests of the Philippine government, 950 Vietnamese refugees aboard the freighter Tung An have settled into a life of boredom and waiting.

A Philippine navy vessel makes its twice-daily visit to bring food to the hulking black freighter. It's a typical day.

Several "boat people" lounge around a radio. Here and there a card game is underway. Women write or read letters. Hair is being shampooed, babies bathed, fingernails manicured. Boys fly a kite.

Leaning on rails, dozens simply stare toward the sea.

"We are hungry," a refugee shouts to a photographer, but there are few outward signs of it. Women are cooking rice gruel. Boys dive into the bay's dirty water, scrape shellfish from the

freighter's hull and return to the deck to sort their treasures, separating barnacles from mussels. Two or three hours of diving yield four liters of mussels.

Life has been this way for the Tung An "boat people" since Dec. 27, when the Hong Kong based freighter chugged into the bay three days after it was refused refugee at Brunei.

There are some signs of change. A flat-bottomed navy boat is moored alongside, giving the refugees room to spread out, and there are fewer people—the Tung An carried 2,318 passengers when it arrived. Multi-colored tarpaulins supplied by the navy provide makeshift shelter from the tropical sun and the almost-daily rains that foreshadow the oncoming monsoon season.

The refugees and the Philippine marines assigned to guard them have painted graffiti on the hull. Over a painted "Dec. 26, 1978," the Tung An's arrival date, there is a small heart, pierced by an arrow.

Hanging over the rails are ropes with plastic bags, some empty, some with rice. Many of the "boat people" have set aside private areas, where they store extra food and personal items. Most have tin cans on strings to bring aboard water for bathing.

In January, Filipino public health officials worried that hygiene aboard the ship was so bad that epidemics could result. Disinfectant sprays and treated water were provided, and a public health doctor said Wednesday that the danger has passed.

"There is a big improvement compared with the first few months," said Dr. Antonio Amparo. "Many were suffering from gastro-intestinal disorders. But they now have a lot more room, and there's not going to be any serious disease problem."

Many of the refugees have open sores on their arms and legs, which Amparo said are boils caused by lack of personal hygiene.

A woman whose family identified her as Mang Ng sobs in pain with a swollen right arm which she says she broke in a ship-board accident. Her family says there is no money for medical assistance, but Philippine government officials say they were not told about the injury and will treat her without charge, as they have done for hundreds of others.

President Marcos' government at first took a hard line with the Tung An, refusing to bring any of the refugees ashore except to take resettlement flights out of the country or for medical treatment. The captain and crew face charges of violating immigration ports laws and are ready to stand trial.

The restrictions on the refugees have eased, although there has been no official announcement.

More than 600 of the Tung An passengers have gone on to new homes in other countries. About 575 are at a suburban military camp, undergoing final processing for resettlement. The ones still on the ship are those who so far have been unable to prove links with other countries.

During the many months living on the *Tung An*, I witnessed many sordid scenes, caused by so many people being cramped together in a limited space. Some made more of an impact on me than others. In particular, four memories remain vivid in my mind.

In the first one, we witnessed two young women prostituting themselves for food. Both in their late teens, they lived on the lower deck right below the opening by my grandparents' location. Almost every night they made visits to the captain and crew's quarters wearing revealing clothing and high-heeled shoes. They wouldn't return to their family until late at night or sometimes the next morning with food for their family. On most evenings I would hang out on the upper deck, since below decks was humid and hot. As I sat by the hatch close to my grandparents' location,

I would see them climb the stairs. Other kids and I would follow them toward the crew's quarters in the stern. Usually, some sailor would open the door to let them in.

I was puzzled about what went on during those visits. My curiosity became an obsession when I heard them discussed as part of the daily gossip. People were saying that these girls sold their bodies for food. In my ignorant twelve-year-old mind, I didn't understand the concept of prostitution. How could a woman sell her body when she has only one body? What is prostitution? My parents and relatives became concerned about my fascination. Mom said in a stern voice, "No matter how hungry we are, you do not need to prostitute yourself for food. We may be starving, but we have dignity and pride. That kind of behavior would bring shame to the Ung family."

I had no idea what Mom was talking about, but I responded, "I understand."

The second memory was more fearful. One night a group of four to five young men came to our area and demanded access to the ladder leading to the holds below us. I was frightened because they had gangster-like manners. We had to move our belongings quickly for them to access the ladder. The young men removed the flour bags around the ladder and pulled out a metal panel, allowing them to get to the hold below. Two men climbed down into the compartment. Each reappeared with a fifty-pound bag of rice and handed it to the men above. The whole operation took only a few minutes. Clearly, one of those men knew a member of the crew or the galley.

The bags of rice were carried into other areas of the ship, and many refugees fought to get some of the stolen rice. We witnessed the other refugees trying to scoop the last grains of rice out of the bag. My family didn't want to have anything to do with such thievery. Dad said to my brothers and me, "We are not hungry to the point of dying just yet. We do not need to steal rice or fight for it."

The third disturbing situation we witnessed was domestic violence between husband and wife. With so many people on the boat, there was no privacy. Your next-door neighbors could hear you clearly. Verbal fights and disagreements were common. Sometimes the neighbors would join the disputes.

One refugee we called "Fat Man" because he was overweight, which was rare in Vietnam. A person had to be wealthy to be fat. When we left Vietnam, he was slightly obese, but after months on *Tung An*, he lost a lot of weight. Still, the nickname stayed with him. In any case, he was loud and notable because he had a bad temper. The hardship on the *Tung An* brought out the worst in him. He would call his wife names and hit her with his open hand.

One time, however, he started lashing his wife with a belt, which caused her to scream in pain. Other refugee children and I watched in horror as the man beat up the helpless woman. People shouted at her to run away from the Fat Man's reach, but she just squatted down and screamed while covering her head and face. Finally, several men nearby intervened. For hours everyone, young and old, took turns ridiculing him for beating up a defenseless woman.

He continued the verbal abuse, and he promised his wife he would beat her up again, but he never dared because the other men threatened to beat him up if he ever laid a finger on her again. Like all bullies, he was not going to challenge someone his own size.

The scene of a large man beating a woman had a dramatic impact on my view of domestic violence. Afterward, some women tried to make excuses as to why the Fat Man lost his temper, implying that his wife provoked him. I was upset by those comments. I refused to be a victim like the Fat Man's wife, and I felt that no man had a right to abuse his wife or a helpless woman for whatever reason. I said to my family, "My husband better not try to beat me up or slap me around. I might be small, but I'm not helpless. I will leave him no matter how much he loves me or I love him." I also felt that I wanted to be as capable as a male. I was determined to do whatever my brothers could or do it even better than them. I carried that mindset with me since that day on. I would not allow my gender to be a barrier.

The fourth memory I had was of a very different kind of behavior between couples: a young man and woman being intimate with each other. As I have mentioned, each refugee who got in line received a ration of one can of hot water, but Mom expected me to get two cans because I could do so with a little more effort. Getting in line for one to two hours required a lot of patience and physical strength. After a while I took personal pride in my daily task. Some days when I overslept, I felt bad for letting my family down, especially Mom.

As part of my daily routine, by 4:30 a.m. or 5:00 a.m., I got up and rushed to the alleyway in order to be one of the first people in line. I would squat on the floor of the galley half asleep. As the morning went on, more people would join me in line. Lining one side of the alleyway was the wall of the captain's and crew's quarters, and on the other side were a few rooms with no doors where refugees lived.

One morning as I walked half asleep into the alleyway, I heard some unusual sounds. When I reached the entrance of one of the rooms, I saw a man in his late teens lying on his side holding a woman in front of him with a blanket only partially covering him, leaving his naked butt exposed. I stared at them, frozen in disbelief, taken aback by what I saw.

They had not expected anyone to show up so early, but they soon realized I was gaping at them in the doorway. The man quickly covered his behind. However, both of them looked at me with a big grin in their faces. Their response puzzled me for the next several hours. I continued heading toward the front of the line. I couldn't fall back to sleep. Instead, my mind was filled with thoughts of concern. It would be unthinkable for me or my siblings to do such a thing. My parents would disown me if I ever had sex without being married. All my Ung relatives would dislike me for shaming them.

What drove them to take such a risk? I was afraid to tell on them, which would get them in trouble. Premarital sex was taboo and could destroy the woman's reputation for life. Therefore, I kept the secret to myself and never told anyone else on the ship. Each subsequent morning as I walked through the alleyway, I would check on them. Invariably, they would be holding each other while asleep.

Eight months later, Mom and I ran into the couple in the Manila Fabella Refugee Camp. The lady was holding a two-week-old baby girl, born premature at seven and a half months. The couple walked up to me and said, "Do you remember us? Here is our baby girl. You saw us making her."

Mom responded, "What?" with an accusing look at me.

I quickly told her it happened so long ago that I forgot the details.

The couple told us that they had decided to get married and would be traveling to their new country the next day as a family. We were delighted for them, since they said they had both left Vietnam alone without any family members. We said congratulations and wished them well. Seeing them again made me very happy. The situation could have turned out badly, but it became a happy ending for them—and me.

Death of a Young Girl

On many occasions during stormy weather, the *Tung An* refugees were transferred to a larger navy ship, sometimes anchored alongside and sometimes not. It depended on the severity of the storm. With a major storm approaching, the navy ship would go in closer to shore to avoid the open sea.

The navy ship provided the refugees more safety from the storms. We carried all our belongings with us when we transferred back and forth between ships. Each refugee family would rush to reserve a space on the navy ship. Usually, a family member without any baggage went ahead to save a space in advance and the rest of the family followed. Mom assigned me the duty of reserving a space since my brothers could carry more than me.

When we were on the navy ship, we had the luxury of showers and more room for everyone to sleep, lying on our back with leg room and moving about freely. I would walk around the deck to study the ship's weapon system. Each ship, depending on the size, might have different weapons. My friends thought I was weird for noticing the new features. During the evenings and nights, many young people walked about on the deck. Sometimes when the ship took us closer to land, we could see the city lights of Manila.

The arrangement for food on the navy ship was the same twice-daily delivery from Manila. However, the navy ship also had a commissary which sold dry goods. We were able to buy instant noodles, canned sardines, and other items with our U.S. dollars. In an experiment, Dad brought three cans of sardines for one U.S. dollar. He gave Mom one can for her own use, and the other two cans were shared among all the family members. After Mom ate the whole can of sardines and drank a cup of hot water, she was energized, no longer feeling weak or seasick. She was able to sit up and walk about like a normal person. Her sugar level had been low all these months from lack of nutrition. Dad said to her, "You are sick from lack of food." It was a relief for all of us to see Mom functioning normally. Since she had been sick for months, we lived with the constant fear of losing her from some deadly sickness.

By July 1979, after seven months in Manila Bay, a flat-bottomed navy ship was anchored alongside the *Tung An* most of the time, which provided more room for people to spread out. Refugees were free to cross back and forth on a wooden gangplank between the two ships. The crossing was dangerous, because the *Tung An* was lower than the navy ship, and the ocean waves caused quite a bit of up and down movement. For this reason, two Philippine navy officers stood on each end of the gangplank to assist the refugees in crossing safely. My parents would remind us not to go back and forth between ships unnecessarily, especially at night when the water was rougher.

Some of the young adult refugees traveling without their parents did not have such advice. One sixteen-year-old girl traveling with her older brother habitually went back and forth with her teenage friend several times a day. One night after eight o'clock she was crossing from the *Tung An* to the navy ship. I was standing close to the gangplank, so I saw her fall into the ocean. Everything happened so suddenly.

The navy officers quickly ordered that the two ships be separated to avoid crushing her. Within a few minutes three navy divers were looking for her in the water, but after searching for hours they still didn't find her. The very next day, her brother's and her name were called to go to England, but he refused to leave until his sister's body was found. We heard that a few days before the incident she had told her friends that she had dreamed of her deceased parents.

Three days later, her body resurfaced several miles away. Her body was collected from the ocean and brought back to the navy ship. We couldn't recognize her face since her whole body was bloated from being drowned in the ocean. The only thing that identified her was the pink outfit she had on. Her brother left the *Tung An* to go to the Manila refugee camp along with her body.

The death of the girl finally roused the Philippine government to take action. The authorities realized that during typhoon season the remaining refugees would not be safe on board the *Tung An*. Many of the refugees were still living on the upper deck, exposed to the elements. The people on the lower deck would be flooded when it rained. Moving the refugees to the navy ship was not a solution either, since it was not equipped to accommodate over nine hundred refugees long-term.

In spite of objections from the United Nations, Filipino officials hurriedly opened a new refugee camp on the remote island of Tara, one hundred and fifty miles southwest of Manila. The island would provide a safer shelter than the *Tung An*—from the tropical sun, the almost daily rains and the upcoming typhoons. So our odyssey would continue on this remote island in the middle of nowhere. Because it was only a temporary expedient, we would not be there for long. The problem was, we were not any closer to settling in the United States.

Chapter 12

Safe from Storms

Journey to Tara Island

When the refugees heard that the Philippine authorities were moving us to a temporary processing center on land to wait for our resettlement to Western countries, we could only wonder why we were being moved to such a remote island, a three-square-mile speck of land with primitive facilities and no electricity, instead of to Manila.

On August 8, 1979, nine and a half months after we first started our journey to freedom, we were happy to say good-bye to the rusty old cargo ship. As the nine hundred plus refugees filed onto the navy ship transporting us to Tara Island, feelings of excitement mixed with a fear of being abandoned. We were relieved and welcomed the prospect of ending our misery on the *Tung An*.

When we left Vietnam, we thought our voyage would end in the United States. But after living on the *Tung An* for so long, many of us feared that we would be stranded in the Philippines. So while the refugees were generally happy to leave the cramped, fetid *Tung An*, we were also scared that our stay in Tara would delay our processing for resettlement. My grandparents' family, Great Uncle #11's family and my family were still waiting for our turn to emigrate to the United States. Since the majority of the refugees wanted to go to the same country, the system was overwhelmed.

We had waited for months without any news, not knowing whether we had been forgotten in the bureaucratic machinery, and now we were stowed out of sight on Tara Island.

As we prepared to board the navy ship, the refugee mentality kicked in for most of the boat people. All of a sudden we were seized with the fear of being left behind. Carrying all our belongings, we started to rush to board the World War II vintage navy transport ship that would take us to Tara Island. I was shoved and pushed by people all around me. Mom held on to the hands of Kau and Tam for dear life. This mass of human movement from one ship to another was more than chaotic; it was dangerous, especially for the children and the elderly. The Filipino marines used their rifles like cattle prods to maintain an orderly transfer.

The journey to Tara Island took seventeen hours, passing through the South China Sea in strong winds and rain. It seemed like forever compared to the thirty-minute ferry ride from the *Tung An* to Manila. Still, the journey would have taken much longer and been more dangerous on the *Tung An*. The trip in the larger navy ship was relatively smooth. I didn't even get seasick during the journey. The ship sailed all night and arrived the next morning.

Figure 12-1: Filipino marines trying to maintain order as the *Tung An* refugees boarded the Navy vessel for Tara. *The Evening Independent*, August 8, 1979.

I was so excited to see land. The navy ship anchored eight hundred yards from shore, and the seamen lowered the front of the vessel to transfer us to a smaller World War II-era beach landing boat. The beach landing boat was shuttling us to land, with standing room only during each trip. The refugees stepped ashore on Tara for the first time with the music of "One-Way Ticket to the Blues," blaring from the Navy ship's loudspeakers. This song, popularized by the American singer Neil Sedaka in the 60s, was being played for several seamen who were roasting a suckling pig to celebrate our arrival.

Tara Island

For the first time since leaving Vietnam over nine months earlier, we stepped onto solid ground. We wobbled unsteadily on the sandy beach, but we felt immediate relief all the same. Every firm step brought us joy. We screamed, "The floor is not moving anymore! We are not on the boat anymore!"

We could see nothing from the beach but a vast, empty sea. Half a dozen tribesmen had been asked by the authorities to greet us on the beach, but we received an unmistakably cool welcome. The indigenous Tagbanua tribesmen stood silently at a distance in tee-shirts and half-zipped faded denims, watching the navy boats disgorge a horde of thin, wobbly-legged refugees. Populating the island were about five hundred of the nomadic Tagbanuas who called Tara home. The women still went bare-breasted, despite the introduction of Catholicism. Belying their nomadic lifestyle, the Tagbanuas planted crops like cassava and papaya, and caught fish to sell to people on another island three and a half hours away by small boat. The tribe was also known for its peaceful ways. We later learned that the Tagbanuas were afraid of us because, in their words, we were "killers who came from the war." The Tagbanuas feared that we would settle on their island and take away their lands, leaving them impoverished. In response, the Filipino authorities sent navy officers to dispel these suspicions.

The refugees settled into eleven prefabricated buildings and six long open grass huts. The buildings were made of bamboo, plywood and sheets of galvanized iron, situated on twenty-four acres shaded by coconut trees. Filipino authorities estimated that Tara could accommodate 7,000 refugees if need be. The eleven prefabricated buildings had more than enough room for all of the families, in welcome contrast to the accommodations on the *Tung An*. Filipino officials told us to watch out at night and lock our doors to be safe from intruders, both human and animals.

The refugees, concerned about their security, chose not to spread out and occupy all eleven of the buildings, believing it would be safer to stick close together. The more superstitious among us also had to watch out for another danger. The islanders said tribal spirits lived in the treetops.

Figure 12-2: Tara Island, Philippine (Image: Terra Metrics and Goggle Earth).

A short distance from our building was an administrative center, with a medical clinic, offices for the officials overseeing the refugees and a row of western toilets. The Filipino officials lived close to the center, separate from the refugees, and our day-to-day interaction with them was rare. We did not interact much with the Tagbanua tribesmen, either, since they lived in the mountains along the northeast coast. a three-hour hike away.

My grandparents' family and Great Uncle #11's family were placed in different buildings, in close proximity to ours. Each family was able to get their own space, with plenty of room to spread out. However, we were used to being close, not only with our own family but with other people that we hadn't known prior to the journey. We felt unsafe physically and psychologically having too much space separating us. We needed to be able to see, hear and interact with them in order to feel secure. Our family reserved enough room, with two bamboo mats and an area to store our belongings, to allow each of our seven members to sleep lying flat on our backs. While we slept, my younger siblings and I would fight to sleep close to one or the other parent. Since I was the second oldest, I had a low priority. That worried me, because

I heard a rumor that the Tagbanua tribesmen wanted to kidnap girls at night and turn them into sex slaves in the mountains. Although we closed the windows and locked the two doors at each end of the buildings, I asked my brother Buu to alert my parents if I was missing in the middle of the night.

One tremendous boon was the wells with hand pumps for our water. We pumped water into our buckets for our bathing, cooking, and cleaning. There wasn't a dedicated shower area, just several changing rooms. The females would pump buckets of water from the wells and wash themselves in the changing rooms. Males just rinsed themselves next to the wells and changed their clothes in the changing rooms. A large structure was built next to the river with a platform as toilets for males and females, but that was pretty disgusting. The human waste of 914 refugees just washed downstream. Often, we saw mackerel fish in the river coming up to the surface to eat our solid waste. So it's not much of a surprise that when the tribesmen came to sell mackerel, most of us refused to eat them.

Each family received mosquito nets, blankets, bamboo floor mats, slipper sandals, and flashlights. The island had no electricity, so the flashlights were needed in case we had to use the toilet at night. Pots, pans, bowls, spoons, and forks were handed out to each family for cooking their own food.

The food provided for the refugees was limited to available dry goods, and that supply was constrained by how much food could be shipped from other islands in the Philippines. We used the six long grass open huts as common areas, mainly for food storage and cooking stations. Each day volunteers would manage handing out canned goods—pinto beans or green beans—and dried goods such as dried instant noodles, dried fish, dried shrimp, and once in a while, fresh vegetables such as cabbage. Since we had no electricity, fresh vegetables were hard to keep for a long time and were rarely included in the food shipments.

The refugee families cooked their food either in the common cooking area or created a makeshift kitchen of their own, with a variety of rocks arranged as a stove. Most families were able to set up a small cooking area under the coconut trees, using stones as makeshift hearths and dry branches and brush for cooking fuel. I was able to help Dad to find some nice-sized rocks and other items on the island for our family's kitchen, located in the shade close to a coconut tree. Grandfather made bamboo chop sticks and cooking utensils from some nearby bamboo trees and gave us a set. We created our own cutting surface from a dried wood trunk.

I was responsible for collecting food each day and cooking meals for my family under Mom's guidance. The meals were simple, since we didn't have many choices. For breakfast we had rice porridge with dried fish. For lunch and dinner we had instant noodles. Every day it was almost always the same thing: tasteless rehydrated noodles.

Even so, we had much more freedom on Tara than we did on the *Tung An*, including access to local fish, plants, and fruit. We had heard about a small community in the mountains behind the refugee camp where we thought we might be able to buy spices and supplies. However, the village was more than an hour away from the camp by foot, and the refugees were concerned that the Filipino authorities overseeing the camp would disapprove of the endeavor viewing it as "too dangerous." Early one Saturday morning, a group of men, including Dad, made the scouting trip in secrecy. It took six hours, including a lunch break, but Dad and the other men returned successfully in the afternoon with various goods.

The tribesmen gradually got wise to our ways, and as opportunistic entrepreneurs they learned to come by the refugee camp and sell us items that we might need. We no longer needed to make those long trips ourselves. Tribesmen often came to sell fish, young coconuts, and mature coconuts. Although we were refugees, Dad and other families had enough U.S. dollars to buy a few items here and there. One time a tribesman sold us four salt water angel fish, with bright white-yellow and white-blue coloring. Dad thought it would give us a chance to eat a different kind of fish. As it turned out, these fish were pretty to look at but not so great to eat. The fish tasted like jelly and had no meat on them.

The Filipino officials had recognized from the beginning that the refugees would need activities to keep them busy. We heard of plans to open classrooms that would teach us to plant crops. Until they started, we had plenty of time for conversation and time for the adults to pass on their knowledge to the younger generation. We used our imagination to come up with interesting and helpful ways to spend our time.

We were free to roam around the tiny island, with its beautiful jungle foliage and white sand beach with mountains in the background. I was not surprised to find out in later years that Tara Island became a resort destination. Num, Buu, Dad, and I would go to the beach for a swim after lunch every day. From the refugee camp, it was only a short walk through the bushes to the beach. I had my first swimming lesson from Great Aunty #11 and Dad. My grandparents, Mom and her siblings didn't know how to swim. My grandmother believed that people drowned in the water all the time, whether it was a lake, river, ocean, or at the beach. Therefore, her adult sons and daughters grew up thinking that swimming or playing in the water was dangerous. My grandfather had no opinion and didn't object to her fears. Therefore, Uncles Sanh, Han, and Aunty Ngoc didn't even try to learn how to swim in Tara's safe, shallow, calm, and warm beach water.

There were plenty of trees and bushes on the island, and one day my grandmother, Great Aunty #11, Mom, and I strolled around the vicinity close to where we lived in search of edible plants and fruit. It was one of my first memories of the older generation passing on their knowledge to me. Grandmother and Great Aunty

#11 pointed out what was edible and what was not. Among the edible plants and fruit we saw a tamarind tree full of fruit, chili plants, and some edible green plants among the ground cover.

Learning from Failures

Although we had limited resources, I enjoyed the challenge of coming up with ideas to create simple things. In particular, I learned how to make dried coconut snacks from coconut meat and sugar. Soon I was telling Dad to buy coconuts so I could make the dried coconut sweets. I learned to crack open the coconuts with a rock and a knife. I would cut the coconut meat into thin slices, each one the length of my pinky. Then I would slowly cook the coconut slices with water and sugar until the water evaporated, using low heat, which was not easy to control with a wood-burning fire.

I was very proud of my cooking experiments. One day I had the desire to make chili paste. Chili plants were abundant on the island, and I thought we should take advantage of them to spice up our tasteless instant noodles. I asked Grandmother how to make the paste. The next morning I set out to pick two handfuls of chilies. I found a flat surface to chop them into small pieces, after which I planned to cook them into a paste. The problem with my plan was that I didn't have any protection for my hands. As a result, when I handled the chilies, I burned both of my hands bright red. From my hands up to my elbows, I felt a painful burning sensation. We had no ice, so I just soaked my hands in water for hours, changing out the water several times as it got warm from the heat in my hands. It took a couple days to recover from the chili burn.

Because there wasn't much to do on tiny Tara Island, we talked a lot, and most of our conversations revolved around food. My mother's family used to live by the sea in North Vietnam, and my grandmother used to catch little sand crabs to make crab paste. She told me how to catch them. She said, "Close to dawn when the sea water rises there will be many little crabs on the beach. If you watch where the crabs go, then scoop the sand around them into our red bucket, you will be able to catch them. Then you separate the crabs from the sand. The little live sand crabs can be cleaned and smashed into paste." Late in the afternoon one day, Mom and I tried to catch some sand crabs. We were not successful, catching only a few. Grandmother said that we had to wait till close to sunset for the high tide water to come in.

The next day, I was determined to catch some sand crabs. After my swim at the beach, I went back to the camp to get our red bucket. I walked out to the beach by myself, wanting to try again. I was so intent on my mission that I forgot to tell anyone about my plan. I waited at the beach for a long while. Then, as I saw the water rise on the beach, I followed my grandmother's instructions.

I was so focused on catching sand crabs that I was not aware that the sun was starting to set. Then the winds picked up and I started to get cold. The sky darkened rapidly as the sun went down. Because I had no light, I realized that I needed to head back to camp as soon as possible. The path back to the camp was a small unpaved trail through the bushes, and in the growing darkness I lost my way. I was terrified by the thought of being kidnapped by the Tagbanua tribesmen and becoming a slave, or being raped by navy officers without anyone to hear my screams. When I realized that I was lost, coming out at a different part of the beach, I headed back to our swimming area. I hoped Dad would come there to find me. I settled down behind some bushes, prepared to spend the night.

At dinner time my parents couldn't find me. No one knew where I was, because I hadn't told anyone about my grand plan to catch sand crabs. My parents became very concerned. Dad interrogated my siblings and the kids in the camp to find out if they had seen me. He had a suspicion that my grandmother was involved, especially after my chili experiment. He went to my grandparents' building and talked to them. Grandmother told him that I had asked her how to catch sand crabs the day before.

He was very upset with her for not making it clear that I couldn't do this by myself. Then he and a few other adults set out with flashlights, calling my name, "Nam Moi, Nam Moi." As they approached the beach, I could hear them calling. I responded back by crying, "Baba, I am here at the beach." When they reached the line of sand, I was standing there waiting for them, terribly relieved.

The search party was relieved as well to see that I was unharmed. Dad admonished me, "You should have told someone where you were going and what you were up to." I acknowledged my error, and we walked back to the camp, guided by the moon and our flashlights.

Once during our stay on Tara Island, we held a celebration to honor the workers who oversaw the needs of the refugees. My friend and I heard about it from the women working in the kitchen. As part of the celebration everyone would be allowed to have coffee, tea, and pastries, starting at 7:00 a.m. and continuing all day until 9:00 p.m. This was pretty exciting news, and my friend and I started counting down the days.

When the big day arrived, we decided to drink as much coffee as we could, since it would be free all day long. I got up really early on that special day and had my first cup of coffee ever, a little past 7:00 a.m., along with some cookies for breakfast. We were determined to maximize our coffee consumption that day, because it was FREE! I drank the first few cups of coffee like it was water, one right after the other, even though I had never had coffee before.

After our third cup of coffee, though, my friend and I were no longer enjoying it anymore. My friend said, "I don't want to drink any more coffee. It is making me sick." However, I wanted to follow through with my grand plan, and I forced myself to continue drinking one cup after another. Even before closing, I worked really hard, trying to drink my last cup of coffee before 9:00 p.m.

That night my coffee overdose caught up with me. Most refugees were in bed around 9:30 p.m. and would sleep through the night without going outside to use the restroom until morning. The doors in the building were locked at 10:00 p.m. Around 11:00 p.m., I was experiencing severe abdominal pains, and I needed to use the bathroom in the worst way. All of the coffee I had drunk during the day was wreaking havoc on my stomach and giving me a bad case of diarrhea.

With no electricity, it was very dark outside, filled with an ominous assortment of animal and insect noises. We had been warned not to go outside at night, in case we encountered snakes, insects, or wild animals roaming about, looking for food. The restroom was a five-minute walk from the camp, without lights. Most of the refugees would not even drink water after dinner, and they always remembered to relieve themselves before bed.

I had never gone out at night to use the restroom. But now I was in such pain that I had to go, and urgently. I woke up Mom and told her that I needed to use the restroom. She told me to dig a hole close to the bushes outside our building instead of trying to make it all the way to the toilets. Then she went back to bed. As I walked out of the bungalow, I heard many strange and spooky animal noises. I tried to follow Mom's instructions, using a stick to dig a hole. But between my upset stomach and my fear of an animal attacking me, I almost messed my pants.

That night I was assaulted by waves of diarrhea and had to relieve myself two more times outside the bungalow. That was an experience I have never forgotten. I was so tired, but my eyes were wide open from the coffee and I couldn't sleep all night long.

The next day, I just lay on the floor of the bungalow, extremely tired but unable to fall asleep. Mom asked me what had happened. I told her about my experience the night before. She told me that I had waited too long before I dug the hole, and that I had been lucky I made it.

I took her advice to heart. The frequency of my diarrhea was not as severe as the night before, but it was still a problem, along with an upset stomach. To be safe, I decided to dig several holes with markers to find them easier in the dark the second night.

Fortunately, I only had diarrhea once that night. Although I was still scared to be out in the open at night, my outing was much faster the second night, using my improved process. On the third night, I was finally able to sleep for a couple of hours. Altogether, my experiment with coffee caused me three sleepless nights and three days of extreme pain and stomach distress. I felt like the walking dead, unable to sleep, think, or function normally. I have never had a cup of coffee again since that first time. Even to this day, trying even a little bit of caffeine causes me stomach discomfort. Is it real or is it just in my head? Both have the same effect on me. Therefore, I stay away from drinking coffee.

After three months on Tara Island, in November 1979, our names were finally called to be transported to Fabella Refugee Processing Center in Manila, in preparation for our resettlement in the United States. Great Uncle #11's family had been called to Manila a few weeks before us. My grandparents' family

Figure 12-3: Maternal grandparents' family in Bataan Refugee Camp, 1980.

stayed behind on Tara Island for an additional four months. They ended up being transported to Bataan Island for processing instead of Manila and continued to wait for the United States to accept them for resettlement. A family picture was taken in front of my grandparents' living space in Bataan, starting from the left, Aunty Ngoc, Grandmother, Grandfather, Uncle Sanh, and Uncle Han.

We were excited to leave Tara Island and our refugee experience there behind. Moving to Manila was the final stage of processing and wrapping up bureaucratic requirements before immigrating to the United States. We were one step closer to reuniting with my siblings. We were entering our final days in Philippines as refugees.

Chapter 13

One Step Closer to Freedom

The Philippine government moved us to the Jose Fabella Refugee Processing Center for several reasons. The center allowed the government to (1) hold the refugees long enough to complete tuberculosis testing, (2) wrap up bureaucratic requirements before sending the refugees to their resettlement destinations, and (3) give the refugees a head start on second language training, which in our case meant English lessons.

By the time we were sent to Manila, close to a year had passed since we had left home. The processing for resettlement continued at a slow pace. We still had to figure out how to get by, day to day, because we would wait in our new location for months. Some people, we learned, had lived at the refugee camp for as long as several years. They built wooden huts for housing while they waited for the bureaucratic wheels to roll.

The land surrounding the refugee camp in Manila was mostly vacant in 1979. Here and there we saw small huts where poor Filipino families lived with their shirtless and shoeless kids. They often scrounged for used tin cans, glass, and rubber.

When we arrived, Great Uncle #11 helped Dad purchase a wooden hut that had been left behind by another refugee family. For $150, Dad bought us ten feet by ten feet of living space with a seven-foot ceiling. This investment was financed by selling a portion of a gold necklace Dad had brought with us. He still had some money left over to spend here and there.

The hut's construction was very primitive, with wood panels, nails, and hinges. It contained two wood panel shelves, four windows, and a door. The hut was built on the cement foundation of a torn-down building. Ours was one of many huts built on similar foundations. Each window was made of a wooden panel and two hinges, with a wooden stick to prop the window open. The windows were doubled up side by side, so that only two walls had windows. A seven-foot by ten-foot bottom panel covered most of the floor, with the rest exposed cement. A three-foot-wide panel was added to top of that, and we used the area underneath it as a storage area for our clothing, luggage, and other belongings. Dad and Buu slept on a raised wooden shelf and everyone else slept on the wooden platform. We cooked on the cement part of the floor, using a propane burner. Despite the cramped quarters, we had to leave enough space to allow the door to open and close.

In the back of the camp was a two-story building which housed both refugees and government offices. The offices were located on the bottom floor, and those refugees without money to live in individual huts occupied any free space they could find in the building. We were more fortunate than most, living in an enclosed hut. That not only gave us privacy, but also allowed us to lock the place up, so we did not need to guard our belongings all the time.

Behind the central cement building were ten individual western toilets with doors, along with several changing rooms. On one side of the building was a common area with faucets and running water, where each refugee family came to do their cleaning and washing. In the late afternoons, many of us would wash ourselves with our clothing on and afterward use a changing room or toilet room to change out of our wet clothes. Women and girls used the area also to clean vegetables or meat in the morning or late afternoon, in preparation for cooking lunch or dinner. This was the only place we could get water in the refugee camp.

In the middle of the camp was a gazebo area with a nineteen-inch color television. This was the most popular area for the refugee children, both for watching television shows and as a shaded rest area from the sun after running about in the open field of the camp.

Daily Life in Fabella Refugee Camp

On our first day, the authorities distributed small bags of rice and cookware with propane burners, cooking pots, and utensils so that new incoming families could cook their own meals. We also received mosquito nets, light blankets, and sandals. Our family was given a little booklet with Dad's name, indicating there were seven people in the family. This booklet was our passport required to collect food, cookware, or other provisions at the camp.

Figure 13-1: Mom (Kieu) and Dad (Ly Sang) inside the Fabella Refugee Camp in Manila, 1979.

Every morning, each refugee family lined up with their passport booklet to collect groceries for the day, usually one type of green vegetable and one type of meat, chicken, pork, or fish. The amount of food was apportioned according to the size of the family. For example, a family of seven people would get either three larger fish or four small ones, equating to half

Figure 13-2: Family and friends inside the Fabella Refugee Camp in Manila, 1979.

a fish per person. Just because of our improved diet alone, life in Manila was much better than on the *Tung An* or Tara Island. We had fresh vegetables and meat daily. The groceries distributed to us were similar to what we would buy back in Vietnam, except it was freely distributed.

At age twelve and a half, I took on the responsibility of collecting the groceries each day and consulted with Mom on how to prepare lunch and dinner. Since we only had one type of meat and vegetable, we had to be creative in order to cook two different dishes for lunch and for dinner. Although Mom was training me to be the cook of the family, determining the types of dishes to cook each day involved a family discussion. After all the food was cleaned, chopped, and ready for cooking, Mom instructed me every step along the way until I mastered each dish. She couldn't read or write, and I also had a hard time getting clear verbal instructions from her. Sometimes I became so frustrated, I would ask her to cook the meal while I took notes.

For breakfast we usually ate rice porridge with salt, or food left over from the night before. By lunchtime, we were hungry and very much looking forward to eating what we considered the first real meal of the day.

Each night I had dinner ready at 5:30 p.m. so that we would have enough time to catch the *Popeye, the Sailor Man* cartoon show that came on nightly at six o'clock. The gazebo was usually packed with kids and adults, with the kids squatting down on the cement floor and the adults mostly standing up in the back. Everyone loved to see Popeye saving Olive Oyl from the villain, Bluto. The Popeye shows gave us hope that everything would be okay in the end. Other cartoons were big hits for the kids too, even though it was hard to sit for a long time on that cement floor with the small television up high. I couldn't sit for a two-hour show without one of my legs or bottom going numb or my neck getting tired from being tilted.

A half hour walk from the camp was a supermarket where we went to buy seasonings for our meals and a few other everyday necessities. That was our introduction to a supermarket. In

Vietnam, we selected our groceries daily at an outdoor market. An indoor supermarket where we put whatever we wanted to buy in a cart and paid for them by the entrance was a foreign concept for us. The first time we visited the one in Manila, it felt like being at an amusement park. We wanted to take turns pushing each other in the cart around the store, but my parents wouldn't let us. I pushed the grocery cart around the first time, and as we shopped, I checked out all the foreign foods, especially the chips. Each night my parents, younger siblings, and I strolled to the market and tried to learn names of products as part of our education for the West.

My parents had a few hundred dollars left from the gold necklace they sold, so we could occasionally afford to buy a few things, like spices for cooking. As a special treat one very hot night, Dad bought us ice cream at the market after we pleaded with him. As children we were very curious how chips would taste, but my parents refused to buy junk food with their precious U.S. dollars.

Our ability to use the supermarket made us better off than many of the people living around the camp. Walking back to the camp, we saw poor Filipino families who were much worse off than we were. Boys were naked from the waist up with bare feet. Everyone, young and old, was very thin, with only skin and bones showing, like what we looked like on the *Tung An*. Their huts were built on dirt, not on cement, constructed with wood panels so worn out by the rain and sun that we could see inside. It was hard to image that native Filipinos could be worse off than the refugees. Compared to them, we lived in luxury. Our food was provided to us, we were safe from the rain and the sun in our enclosed huts, and we had slippers and clothing to wear. My parents said to us, "We are so fortunate being able to get meat and vegetables every day and to be able to buy a few things as well at the supermarket."

While our living situation had greatly improved from the months on the *Tung An*, even in Manila the basic need to use a toilet was an inconvenience and took planning to avoid undesired results. There were no outhouses close to our hut, and we had to walk over five hundred feet to the back of the central two-story building. Women and girls were very careful about not drinking water after four p.m., since using the toilet at night was an ordeal. Having to go in the middle of the night meant you had to be accompanied by another person to walk all that way. Most males didn't worry about that; they just urinated in the bushes or at the edge of the camp property.

Another downside was the rats. They were everywhere in the camp. I had had an irrational fear of mice even in Vietnam, but my fear of rats intensified at the Fabella Refugee camp. Seeing rats the size of cats freaked me out worse than seeing dead bodies floating in the ocean. The rats usually came out at night en masse, prowling for food. Because our hut had holes big enough to let rats in and out, I had many discussions with my parents about fixing the holes and eliminating the rat invasions every night, since I lived in constant fear of them. Dad and Mom were focused only on the idea that we could resettle to the United States any day now, and they refused to put any money into rat-proofing the hut. I had to adapt by putting a sizable rock on top of the pot cover to prevent the rats from getting into the food. But they were smart enough to knock off a rock. It was not unusual to hear rats rustling about, getting into our pots and pans at night.

At night all seven members of our family slept lined up in one direction, with five people on the bottom panel and two people on the top panel inside two separate mosquito nets. Usually Dad and Buu slept on the top panel. Occasionally, Kau slept with Dad under one mosquito net. I slept on the bottom panel under another mosquito net, wedged in between family members because of my fear of the rats.

On one occasion, while I was sleeping, I was awakened by something pulling my hair. I thought it was Tam or Kau, playing with my hair because they couldn't sleep. I said, "Please stop playing with my hair, I am sleeping." When my warning had no effect, I finally opened my eyes and saw my family was sleeping soundly. One of the rats roaming back and forth had crawled into my hair.

At that realization, I screamed so loudly that I woke up everyone in our hut and even the neighbors too. My nightmares about rats had become reality. The next morning our neighbors asked my parents what the screaming was about. They thought if we were going to survive at the camp, I needed to overcome my fear of rats. Instead of overcoming my fears, though, they intensified to the point of becoming a phobia.

When my parents refused to take action, I took matters into my own hands. I was determined to block the holes in our hut and eliminate leftover food. To block the holes, I scouted the camp for big rocks or cement pieces from the demolition of an old building. Of course, I couldn't carry them alone, and I sought help from my brother Buu. We worked on the "no more rats" project for a couple of days. Although my plan worked, in order to sleep securely at night, I came up with a plan to reinforce the space above my head and below my feet so the rats would never be able to touch me again.

Other kids at the camp were more aggressive about the infestation. They sometimes caught rats and burned them with gasoline. I couldn't believe how people could be so cruel to animals. I had a fear of rats, but I thought killing them inhumanely meant that we were not any better than the animals. Those images of rats and the ways the refugee kids tortured them in the camp had a big impact on me that has never gone away. I can't even look at images of rats, mice, squirrels, or other rodents without feeling very afraid.

Luckily, many aspects of living in the camp were not so repulsive. In one nightly routine Filipino vendors would bring their cooked goods in insulated baskets, selling food like meat buns, corn, or cooked duckling eggs. People in Vietnam believed fertilized duck eggs were especially good for one's health. The duck egg vendor would come almost every night with the same product. Other vendors brought different items each night. The vendors tried to sell the snacks directly to kids, hoping they would ask their parents to buy the products. My parents wouldn't buy anything from those Filipino vendors, though. They said that we could have leftover food from dinner. They didn't want to waste our precious money on snacks.

Refugee Processing

After the first week of living at the refugee processing camp, we were transported by bus to a medical facility in town, along with other refugee families. Before we could resettle in a Western country, we had to get a tuberculosis test and a physical checkup. We had a total of thirty to forty people, about six or seven families. After we arrived, the officials took a roll call of each family.

Each of us was given a tuberculosis skin test. All females were asked to follow a woman official into a room. Everyone was asked to take off all of her clothes, and we walked from one side of the room to the other. All the males had to follow a male official to a separate room, where they had to perform the same physical exam. They also checked all of the females' hair for lice.

When the official called my family's name, I was standing nearby and noticed the photo of my family with Dad holding the sign "Ung Ly Sang, Family of 7." I waited for an opportunity to discreetly ask her for my family picture. Since my English skills were limited, I told her, "I want it, please. I want my family." She paused and looked me in the eye. I repeated myself. She surreptitiously removed the paper clip and gave me the photo. I hid it under my shirt and didn't tell anyone until I got back to the camp. If other refugees had found out about it, they would have demanded their own photos. I wasn't going to risk losing the most valuable memory of our journey, one I could show my siblings and my kids someday.

Fortunately, I didn't have lice in my hair, because anyone who didn't pass the physical checkup was retained longer in the camp. However, within two weeks of playing with other girls, my hair became infested. My parents were very upset with me, and I had to listen to a daily lecture. Dad told me that we had come such a long way to get to this point. We were mere weeks away from reuniting with my older brothers and sisters. Yet they would not take us in the United States with lice on my head; I had better make it a priority to get rid of them. To do that, I had to comb my hair with a lice comb in the sun over a clear surface each day, and then crush and kill any lice with my thumb nails. I had so many lice on my head that Mom's head got infested too.

Getting rid of those lice was a major project for my family and me. As part of that effort, my parents insisted that I get my hair permed to kill all the eggs too.

To get our hair permed, we had to go to Makati, a town twenty minutes away from camp by tricycle. One day Mom and Great Aunty #11 asked me to take them to town to get our hair permed. I said I didn't know how to speak enough Tagalog or English to get them to town. They said to me, "We are blind and deaf. We are relying on you to get us there and back. Even if we get lost, you know how to get a taxi back to the refugee camp." Although I didn't know much English, I was supposed to be the spokesperson for us.

My brothers Buu and Num started laughing like it was the biggest joke. Buu said, "Will Dad have to come find you again?" Just in case we got lost, I wrote the address of the refugee camp on a piece of paper. Then Mom, Great Aunty #11, Aunty Cun Kieu, Tam, and I took off.

We were told by people at the camp that the ride to town cost between one and two pesos. After a short walk outside the refugee camp, we would be able to hire a Filipino man on a tricycle to take us to Makati. Most Filipinos knew a little bit of English, enough to communicate. I asked a man on a tricycle, "How much to go to town?"

He said, "Two pesos."

I didn't know how to say one and a half pesos, so I said, "One peso" and I used my fingers to gesture half by using one index figure to cut the other index finger in the middle.

He said, "Okay, one and a half pesos." We all laughed out loud getting onto the tricycle.

Five of us squeezed into a tricycle with three people on the seat, and Cun Kieu and Tam sat on the two adults' laps. Mom and Great Aunty said, "You are very resourceful. We didn't make a mistake bringing you along."

That small bit of success encouraged me for my next task. We went into a salon in town and asked for the cost of a perm. I asked, "How much?" and used my fingers to curl my hair. The hair stylist told me the price in English, but I didn't understand. I used my hands to gesture asking her to write it down on paper. My English was so poor that I struggled to communicate even with simple words.

We all got our hair permed and cut that day, but afterward I told myself I had to learn more English so that I wouldn't struggle as much the next time around.

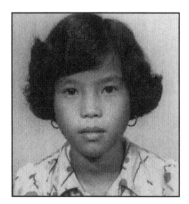

We discovered other reasons to go into Manila. We found out that a large Buddhist temple in town served free vegetarian food during the full moon or new moon celebrations and food offerings to

Figure 13-3: Nam Moi, 1979.

the gods and goddesses. A few women at the camp took buses to the temple and stayed for lunch. Mom and I went with them the first time.

Walking into that temple was like being at our temple back in Vietnam, with the same gods and goddesses. The only differences were that the Philippine temple was cleaner and the people were more organized. We knelt down to pay respect to each of the deities, and thanked them for our safe journey to freedom. Most of the people in the temple were Filipino of Chinese descent. They knew we were Chinese-Vietnamese refugees, and they were very nice to us. We came back to the temple a few more times during our stay.

Preparing for Life in the United States

The refugee camp offered English classes on Sundays from 9:00 a.m. until noon. The problem was, the program was sponsored by one of the Catholic churches in Manila. Most Vietnamese refugees of Chinese descent practiced Buddhism. They were not interested in learning about the Catholic religion, God or Jesus, and they feared if they attended the English classes, they would be converted to Catholicism against their will. As a result, very few of the refugees participated.

I knew the routine very well. Every Sunday a bus load of Filipinos in their late teens and early twenties came to the camp, including some of Chinese descent. They held a service that included a morning mass, with the church volunteers talking about Jesus for an hour. Then the English classes were taught, divided into sections for children and adults.

It was my first taste of any religion other than Buddhism, and the first time I heard about this great person named Jesus who was also God. When I was in Vietnam, some of our neighbors went to church, and they chanted passages from the Bible out loud, but I couldn't understand the meaning or the words. In the Manila refugee camp I didn't enjoy the Sunday morning masses, and I wasn't interested in the concept of God. Listening to someone preach about God and Jesus in a language I didn't understand felt like torture.

However, my attitude changed after my stumbling experience in town, when I hadn't been able to communicate in English. After that, I became serious about learning English, and tried to improve in any way that I could. From that time on, I never missed a Sunday class.

The volunteers had other inducements as well. Some Sundays they brought sweets to pass out to all the children after class, and other times they brought toys. One time they passed out shoes. We all lined up for those, but we were disappointed to see that the shoes for boys and girls were the same design. They looked more like shoes for boys. Buu and I each got a pair of shoes with blue fabric on top and a white rubber bottom. I was disappointed with my boy shoes, but I told myself, it was better than none at all. Tam got a pair of white and red tennis shoes, and Kau got a pair of blue tennis shoes.

Several times they brought a truck load of used clothing for the refugees to pick from. I didn't find anything for a teenage girl like me, but fortunately, I was able to pick out a few articles of clothing for my brothers and sister. I found a nice red dress for Tam and a green-striped shirt with a pair of gray pants for Buu. I was able to find a few sets of clothing for Kau, including a pair of overalls that featured patches. He wore them on our trip to the United States.

Since the French had occupied Vietnam for many years, we referred to Christmas as Noel. We were very excited to participate in the Noel festivities by the volunteers. They sang songs and provided snacks and drinks. At the time, we didn't understand the concept of exchanging gifts during Noel. The Sunday before, the volunteers brought toys for the children in the refugee camp under the age of six. Since I was going on thirteen and Buu was eleven, there were no toys or gifts for us. We didn't care that much, because we were very aware of the fact that all the material goods we had obtained would soon be worthless. Just like our toys in Vietnam, we would not be able carry them to our new home.

We also heard the volunteers were offering to take pictures of each family as part of the Noel celebration. I told my parents about it, and we wanted to take a family photo in memory of the Philippines, our adopted country for over a year. For days we wondered what to wear for the family picture. Fortunately, most of the children had something to wear from the donations. Tam wore her red dress. Kau wore a T-shirt and a pair of gray pants. Buu wore his green-striped T-shirt with a pair of long gray pants. Num had a nice shirt with a pair of black pants. My parents could still fit into their clothing from Vietnam. Since we hadn't bought any new clothing yet, I wore the best clothing that I had at the time, which meant the least worn out. It was a beige pajama-like outfit which Zenh had made me for the 1978 Chinese New Year celebration. I wore it along with my blue shoes.

On the day of the picture, Cun Kieu wanted to have a picture taken too, but her parents, Great Uncle #11 and Great Aunty #11, refused to have anything to do with picture taking or getting in line for hours. Cun Kieu was so upset, Dad offered to include her with our family. Although her red dress from Vietnam was a bit short, it was not obvious when she was sitting down. She did have to wear her slippers since she had not gotten in line to get a pair of new shoes. Each child had to be present when they

Figure 13-4: Family picture with Cun Kieu in Manila, December 1979.

passed them out. In my family, I made all the arrangements for younger siblings, since my parents, like Great Uncle #11, did not want to be bothered by waiting in line for hours. At last, all eight of us got our picture taken. The volunteers handed it to us the following week.

We soon were joined by other members of our family. Uncle Hai, Aunty Binh, and Lac had been staying at the military refugee camp since leaving *Tung An* in March 1979. The Filipino government decided to close that camp and transfer all the refugees to the Fabella camp by the end of 1979. When Dad heard the news, he reserved the hut next door to us for Uncle Hai's family. The cost of the hut was $120 dollars, with a smaller living area than ours, only capable of storing a bunk bed. They moved to the Fabella camp shortly after the New Year.

Since Uncle Hai and Aunty Binh had been living in Manila for over nine months, they had enjoyed more freedoms. In particular, Aunty Binh learned to knit and crochet with yarn that she purchased in town. When they moved next door to us, she taught Mom and me how to make hats, scarves, and sweaters. Mom proved better at knitting, while I preferred crocheting. As part of preparing for our new lives in the West, many female refugees took up knitting or crocheting. Mom and I went to town to get knitting and crocheting tools and yarn. We spent most of our free time weaving a hat and scarf for each of us. We would have knitting get-togethers. Mom's handiwork was more consistent and her designs were more complex. I made a lot of mistakes on my first hat, but the subsequent ones had fewer mistakes and required less rework.

In less than two months, I made four hats and two scarves for my siblings. Crochet, crochet, and more crochet was my world as the date approached to migrate to the United States. Mom knitted a few scarves, hats, and a sweater. Refugees with money could also order a knitted sweater, hat, or scarf from the refugees whom had lived in the camp for a couple of years while they were waiting for a Western sponsor. Between Mom and me, we made enough hats and scarves that each person in the family had a set. We were prepared for the cold climate in the United States before the departure date.

Figure 13-5: Nam Moi's handmade hats and scarf, February 1980.

Chapter 14

Transformation

At long last we were told by the Philippine authorities that we would be leaving for the United States in a few weeks. Dad immediately telegraphed our itinerary to my older brothers and sisters in Los Angeles. We were very excited that our family would soon be reunited.

My parents had been very frugal about how we spent the little money we had left. With our day of departure coming up, though, we needed to buy some clothing and shoes. After being refugees for fifteen months, the clothing we had brought from Vietnam was either worn out or not suitable for wearing in our new country. In Vietnam, women and girls wore thin cotton shirts and pants, similar in style to Western pajamas, but what we had was worn out. On the *Tung An* we had gone barefoot. Our shoes from Vietnam had been destroyed by salt water, our slippers from Tara were in tatters, and all we had left were slippers donated to us at the Manila refugee camp.

I was very excited about shopping in town. My parents took all of us to Chinatown in Manila so we could communicate with the merchants. Dad was very good at directions and finding destinations. We took the bus and then walked to Chinatown. As we walked down the streets, people stared at us like we were a spectacle. First, we stopped at a shoe store and tried on shoes. They didn't have some of the sizes we needed, so we had to go to another store to get the rest of the shoes. We also had to purchase a blouse or shirt for each of us.

The shopping excursion turned out to be a whirlwind. In a little over an hour, we were done. That's because shopping with my father was like being on a military mission. We searched for exactly those items each of us needed, engaged the shopkeepers and then bought our shoes and clothes.

Before we returned to camp, we were surprised by an unexpected treat. In front of several stores, cups of pre-made herbal teas were offered for sale. The weather in Manila was hot and humid, even in early February, and we kids were thirsty. When we stopped at one store and asked how much a cup of herbal tea cost, the store owner told us it was free for us. We were very grateful, because my parents were reluctant to buy drinks for everyone, seven of us in all. We drank the herbal tea like we were about to die of thirst. The people working at the store told us to drink some more, but my parents only allowed us to have only one cup each, because they didn't want to take advantage of a stranger's generosity.

As the travel date to United States approached, my parents and the next door neighbor's family decided to visit Manila for the last time with the entire family. Only this time, with our new clothes, we would go as tourists and not as refugees. It was our way of closing this chapter of our lives. The neighbor's family had six children—five girls and a boy. Their oldest daughter was my age and their son was Buu's age. Their younger four daughters were in between Kau and Tam's age. The neighbor's family was also migrating to the United States but not to California.

In early February, Num turned fifteen. As a teenager, he often hung out with other teenagers or young adults without parents traveling with them. He spent most of his time in Manila not with our family but only came home for lunch, dinner, or to sleep at night. My parents worried about him being influenced by other teenagers without parental guidance. They reminded him often not to get in trouble or he would have to stay behind. Num opted out of the outing to Manila with family and friends, which was no surprise to any of us.

All the children were very excited, and we chattered about wearing our new clothes. This was important to us because so many times we had appeared in public as refugees with our worn-out clothing from Vietnam. This time, all dressed up, only days away from immigrating to our new country, our transformation physically, emotionally, and mentally was increasing each day. Physically, it didn't take much for us to transform from a refugee to a tourist. Wearing the newly purchased clothing, we looked like normal people in the Philippines.

Our self-worth and pride showed in our faces and body gestures. Mentally, as each day passed, we counted down to the date of departure. We were ready to start the new chapter of our lives with our family and relatives in the West and leave the hardship and unpleasant memories of the past year behind. Emotionally, as we announced our departure date to the other refugees, we started to say, "Good-bye and well wishes" to each of our friends. We got more excited each day and wondered what America would be like. We wondered if America had Chinese food and people like us.

In the middle of the morning, all the kids went to wash up at the two-story cement building before putting on our new outfits. The two mothers cooked an early lunch for everyone to eat before heading out to town. We still could not afford to buy food and drinks at a restaurant, so this lunch had to last us until we got back to the camp for dinner. With our stomachs full and new clothing on, we were ready to venture out. All fourteen of us took a bus to Manila. Then we traveled by foot to various landmarks in the city such as Manila Bay, the famous water fountain at the United States embassy, Rizal Park, and the Chinese Garden, all in close proximity to each other.

Walking in the hot Manila sun was hard on the children. The youngest in the group were only two to three years old. The Chinese Garden, a large park with benches, swing sets, seesaws, gazebos, and rest areas, was the best part of the day. All the kids enjoyed running freely around the park and playing in the playground while the adults sat on shaded benches under the trees. We spent a long time at the park before heading back to the refugee camp. Our neighbor was able to take some pictures of our visits at the various landmarks with the camera he had purchased a few weeks earlier.

Figure 14-1: Friends and family at Embassy of the USA in Manila, 1980.

Figure 14-2: Playing with friends in the Chinese Garden in Manila, 1980.

Figure 14-3: Family picture at the Chinese Garden in Manila, 1980.

We managed to last throughout the day trip without spending any money on water or food, but we were extremely thirsty by the time we made it back. Overall, it was a fun, memorable trip, a last hurrah in our adopted country.

As part of dumping our refugee baggage, literally and figuratively, we started to give our things away to refugees still remaining in the camp. We gave used items such as old shoes, clothing, glass jars, pots, and pans to the poor Filipinos in the vicinity. They often came into the camp to collect recyclable items such as rubber, metal, and glass for resale and were usually happy to receive donations. All the items we collected from the Tara Island and the Fabella camp were left behind. We only brought our newly purchased clothing and our precious things from Vietnam like photographs and Dad's nice suits. With new waves of refugees continually arriving at the Fabella refugee camp, our hut was in high demand. However, my parents were not interested in making a profit under the circumstances. The people selling the hut preferred to sell to other refugees' relatives or friends by word of mouth, and that's why Great Uncle #11 purchased our hut from us. We sold the hut for $150, the price we paid for it. We were grateful to be able to live in the hut for those three months. To take advantage of other refugees when selling it seemed morally wrong to my parents.

Great Uncle #11's family and Uncle Hai's family were still waiting for their departure dates. Uncle Hai and Aunty Binh would end up having a change of heart about immigrating to the United States when they heard that Switzerland had more social programs for kids with special needs. Lac had speech difficulties and was unable to walk due to her uneven legs and misaligned spine. They were afraid that Lac would not be able to live a normal life without early intervention. After waiting for more than a year in a Manila refugee camp, Uncle Hai's family was accepted by Switzerland. The officials of that country announced that the refugees could leave within days. At that point, it was more important for them to get a new start than to hold out indefinitely for possible resettlement in the United States. They left for Switzerland on March 6, 1980, sixteen months after leaving their home in Vietnam.

Along with a group of 15 refugee families, Uncle Hai, Aunty Binh, and Lac arrived in Switzerland. The refugees were first brought to a temporary refugee camp, where the government provided living arrangements, clothing, and food. Soon, they were transferred to Caritas Lugano, a Swiss organization to help people in need. They received assistance to find a job, learn the local language and the Swiss culture. They were also introduced to a local sponsor family in charge of giving them support of any sort, with which they are still in touch today.

The sponsor family helped Uncle Hai's family to find a place to live and provided all the necessary comforts in starting out their lives in a new environment. The process of integration finally could begin. At the beginning their new life was daunting. Not being able to move around autonomously and encountering the cultural differences on a daily basis made them feel disconnected from their surroundings. It seemed difficult to imagine that they could rebuild a new life. Being one of a few Asians among all Westerners, it felt as though everyone was constantly noticing them. Over time, the local people got used to them and they got used to living in a Western environment.

One of the things that struck Uncle Hai and Aunty Binh the most at first was the high mountains, which they were not used to. Living in Vietnam, they had seen mainly flat lands. At times Aunty Binh felt the mountains were collapsing toward her. After living at the foot of the mountains for many years, though, this fear has become a distant memory.

Living in Locarno, the family learned Italian, the official local language. Uncle Hai and Aunty Binh went to school to learn Italian for many months, which is very different from Chinese or Vietnamese. With the help of the sponsor family, Uncle Hai was

Figure 14-4: Aunty Binh and Lac in Switzerland, 1980.

Figure 14-5: Uncle Hai and Lac at the lake in Switzerland, 1981.

able to find a job with a local company in Losone, producing advanced milling machines. When Lac reached school age, she attended a special school for students with special needs and autism. She continued with her schooling until age eighteen before attending a trade school.

Figure 14-6: Lac in school.

As Lac became more independent, Aunty gave birth to two sons, Liam and Mann, a year apart. Uncle Hai was the single income provider for the family for many years and they had to live frugally. The family lived in a small two-bedroom apartment for over thirty years.

Once all the children were in school, Aunty Binh entered the workforce, taking a job in a large chain clothing store in Locarno.

With a second income they were able to visit family in the United States every few years. Over the years Uncle Hai's family remained close to family and relatives in United States. Although the official language is Italian, the family have continued to speak *Hakka* and Cantonese at home with each other and the children even today.

In April 1980, Great Uncle #11's family of four, Great Uncle #11, Great Aunty #11, Cun Kieu, and Great Aunty #11's mother, immigrated to Los Angeles and reunited with their son Gieng.

We were the first Ung family from the *Tung An* to travel to the United States. Altogether, we spent over sixteen months as refugees. We stayed for over nine months on the *Tung An*, close to three months in Tara Island and over three months in the Fabella refugee camp.

For our trip to the United States, Num, Buu, and I packed our belongings in the brown nylon bags that Mom had given us back home. Mom and Dad packed the things for Tam and Kau in their bags. We traveled lightly, because so much of what we had prized as refugees would be useless in our new world.

Journey to the United States

On February 24, 1980, we had our last breakfast. Our bags were packed and ready to go first thing that morning. We said good-bye to our Ung relatives and friends in the refugee camp before a bus came to take us to the airport. Unlike when we left Vietnam, facing an uncertain future, this trip to United States was filled with the excitement of seeing my siblings again and the hope of a better life in our new country.

The journey to the United States was our first experience on a plane. It was both a novelty and a cause of fear at the same time. The idea of riding on a plane, which we likened to taking a sky bus, was wholly beyond our comprehension. We didn't know what to expect. Weighing heavily on our minds was the possibility of our plane going out of control and crashing somewhere far below.

As our anxieties were building up, Dad reassured us that we were not the first people ever to fly. Everything would be fine. Many people traveled safely by plane around the world every day.

Our flight to the United States took more than twenty-four hours. The United States government paid for our tickets in return for a promise we would pay back the cost within a few years. Our tickets must have been inexpensive because the itinerary called for long layovers at three separate destinations on the way from Manila to Los Angeles.

The first leg was from Manila to Guam with couple hours' layover there. We started the journey with a positive attitude. Although we were nervous, especially during the takeoff and landing, the flight to Guam was relatively short. We were fine for the most part.

The second leg of the trip, to Oahu in Hawaii, was a longer flight, and we had our first meal on the plane. The plane encountered turbulence and we started to get motion sickness. Everyone was sick except for Dad and Num. Mom, Kau, and I were the most nauseated. The food we ate didn't sit well in our stomachs, given our growing anxiety as the plane battled through the storm clouds. Most of the food we ate came right up over the course of the flight. Once we arrived at the Oahu airport, we were relieved to be on solid ground. However, the three of us continued to vomit until there was no more food left in our stomachs. For the next five hours, we waited at the airport, trying to recover from motion sickness.

Nonetheless, we felt lucky to be in Hawaii. Dad said this was one of the most popular places for people to vacation. We hoped to get a glimpse of the beaches or the famous surf, but as we looked out from the Oahu airport, we could only see mountains.

The time came to board for our flight to California. We were no longer thrilled to be getting on a plane after our last experience.

We had to make changes in order to make it through another flight. This time around, we limited our intake of food to items that were not greasy, like bread or fruit. We continued to feel severe motion sickness even with the new strategy.

After more than five hours, my siblings and I thought we finally had reached Los Angeles. Yet we landed in San Francisco instead and had a long layover due to weather issues, which was a big disappointment for all of us. Two people in their early twenties, one male and one female, were overseeing the group of refugees at the airport. They could speak only English, however. Our eyes filled with tears when we heard the announcement. We said to my parents, "We are so close but still not in Los Angeles." At this point we were tired, cold, thirsty, and hungry.

We were told the delay could be as long as eight hours. We sat on the floor of the airport terminal with our belongings lying around us. The time passed so slowly. I kept asking our guides, "How much longer?" For hours their reply was "We don't know, the plane is not taking off yet."

After five hours of waiting, we were told we had to wait three more hours. Many refugee children cried, "Sir, we are hungry." It felt like the *Tung An* all over again. Our two guides felt bad and purchased some Chinese noodles and fried rice with their own money to share among the several dozen refugee children. We all jumped up and down with joy at finally being able to eat. I ran back to where my parents, Tam, and Kau were sitting to tell them. Dad ordered all of us not to participate. "You must not take advantage of the generosity of strangers. We are not on the *Tung An*. We are only a few hours away from reuniting with your siblings. A little hunger now will not kill us. We survived the hardship on the *Tung An*. This is nothing compared to that experience."

Although we disagreed with Dad, since many other refugees were eating the free food, we replied with disappointment,

"We understand." All of us were very obedient children, and we followed our parents' instructions without question. My dad had his reasons for what he did that we didn't understand as children. We did know that our parents had sacrificed a lot for us—their wealth, social standing, and dignity—especially my dad. For the next few hours, we watched these kids and adults chowing down food while our stomachs were growling. We also had to endure the other refugee children telling us how delicious food was in America.

Reunited

When we finally boarded the plane heading to Los Angeles, we started to get excited again. This was our final destination. Mercifully, the plane ride from San Francisco to Los Angeles took only a little over an hour. Finally, we landed at Los Angeles Airport. When the passengers on the plane started to walk off the plane, we grabbed our belongings eagerly. We couldn't wait to leave, knowing my siblings were just outside the gate. I was the first one in line as we walked into the terminal.

My four siblings, Zenh, Hong, Kien, and Xi were waiting patiently for us. I rushed to hug my sisters, Zenh and Kien. I called out each of my siblings' names in *Hakka*, the ones given by the monk after birth. I called Zenh "Phung Chi" because Phung is Zenh's *Hakka* name and Chi means "older sister" in *Hakka*. I greeted Kien "Moi Chi," with tears of joy running down my face. I turned to greet Xi and Hong by calling their names.

I was so relieved to see them again. With my sisters around, the burden of being the oldest daughter was lifted off me instantly. With my older brothers around, I was no longer helpless. The other family members, one by one, walked off the plane behind me and met up with my elder siblings. We all had tears of joy in our eyes as we hugged each other. All those months of hardship as refugees on the *Tung An*, Tara Island, and the Manila camp melted away because our entire family had now safely migrated from Vietnam to the United States.

Zenh, Hong, Kien, and Xi were happy to see their parents again. For close to two years, they had to make decisions without their parents' guidance. Mom and Dad felt complete again with all their children in one place. They had worried that Zenh, Hong, Kien, and Xi couldn't endure the hardships in a new land since they had lived such a prosperous life in Vietnam. Seeing them as mature adults and looking healthy made my parents so happy, especially Mom. In all of our minds were the unspoken words: Dad's plan worked. All eleven of us were healthy and alive in the United States. The way was open for a better life.

A total of three cars came to pick us up. Since my siblings did not own a car, they had asked Uncle Tac's friends to pick us up. The ride from the airport to Chinatown was our first experience of bumper-to-bumper L.A. traffic. Seeing all the lanes of cars completely stopped with their brake lights on, I asked Kien, "Why are we sitting in a big parking lot along with so many cars?"

She told me, "Nam Moi, we are not in a big parking lot but on a freeway with many lanes going in only one direction. We must be in a traffic jam caused by an accident ahead somewhere, since today is Sunday."

I was amazed by all the cars around us and all the roads with no end in sight. We saw many buildings tall and short on our ride home. The stop and go motion caused us to be nauseated all over again with motion sickness. Mom, Kau, and I vomited all the way home for over an hour and a half. Luckily, we were prepared. We had requested that the stewardess on the plane give us extra bags.

By the time we got to the two-bedroom apartment on Broadway in Chinatown, we were very weak and exhausted from the long journey that had started in Manila seemingly days ago. We were greeted by Great Uncle #7's family. Great Uncle #7 had arrived in the United States a couple of months before. On June 6, 1979, Great Uncle #7 had left Vietnam in a thirty-meter long wooden boat along with Great Uncle #6's and Great Uncle #4's families.

Singapore and Malaysia refused to accept them, and their boat was towed out to international waters. After ten days of sailing, they reached the Pulau Buton Island in Indonesia and ended up staying at the Indonesia refugee camp for months. All the Ungs on that boat later migrated to the United States.

Great Aunty #7 had dinner ready for us. It was our first meal at home together in our new country. The meal tasted so good, with various dishes and soup. It was like a holiday celebration back home. We ate like we hadn't seen food for days. Great Aunty #7 and Great Aunty #7's mother kept telling us to eat more. They said, "We have more groceries in the refrigerator for the next meal. We eat every day here like it is a holiday."

In this two-bedroom apartment with one full bath, lined with carpet, we had eighteen people staying. People slept everywhere except for the kitchen and the bathroom. Although it was crowded, it was still better than Manila refugee camp. We'd had only seven by seven feet of the living space in the hut with no washroom or toilet. In this apartment we had a kitchen, dining table, chairs, refrigerator, and a living room with sofas and television. However, since we had so many people with only one bathroom, Dad told us to give priority to the people going to work or school. We must not inconvenience them. We had to use the bathroom in late morning or early afternoon and be mindful not to stay in there longer than necessary. That bathroom was occupied most of the time throughout the day. My parents, younger siblings, and I took our baths in the afternoon. Although the tub had a shower, we did not use it at first. We continued to take baths like we were in Vietnam. It took us a few days to understand how to use the shower.

As part of the requirements for entering the United States, we had to get another physical checkup. After getting adjusted to the new time zone, the entire family walked over forty minutes to a local hospital. Each of us had to take a skin test to check for tuberculosis, and within a few days, we had to walk back to the hospital for a follow-up exam. We left the house early in the morning after breakfast. Since we couldn't afford the bus fare, Dad used a Thomas Guide map to chart a route by foot. It included a walkway above the freeway and through residential areas. Once we arrived at the hospital, we had to wait for hours before the hospital staff was ready to see us. It was close to noon before we were examined. The walk back was hard with empty stomachs and the hot sun beating on us. Altogether we had to make four round trips to the hospital.

We lived with Great Uncle #7's family in the two-bedroom apartment for close to a month before moving into our own home. The transition to our new lives was not over yet. We still had to face all of the obstacles of penniless immigrants in a new land. We never doubted, though, that Dad had made the right decision.

Chapter 15

Starting Over

We started our lives in the United States in severe poverty. We had no means of earning money to support the eleven people in the family. We had to register to receive government assistance. Finally, a check arrived from the government, and our family was able to start our newest chapter as American citizens. At that time, Chinatown and Monterey Park, a suburb east of the city, had a high density of Chinese and Vietnamese immigrants. Alhambra, just north of Monterey Park, at the time had a lower immigrant population, and my parents thought we would learn English faster with fewer Asians around. The population mix in Alhambra changed over the years, though, as more Vietnamese refugees and various Asian minorities immigrated to the United States.

In late March 1980, when I turned thirteen, my family rented a 2 ½-bedroom town house with a bath and a laundry area in Alhambra. The decision to move there was mainly based on the location and the price of the rent. It was close to three bus lines, which went to Chinatown and Pasadena City College, where my siblings commuted on most days. The rent was also cheap due to the poor condition of the place.

We lived on the upper floor of the town house with close to 1,000 square feet. Carpets covered the bedrooms and living room, and the rest of the place had vinyl flooring. The two bedrooms were a standard size with a closet. The half bedroom was converted from a laundry room or pantry with a plastic corrugated door and windows on two of the three walls. This room was only big enough for a bunk bed and a small desk and chair, without a closet or storage space. Kien and I shared the tiny bedroom and stored our clothing in the hallway closet. I slept on the top bunk, with one side and the foot of the bunk bed facing the two windows.

The five boys—Hong, Xi, Num, Buu, and Kau—slept in one room with two queen-size and one twin-size mattresses lined wall to wall. My parents and Tam slept in the other bedroom with a king-size bed and a twin-size bed for Tam. The town house was old and rundown, with old-style window panes and no air conditioning or heating. It was also poorly insulated, and windows covered one wall in the living room, dining room, and kitchen. That meant it was very cold in the winter and hot in the summer. The temperature inside was sometimes worse than it was outside. In the winter especially, we would wear jackets, scarves, socks, and gloves around the house like we were outdoors. Our landlord refused to fix the kitchen counter with its vinyl sheet half peeled off, and the garage was totally damaged by termites and infested with mice. Since we didn't own many belongings, not having a usable garage was not an issue.

We only had the essential items in the house that my parents furnished, an old sofa from a thrift store, a simple dining table with a formica top and four metal legs, ten metal folding chairs, and a bunk bed. The new things we soon purchased were a refrigerator, my parents' king-size bed with a metal frame, a rice cooker, dishes, and a few cooking utensils, including a wok. Zenh had purchased several blankets and bed sheets before we arrived. Although our home was dilapidated and not as comfortable as other people's homes, compared to the refugee hut in the Philippines, we considered ourselves much better off. We were particularly happy to have a place of our own, no longer having to share that two-bedroom apartment with Great Uncle #7's family or having to walk a few minutes to use the bathroom in Manila

Refugee Camp. Best of all, our family was complete again; we were ready to rebuild our lives together.

Once we had a place to live, we were able to enroll in school. Hong, Kien, and Xi transferred from Belmont High and Nightingale Junior High schools to Alhambra High School with Hong in eleventh, Kien in tenth, and Xi in ninth grade. Dad enrolled in a trade school to learn how to operate printing machines. He was soon learning a trade during the day and going to English as Second Language (ESL) night school with Mom in the evenings. Since Dad had learned French before, learning English was not as much of a problem.

Figure 15-1: Dad (Ly Sang) at Night School, December 1980.

Mom, on the other hand, struggled to learn English. She didn't even know how to write the basic alphabet. That quickly became a problem because as a parent in the United States, she had to sign many of our school documents. She wanted to just put an X as her signature, but I didn't feel that would be acceptable legally. I taught Mom how to write her name by using Kau's homework material from kindergarten as a sample. I started with her tracing her name on a piece of paper and then later writing it in free hand without any aid. After a month of training, she finally mastered writing her full name.

Armed with a utility bill with Dad's name, Zenh was able to enroll Num, my younger siblings and me in Northrup Elementary School in Alhambra. Num was slotted into eighth, me in seventh, Buu in sixth, Tam in first grade, and Kau in kindergarten.

Once we were settled, with everyone going to school, Zenh announced to the family that she had decided to move to Seattle, Washington, to live with a family friend and go to school there.

Her reason was the smog in Los Angeles, which caused her eyes to tear up. I was very sad to hear that Zenh was leaving us. I told my parents that she shouldn't be allowed to move away since we had just reunited. My parents said that during the two years we were apart, Zenh had taken on the role as head of the household, responsible for her three younger siblings. She had made all the arrangements for us to come to the United States. Zenh was old enough to make her own decisions.

I didn't understand why Zenh would want to move away. We had stayed together as a family through hardships and good times. As a family we could overcome any obstacles. Our long journey as refugees was proof of that. So I was sad, unable to see Zenh's viewpoint. After a few months without her, however, I came to accept how much we all had grown and changed, especially after two years of being apart. I myself was evolving as a teenager in my adopted country.

By the time we enrolled for classes, we had missed over half of a school year. Num, Buu, and I were behind in all our courses. It was easier for me to catch up in math than other subjects. Our English-language written and verbal skills were sorely behind for our grade level. We couldn't understand the teacher's instructions and were unable to read or understand the class work like everyone else. The school was flooded with Vietnamese immigrants and unprepared to handle the students' needs. There were no formal English as Second Language (ESL) classes until the next year.

In Northrup Elementary school, there were other Vietnamese immigrants who migrated before the big wave of 1980. I was quickly made aware of the social class differences between us and these earlier Vietnamese as well as the Chinese students who didn't have a refugee background at all. My family could only afford a few set of clothes, and we had to wear the same outfits every week. Our parents had to start all over in their career paths.

For the first few months of school, I was depressed and lonely, keenly aware that I did not fit in. I came to understand why my mom said being illiterate was like being blind and deaf. I couldn't understand the written materials in the textbook or the instructions or discussions in the class. For hours I patiently watched all the activities going on around me. Physical Education (PE) was the only class where I could truly participate. During recess, I would go to check on my siblings to see how they were doing. Tam and Kau were in a separate part of the school, where I was not allowed to go. Buu got involved in playing games with other boys during recess. Num started hanging out with his new friends. I mostly paced back and forth or walked in circles in the playground, since my class had no other Vietnamese or Chinese immigrants.

I tried hard to understand and absorb my new environment. It seemed impossible to be as good as a local kid. Luckily, the grading system was by letter grade and not a ranking system from one to the total number of students in the class. It didn't matter. I was sorely behind in all subjects. I told Dad that I was seven years behind in learning the English language. The prospect of going to college seemed out of reach. I felt like I was going to have to give up the dream of getting a higher education.

Dad taught us that we could always find a way to overcome our limitations. He said that I had to spend nights and weekends to catch up in school. That's what he did when he was thirteen, learning the French language for the first time. I knew Dad was right. I had five years before I would go to college and I couldn't waste any time. I learned English in every way I could: watching the news or commercials on TV, or singing along to the music on the radio. I also had a good example right in my own family. Hong was able to test for high school graduation credits in math and science in order to qualify for a high school diploma. He completed high school in less than three years.

The focus for all of us was to get a high school diploma and continue onto higher education. Dad projected confidence and a positive attitude in our ability to achieve in school. In his mind, failure in school was not an option. My parents demanded that we do well because otherwise we would waste the precious gold that had been paid for the opportunity to emigrate to our new land. We did our homework on the dining room table before and after dinner, as we had in Vietnam, except we were all on our own.

To help us focus in school, Dad imposed a rule that the television had to be off from Sunday after dinner through Friday before dinner. This rule applied to Mom as well, which meant that no one was allowed to turn on the television for any reason. On several occasions we disobeyed Dad's rule, watching the Superman movie and the Shogun television series while they were at night school. On those occasions we were careful to turn off the television minutes before our parents were expected to come home. Kau was not interested in watching, since the Shogun series was four two-hour shows beyond his comprehension, and he told on us after we watched the first time. After our parents arrived home, he said, "Everyone watched television except me. I told them to turn it off because Dad said no TV during week nights. They didn't listen to me and continued watching."

Our parents didn't take any action to discipline us, however. Kau was shocked and felt that our parents didn't believe him. He dragged Mom's hands to feel the heat on the back of the television after being on for over an hour.

Mom said to us, "Doing well in school will only benefit you. You shouldn't get distracted by other activities."

The next night, we gave Kau a hard time for being a snitch. Kien, Buu, Tam, and I ganged up on him, putting ice on his chest and belly while pinning him down on the floor. That night he was quiet when our parents came home but looked unhappy. We were also smarter in turning the television off earlier than the night before, to allow it to cool off.

Early Struggles

The money we received each month from government assistance was just enough for food and a few necessities. We had to live within our means. Since food was our biggest expense, we found ways to cook inexpensive meals that could feed ten people. My parents, younger siblings, and I walked to the grocery store, and I helped plan meals for the family. We calculated the cost to cook each dish and then chose the least expensive one. Mostly, our meals consisted of a lot of vegetables such as carrots, potatoes, cabbage, and a small amount of chicken or meat. We couldn't afford meals like pork chops, steaks, or seafood. Since most of us were growing teenagers, we could eat one to two pork chops or steaks apiece. Yet a few expensive meals like that would blow our budget for the entire month.

Our favorite meal was soup and noodles for brunch on weekends. Mom would cook a big pot of pork bone soup with ground pork, crab paste with eggs mixed together and fresh tomato chunks, which we ate with rice noodles. In Vietnam we called it "*bun rieu.*" A woman used to sell it on the street by our house.

Figure 15-2: Mom (Kieu) and Dad (Ly Sang) in Alhambra house, 1980.

During our early days in Alhambra, we walked or took public transportation everywhere. Within a ten-minute walk in three different directions, we were close to three bus lines with various connections to and from the different sections of Los Angeles. It was convenient for Hong, Kien, and Xi to take buses to work. Hong worked in Monterey Park at the Man Wa Supermarket, packing groceries. One time he saw a famous Hong Kong actor, Jackie Chan, shopping. Hong was very excited about telling the family that he saw Chan in person—only to find out that we didn't know who Jackie Chan was.

Xi and Kien took buses to work in Chinatown on the weekends. Xi worked as a parking lot attendant at the East-West bank for over four years. While he was not busy, he would use the down time to study. Kien worked at a jewelry store, and as part of her job of buying and selling gold, she tracked the daily price of gold. The value of gold was very important to our family. If our parents hadn't had the foresight to invest in gold, we wouldn't have been able to emigrate at all. Talking about gold prices and the importance of saving and investing were common topics at dinner.

Although we could take Metro bus line 76 four stops to visit the Diep family and Phuong, our neighbor from Vietnam, now living in San Gabriel, my parents, Buu, Tam, Kau, and I would walk over every few weekends on foot. Bus fares for the six of us could add up over time. Dad said walking was good exercise and we could also see more things that way. On the night we planned to visit the Diep family, we would have dinner early and walk the forty minutes to their house. We would visit for an hour or so and then walk back home. When we went to Chinatown to visit relatives, however, it was too far to walk and we had to take the bus.

Walking seemed to take too long, and after several months Buu and I asked our parents to buy us a used bike to ride around the neighborhood. We knew of a thrift store on Main Street, because Buu and I would go window shopping there on weekends. One day we saw a $12 used bike along with a pair of $2 roller skates. My parents often took walks after dinner with my younger siblings and me, and on one of those walks we were able to convince them to go to the thrift store, twenty minutes away. While we were walking, we told our parents about the $12 bike that had just come in last week. Inside the thrift store, Buu and I took turns demonstrating for our parents by sitting on the bike. We begged and pleaded for that used bike. Since we had arrived in the United States, we hadn't asked for anything from our parents. Buu and I promised we would share the bike with our other siblings.

Kau saw a tricycle in the store for five dollars, and he said that he and Tam could share the tricycle. I wanted a pair of roller skates too for just $2, but Mom said the roller skates would be too dangerous and we could get hurt. Mom had been taught by her mother to be cautious about everything. Any activities, especially sports, swimming, or any kind of play, even being in a crowded place, were dangerous. I told Dad that the $2 pair of roller skates was much better than the one he had bought for Xi in Vietnam.

The roller skates we had in Vietnam were made out of plastic. These roller skates were like a pair of shoes with rollers on the bottom. Dad saw how excited we were and decided to buy the bike, tricycle and the pair of roller skates. They kept us busy on the weekends and the long summer days.

Figure 15-3: Tam and Kau on the tricycle, 1980.

Since our money was so limited, we couldn't afford to get our hair done at a salon. The first haircut and perm I had in the United States was at someone's house, the way most new immigrants we knew from Vietnam did. Dad took us by bus to a house in Lincoln Heights to get Mom's and my hair done. I requested a perm and a cut. I explained that my haircut had to be layered since I have thick, coarse hair. Instead, the lady hairdresser gave me a bob cut, straight across two inches below my ears and a straight bang above my eyebrows. My hair looked like a broom. The woman was not interested in spending any more time on me with other customers waiting to get their hair done. I pleaded with her to layer my hair in order to reduce the puffiness, but she refused and demanded that I get off the chair. Getting angry, I told her that my mom was paying her to make me look good, not look like a broom. My words had no effect on her. I got so mad. I made a scene with everyone watching me. Embarrassed, my mom apologized for my inappropriate teenage behavior. Not to be deterred, I told the hairdresser in an outraged voice, "If you ever sit on my chair for a haircut, I will give you the same treatment as you gave me." I got off her chair and started tearing up while sitting in the corner, waiting for Mom to be done.

At age thirteen, having a terrible haircut felt like the end of the world. I didn't want to go to school looking so awful. I ended up cutting my own hair, learning how to layer my hair with the aid of mirrors placed all around me. I continued to experiment with my hair for the next few weeks. We never went back again to the hairdresser, working out of her house without a license. Mom started giving haircuts to Dad, Buu, Tam, and Kau at home. It was not hard to convince them to give me a chance to practice on their hair. Using my new haircut as proof, I told them that I couldn't be any worse than Mom.

Although my older siblings were reluctant, my younger siblings were convinced and allowed me to cut their hair. However, Dad insisted that Mom continue to cut his hair. My haircutting skill improved quickly with more practice, and I was soon able to train Mom on how to give Dad a better haircut. At age 16, I registered for the beauty school program at the high school. This program was sponsored by the state of California to provide low-income students with a trade after high school. I spent three hours each day from Tuesday to Friday after school and all day on Saturday attending the John Regel Beauty School in Temple City. My older siblings' attitudes changed once I got formal training, and they started to request that I give them haircuts. For the first year I gave them a hard time for not believing in my ability to cut their hair before. With more opportunities to cut hair, I continued to experiment with various hairstyles, giving my siblings the latest hairstyles of the 1980s. Xi and Buu had various versions of a mullet haircut, since they were more willing to try new hairstyles. By the time I graduated high school, I also graduated from the John Regel Beauty School. I had to earn 1,600 hours of beauty school in order to qualify for a cosmetology exam and to obtain a cosmetology license in order to work at a salon. The summer of

1985, I passed the exam, using Mom as my model, and was able to work at a salon.

During our first Christmas in Alhambra, we watched our neighbors decorate their houses with lights, and we could see their Christmas trees through the front windows. We were filled with curiosity and fascination. Everyone rushed around buying things and wrapping gifts as part of getting into the holiday spirit. We thought it was more like a shopping holiday and didn't understand the true meaning of Christmas. Not used to celebrating the season, we didn't have the money to buy a Christmas tree or lights to decorate our home. Kau begged our parents to buy him a small Christmas tree so we would not be the only house without Christmas decorations. My parents didn't see the point of spending their limited funds on decorating the house. In their minds, it was a waste of money. Since it was our first Christmas in the United States, we didn't know what to expect.

We had two weeks off from school, a mini winter break with nothing to do. After dinner, we would walk around our neighborhood to see each house decorated with lights, sometimes accompanied by figurines and statues. On Christmas night our next door neighbors, living in a four-unit complex, had a big party with food, drink, and music. We watched from our windows with curiosity. My younger siblings and I would announce to the family what we observed. Our neighbors' enjoyment was utterly foreign to us.

The day after Christmas, many people dumped their Christmas trees by the curb, as though they couldn't wait to get rid of them. I told Kau, "Let's go Christmas tree shopping."

As we walked down the street, I told him, "You can have any tree your heart desires. We have so many to choose from." Kau was pleasantly surprised seeing so many selections, and they were all free. After many debates and discussions, we decided a small artificial tree would best fit our house. We found several that were being discarded, but we chose a three-foot tree. Now we needed Christmas lights to go with it. We continued walking, checking the bags lying on the sidewalk with mostly broken ornaments. Finally, we found a string of Christmas lights with a few lights missing. We brought back the Christmas tree and lights, joyful like we had just won the lottery. We displayed the tree proudly in the corner of the living room closest to the street. We still didn't have any ornaments, though.

Luckily, in school my younger siblings and I learned how to make ornaments with toothpicks glued together as a picture frame with pictures we cut out from advertisements of things we liked. During our time off from school, making ornaments was a good project to keep us busy. Our Christmas tree was soon decorated nicely with lights and the ornaments we had made. We noticed that some people in the neighborhood still kept their house decorated with lights and Christmas tree until after New Year. For a few short days we were proud of our Christmas tree decoration and no longer felt left out. We liked our tree so much that we kept it on display for the whole year until the following Christmas. Only after New Year of the following year were we ready to put it away.

Teenage Years

My maternal grandparents immigrated to Los Angeles in July 1980 from the Philippine Refugee Camp. Once we arrived in-country, they were able to prove they had relatives living in the United States. It took five months for refugee processing before they arrived. Our house was too small and couldn't accommodate my grandparents' family for long. Dad had already arranged to rent a place for them in an apartment complex in the city of Van Nuys where Great Uncle #4, Great Uncle #9, and Great Uncle #11 lived. They moved into an apartment with two bedrooms and one bathroom in the same complex as our other great uncles.

The rent in Van Nuys was cheaper than our town house in Alhambra. Since several companies were hiring, Uncle Sanh got a job working as a technician, testing electronic boards, within a few months. Aunty Ngoc and Uncle Han started high school in the fall. Grandfather Liam started working at a mattress factory. Dad would take us by bus to see our great uncles' and grandparents' families in Van Nuys every few weeks. Once we owned a car, we would go more often. For a few summers, my brother Buu and I would spend a week with my grandparents and hang out with Great Uncle #9's children and other cousins our age. We called them uncles and aunties even though several of the children were younger than us. In the hierarchy of the Ung family, they belonged to the Menh generation.

My parents relied on rigid processes and rules to manage their large family. One rule was that we must be home to eat dinner by six thirty every night regardless of the day of the week. Mom said it would be impossible to manage the food portions if some of us ate at different times. During the day, we all had our own busy schedules, but we made it a priority to be home for dinner. If anyone wasn't home on time, that meant they wouldn't eat. At best they would have leftovers, but that was only if there were any leftovers. Since most of my siblings were growing teenagers, we didn't want to miss dinner by being late.

Figure 15-4: Family picture with maternal grandparents' family, July 1980.

Dinner was more like a family meeting with Dad as the head of the household and Mom as his right-hand person. My parents never contradicted each other. They might have disagreements, but they resolved them privately and never in front of us. At dinner we would share our stories of the day and make any request we had of our parents or sometimes siblings. My parents also used dinnertime to talk to their children. Dinner was a special time together as a family.

During our first summer in Alhambra, Buu and I hung out with some friends we met at school. They were a brother and sister close to our ages, also Chinese immigrants from Vietnam. My friend Huong was in eighth grade and I was in seventh grade. She loved to dress up and put on makeup. Her parents were seamstresses and made her many fashionable clothes.

That summer we spent many days together at her apartment complex and rode our bikes all over Alhambra and San Marino. When we ran out of ideas or places to go, Huong would suggest picking fruit from homes in her neighborhood. The first time I brought fruit home, Dad told Buu and me not to take any fruit from people's yards, not even the fruit that fell on the ground. When I told Huong about my dad's reprimand, we continued to pick fruit from people's yards for Huong but we didn't bring any home.

I remained unhappy about that, and then the issue came to a head. One day Huong suggested that we hang out at a department store in Alhambra. I later learned that Huong loved makeup but wasn't able to afford it, so she would steal. While we were looking around, she came up to me with a lipstick and shoved it in my front pants pocket. She was very bossy and took advantage of our being new to the United States. I argued with her about taking the lipstick. I told her, "I don't steal."

She said, "The store security guard was watching me. Put this in your pocket and I will get it later."

I knew better from my parents. When Huong was walking away, ready to leave the store, I put the lipstick back on the shelf and made sure she hadn't shoved anything else in my other pockets. As I walked out the store, a security guard pulled me over to the side and accused me of stealing. He asked me to empty my pockets. I followed his instructions, but my pockets were empty. He looked puzzled and asked a female cashier to search me all over, including my shoes. I told the security guard, "I am not a thief and I don't steal." He let me go after the female cashier couldn't find anything on me.

Buu was waiting for me by the door, but Huong and her brother had taken off. While Buu and I rode together on a bike, I told him that we should stop hanging out with those two. It was a close call, and we could have gotten into trouble with the law and our parents. From that day on, we stopped seeing them. When I finally attended high school a year later, I distanced myself from Huong. She was only interested in boys and being popular in school, anyway. Getting an education was not a priority for her, which was the exact opposite of me.

In the school year of 1980-1981, I was in eighth grade. By that time Northrup Elementary School was more prepared with ESL classes after handling an influx of Vietnamese immigrant students. I was so advanced in my studies that I was pulled out of my class and asked to be a translator for the new Vietnamese female students. I told the ESL teachers that because my Vietnamese was limited, I would be unable to do that.

They asked, "Aren't you from Vietnam?"

I replied, "Yes, but I mainly spoke Chinese in Vietnam. Whatever I learned there in a couple years of schooling, I forgot."

One of the teachers said, "You know more Vietnamese than we do," and insisted that I explain to the new students their class schedule, including recess and lunch.

I introduced myself to two Vietnamese girls and said, "My name is Lin."

One of the girls said, "Len?"

I told her, "No, Lin."

She responded, "We'll just call you Len. That is close enough."

From that day on, I had a new name, Len. I since have been called Len by my Vietnamese friends in elementary school, high school and even today. When I get a phone call and someone says, "Hi Len," on the phone, I know the caller is an old friend from school.

I spoke to the new Vietnamese students with my limited Vietnamese, and they struggled to understand what I was saying, especially about lunch. I told them that I would show them instead of trying to explain in words. We met for lunch the first day and then every day from then on.

A few more Vietnamese students enrolled at Northrup in the following months. My Vietnamese improved quickly because these new friends would only speak Vietnamese. My family was amazed about how my ability to speak Vietnamese improved more in the United States than in Vietnam.

The eighth-grade class field trip near the end of the school year was the biggest event at the school. The eighth-grade students held various fundraisers throughout the year to reduce the cost of the trip. The final cost for each student was $50 for the week-long field trip with everything included. Hearing how excited all the eighth-grade students were, how much they were looking forward to the trip, got me excited and curious too. I had never been on a field trip or away from my family. None of my Vietnamese friends could afford to go.

Therefore, I was both excited and anxious at the same time when I told Dad about the trip. He shared with me his experience when he started French military boarding school. It took him awhile to get used to living away from his family at age thirteen. He remembered some of his classmates struggled with being away from home, which had a negative impact on their schooling. He said that it had been a good experience in learning to be independent.

To my surprise, Dad approved of my going on the trip. Fifty dollars was a lot of money for our family in the early 1980s. My siblings, and Mom, said that I shouldn't go. Fifty dollars could buy us many meals. Dad continued to support my desire to be away from the family for a week and have fun learning new things outside of the classroom environment. The next year he offered the same opportunity to Buu, but he was not interested.

I knew that my family had to make sacrifices because of the cost of the trip. I felt privileged and fortunate, especially since none of my friends could afford it. I went on the trip eager to learn what Americans did. For the first time I had to speak only English to all the people around me, and I ate American food for the whole week. I adapted well and had a lot of fun. Among the many first-time experiences, I learned archery, canoeing, hiking, and dancing.

The only annoying part was dealing with some of the male students. In most physical activities the male students felt the need to look down on females. While we were playing in a stream with our bathing suits on, a group of boys sat nearby, watching and commenting on our figures, making sure we could hear them. At age fourteen, I found boys annoying and I disliked dealing with their immaturity and inappropriate behavior.

My friends and I were teased by mostly Vietnamese boys daily during recess and after school. One day after school, two of the boys walking in front of us as we went home began singing, "Hey, tigers from Asia. They are mean and deadly."

I had had enough and told my girlfriend we should catch up to them and hit them with our history books. My girlfriend and I snuck up closer and hit them hard with our history books on their heads and backs. We caught them by surprise. They didn't expect that at all. We told them, "We don't like you teasing us. You must stop. You got that?"

We didn't stop hitting them until they responded, "Yes, we got it."

From that day on, we got the reputation as the mean girls from Asia. Still, the teasing stopped. Our plan worked. However, these boys told all their friends in high school not to interact with us. They said that we might look pretty, but we were mean inside. The word must have spread, because for the most part, Vietnamese boys in high school left us alone.

On the last night of the field trip, we had a dance party with music and disco lights. I danced for the first time with my classmates, free style, to seventies music. For a few hours I didn't feel the social differences between the other students and me. We were all the same, kids having fun dancing together. The experience was liberating. The positive energy from dancing, from moving our feet to the beat of the music, allowed our mind to run free of the worry of not being good enough. I felt a oneness with the people on the dance floor. Even many years after that first experience, I still enjoy dancing and letting my spirit run free.

Near the end of the party, the teachers insisted that all the students had to experience slow dancing with the opposite sex. I thought, "There must be a boy that I could dance with. I just need to pretend he is Buu." When a teacher came and paired me up with a boy, my heart started racing. Everything around me went out of focus. After the music stopped, I thought, "I survived slow dancing with a boy without tripping or stepping on his feet." I felt relieved, and my heart slowed down to normal.

The next day, the bus took us back to school. When I got home, Mom asked, "What did you learn? Was it worth the money we spent?" I told my family that I had learned a lot. Dad noticed the changes in me even after only a week being away. He told me that the experience would help me build self-confidence.

On June 1981, I completed eighth grade. For graduation, girls had to wear a dress. My sister Kien didn't have one that I could borrow, and buying a new dress to wear only once seemed to be a waste of money. Kien asked a friend of hers if I could borrow a nice dress and shoes for graduation. Her friend loaned me a purple dress with white lace on the collar and a nice pair of shoes that went with the outfit. Ironically, one of the ESL teachers commented that I was the best-dressed person at the ceremony.

Figure 15-5: Nam Moi's 8th grade graduation, 1981.

My friends and I tried to find ways to have fun inexpensively. We were not interested in boys. They seemed to be too complicated to understand. Playing basketball or volleyball during recess and after school on Fridays was one way, since participating in those sports didn't require any money. In high school, we recruited enough girls to have five people on a side to play basketball. I continued to play every Friday after school for the first two years before starting beauty school. We were the only female team in the playground. After several games we would gather enough money to buy French fries to share among all of us. We usually bought two orders of fries at Rick's Burgers, a block from the high school, and shared them among the ten girls.

After a few years, my parents saved up enough money to buy a used car. One weekend Dad went with a car dealer who had been recommended by a family friend to the car auction center in San Gabriel. He bid on a car that was within his price range, less than $5,000. We were excited by the prospect of owning an automobile. Right before noon, Dad drove a yellowish brown Datsun 210 into the driveway. Our family was happy about the new car, but my siblings and I didn't like the color.

Dad explained, "We got a good value, paying only $4,000 because not too many people were interested in a car this color."

We were hoping to get a car like the red and black one in Xi's picture. Disappointed, I said to Dad, "The color looks like the color of a monk's robe."

Mom responded, "As long as the car is reliable, we shouldn't care too much about the color." She was right: we were happy to have a car in the family.

Now that we owned a car, Hong, Kien, Xi, Num, Buu, and I wanted to get our driver licenses. By the summer of 1984, we had seven drivers and one car. To put some order in sharing the one car between seven drivers, Dad announced the guidelines at dinner when everyone was present. Priority was given in order from the oldest to the youngest, using the car for work, school, and then play. With these guidelines we had to work out the schedules among ourselves. That was Dad's approach to managing his children. We knew not to get our parents involved with our disagreements. We would get lectured or we'd had to live with the decision they made.

With these guidelines, of course, Num, Buu, and I had no priority at all. It was impossible for me to use the car. However, one weekend afternoon I wanted to use the car for a few hours to see a movie with friends. I asked Kien's boyfriend to pick her up after work and he agreed. Xi was the only one that needed a car for work that day. After work he was going out with a female friend to a movie. I suggested that his friend pick him up at work and take him home to clean up before heading out. Buu and I agreed to keep his friend entertained while she waited for him.

Xi said, "She is a terrible driver. Also, I asked her out and I don't want her to drive."

I pleaded with him to explain the situation to his friend. He did and she agreed to drive. Yet I learned something from having to make all the arrangements. I was receiving early training in coordination between people to accomplish a goal. These skills in coordination would help me when I became an adult.

As we became more Americanized, we wanted to fit in like everyone else. We had forgotten about our parents' sacrifices. At age sixteen, several of my elementary school friends and I started attending beauty school. On Saturdays, we had training from 8:00 a.m. to 5:00 p.m. As part of the training, we had to work on each other's hair, nails, and makeup. We made each other look our best, but then we were all dolled up with no place to go. We tried to find things to do, like having a party at a friend's house. When I didn't go out with my girlfriends, I often would go to a house party with Xi. He knew a lot of people from working at the bank as the parking lot attendant, and he often got invited to parties.

My parents disapproved of their children being out past ten o'clock on the weekends, even though on weekdays we were good about doing our homework and staying in. We asked our parents to extend the time till midnight, but Dad held firm to ten and Mom couldn't budge him. By ten o'clock, our front door was locked, including a metal chain lock, and my younger siblings, Kau and Tam, were not allowed to open the door for us. Being teenagers, Kien, Xi, Num, Buu, and I rebelled against Dad's unreasonable demand. I wished Dad would compromise because 10:00 p.m. was so early, my friends wouldn't take me home.

For their part, our parents wished that all their children would be like Hong. For the first two years of college he attended Pasadena City College while living at home. He spent most of his free time studying or working at the Best Western Motel in Pasadena as the night attendant. He had no desire to party or hang out with friends at night.

The first time I got home late, at 11:00 p.m., happened after attending a friend's birthday party. The door was locked and I had no key to open the door. My parents and Hong were the only ones with a key. I knocked on Hong' bedroom wall, asking him to open the door. After fifteen minutes of knocking, he finally woke up and opened the door half asleep. I was greeted by his raging anger.

Kien and my other siblings typically came home after me, and I was able to open the door for them. I realized that I had to develop a strategy to open the door because I wasn't asking Hong again. I asked Xi if he knew someone with a hotel key like a credit card. He got me a used Las Vegas hotel key card from a worker he knew. When my parents weren't home, I tried to unlock the door with a hotel key card. I wiggled the door to get enough space to wedge the key card in to slide the door lock open. I was elated by my success because I knew I could do this time and time again.

However, I still had to open the metal chain lock from the outside. For weeks I tried various ways of lifting the metal chain with a stick, a knife, or the key card. None of those techniques worked. As I studied how the chain lock worked, I realized the door had to be almost closed in order to get the chain off. A rigid object such as stick would not work. I needed a string to yank the chain while the door was almost closed. The string had to be strong and thin, I told my siblings. Xi thought the dental floss would meet the criteria I needed. Sure enough, I was able to loop the dental floss around the metal chain and lift it high as I closed the door—until the chain slid out of its track. Now I was able to get the door and the metal chain unlocked from the outside. Once we were able to open the door without a key, Dad's rule had no effect on us.

Staying out late is how I met my first boyfriend. As part of our routine, Xi and I would walk into a party together. For the first hour he would introduce me to his friends and we would hang out together. Then Xi would go off to different rooms, talking to friends. At one party on a fall night in 1984, I discovered that Xi was nowhere to be found. I was stuck at the party.

Quoc, the younger brother of one of Xi's friends, came in later with his friends from another house party. We had met casually in school, but he was a grade lower. We heard shouting on the front lawn between a Vietnamese and Chinese teenager, and I went out to see what was happening. The Vietnamese teenager was not a friend of the party host. Also, there was always simmering tension between certain Chinese and Vietnamese teenagers in high school. I later learned that the Chinese teenager had been fired earlier that night from his job at a restaurant.

When Quoc saw me on the front lawn, he was concerned and ordered me to go in. He said, "It is dangerous out here. A fight may break out soon. You must go inside."

I responded, "You can't order me around."

So he pushed me into the house instead. Once we got inside, Quoc asked, "Why are you still hanging around? It is close to one o'clock in the morning."

I explained, "I came with my brother Xi, and I am waiting for him to take me home."

As it turned out, people at the party separated the two teenagers before their argument escalated into a real fight. Quoc and I ended up talking for the next two hours before Xi finally showed up to take me home. Quoc told me before we parted, "You are all right. You're not like what people said about you in school. I enjoyed talking to you."

From then on, Quoc would walk me to my classes and wait with me for the van that took me to beauty school. A few months later, he invited me to the senior prom. Wanting to fit in, my girlfriends and I didn't want to miss the experience of a prom. However, I didn't have the money to buy a formal dress, which cost close to a hundred dollars, not including the cost of high-heel shoes. Unlike my friends with older siblings who worked or parents with the means to pay, I remembered Dad's advice that there is always a way to overcome our struggles. I decided to borrow a formal dress that Zenh had worn at her wedding banquet. After I called her, explaining my situation, she agreed to mail her dress and shoes to me. I also asked my teacher at the beauty school to do my hair and makeup on the day of the prom. Soon I was all set.

Figure 15-6: Nam Moi's senior prom, 1985.

That night I was tremendously excited. I was going to a prom like a regular American teenager. I didn't know what to expect, except for lots of dancing, which I knew I would enjoy. Quoc came to pick me up in his father's Buick. We met our friends, one of whom owned a camera to take pictures to commemorate the event.

In May 1985, strapless prom dresses were in style, made popular by the movie *Sixteen Candles*. Zenh's dress was one of a kind, personally designed by her. Yet instead of feeling special, I was sad because I didn't fit in like everyone else. When anyone asked me, "Where did you buy the dress?" I said, "My sister designed it," hoping they wouldn't say anything about it looking old-fashioned.

Yet that dress turned out to have a big advantage. I arranged to sit with a group of my friends at a table. As the music started, people flocked to the dance floor. After a song or two, the girls wearing strapless dresses realized they were not designed for the jumping and kicking we did to eighties songs. They had to grab onto their dresses to stop them from falling down their fronts. While my friends had to sit down or used the restroom to adjust their dresses, I kept dancing up a storm. My friends started telling me how lucky I was able to dance freely. I laughed at myself for worrying about my dress being different. In the end, my sister's dress turned out to be perfect for the occasion.

By this time my parents were concerned that my siblings and I were having too much freedom in our adopted country. They often reminded us that the ticket out of poverty was through higher education. Dad said to us, "You must go to college and get a four-year degree. You can choose any major that you like to pursue." That was Dad's expectation for all the sacrifices they had made. Mom would say to us," We did not come to America so you could party and have fun. You have to find a way to earn money for a living. We don't have the money to support you now, like when we were in Vietnam."

My parents put all their hopes and dreams on their children. Dad struggled to find a job, but he thought like an entrepreneur. If one of his nine children made it, he would already get back more than his investment he had made in us.

Although my siblings and I went out almost every Saturday night, we kept our focus on school and getting good grades. One by one

we graduated and earned
a diploma from Alhambra
High School. Starting with
Hong in 1981, Kien in 1982,
Xi in 1983, Num in 1984, I
graduated in 1985 and Buu
a year later. Kau and Tam
would graduate many years
later.

Figure 15-7: Buu and Nam Moi at high
school graduation, 1985.

American Dreams

My siblings and I felt a lot of peer pressure to start working
immediately in order to earn money to acquire the things we
wanted and to take trips. Many people we knew from high school
did not go to college but got jobs right away and bought a car.
In my senior year, I started giving haircuts and perms at people's
homes. During one of our family dinner conversations, I told my
family that I wanted to open a salon after getting my cosmetology
license and start earning money. Dad said that I could do better
with a four-year degree than being a hairdresser. He said if I still
wanted to own a salon after getting a college education, he would
support me, but I had to get a college degree first.

My first choice was California State University, Los Angeles,
since Kien and Xi were going there and most of my girlfriends
were planning to attend. It was only a few miles from home, so
I could take a bus to and from our house. My second choice was
California Polytechnic University, Pomona, to which some high
school boys I knew were going and majoring in engineering. Yet I
didn't own a car for commuting daily, and my parents would not
permit me to live in a dorm, so that was not a viable choice.

Seeing that I was having too much fun hanging out with friends,
my parents and older siblings thought it would be good for me
to stay with my grandparents Vu since they had moved from
Van Nuys to Reseda, only a few bus stops from California State
University, Northridge. Mom was adamant that I had to live with

a relative's family. I had no choice but to attend California State University, Northridge (CSUN).

In the summer of 1985, I worked at the salon as a hairdresser for $30 dollars a day, plus any extra money if I gave haircuts or perms. The salon was managed and owned by a husband and wife team of licensed hairdressers. I worked from Tuesday to Sunday, 8:00 a.m. to 7:30 p.m. with half an hour lunch. Some days I had to stay late if we had a customer coming in after work for a perm or color. Other days I could go home as early as 6:30 p.m., which was unusual unless the owners had somewhere to go. My main job was washing customers' hair, wiping the floor and putting on perm rods, cleaning the counters and keeping up the salon. Often, a large family would come in with several kids. I said to the owners, "I can cut one of the kids' hair," but they rejected my requests time and time again. I felt that they were not honoring their end of the agreement. I was working for less than minimum wage. I later realized that the salon owners had no intention of letting me earn extra money by giving haircuts or perms. I thought to myself, Dad was right. Working long hours, being on my feet all day, I could do better than being a hairdresser.

I was accepted at California State University, Northridge. Being a carefree teenager, I was oblivious to the challenges that I would be facing during the first year of college. I was leaving my family, living with grandparents, transitioning from high school to college, away from my friends. That fall I moved in with my grandparents Vu's family, living in a three-bedroom rental house. I shared a room with Grandmother Qui and Aunty Ngoc. Grandfather Liam shared a room with Uncle Han. Uncle Sanh and his wife lived in the third bedroom. Aunty Ngoc and I shared a bunk bed with me sleeping on top.

Living with my grandparents' family was a culture shock for me. Grandmother Qui was not only old-fashioned, she was also totally unreasonable. She had a strong will and she was vocal about her opinions, with little tact. In her mind, a young girl like me should find a good husband and start a family as soon as possible. She voiced her disapproval of my studying after everyone in the house went to bed because I was wasting electricity, since the light was on only for me. She would lecture me every single night when I came in late. I got so tired of her lecturing me, I brought a flashlight to read at night. She didn't understand why I was getting a college education and had to study so hard each day. I told her, "Times have changed. Women cannot solely rely on their husbands. Women must learn to take care of themselves or they won't find a husband." Grandmother was happy at least to hear that finding a husband was a priority to me, and gradually she began to accept my reasons for getting a higher education.

Grandmother was full of restrictions for me, especially since I was a female. I could only eat during the three main mealtimes of the day, breakfast, lunch, and dinner, always with the family and never alone. During my first meal together with the family, I sat down after setting the table and getting rice for everyone. I was seated in the corner, allowing others easy access, when Grandmother yelled at me, "Why are you sitting in the back? How are you going to serve your uncles and Grandfather if they need water or rice?"

I replied, "What is wrong with them getting up and doing it themselves?"

Qui said with a disappointed voice, "Your mother did not teach you any manners. How are you going to find a husband?"

I had no freedom with Grandmother Qui constantly watching me and judging my every move in a negative way. Although Aunty Ngoc was only two years my senior, Ngoc was Grandmother's youngest and favorite daughter. She could do no wrong in Grandmother's eyes. Grandfather Liam was more reasonable.

Every day I looked forward to my nightly shower. It was my sanctuary, being alone in a room with hot water running down my body, washing away my sadness. On one occasion, though, I took a longer shower than usual. When I got out, I was greeted by Grandmother yelling at me, "Nam Moi, why are you taking so long in the shower? Were you working in the fields today? You are wasting water."

I thought, "I have to give up my only escape too." That night I went to bed crying. I lived with a grandmother who hadn't treated me like her granddaughter during the starving days on the *Tung An*. Although I had endured many hardships up to this point, my family was behind me. They were my support group and safety net. We shared our struggles together. Now and then I complained about Mom being old-fashioned. Yet compared to Grandmother, Mom was avant-garde.

I realized that I shouldn't have agreed to live with my grandparents. Near the end of the first semester, my relationship with my grandmother took a turn for the worse. My professor in calculus recommended that the class form a study group to prepare for the final exam. I volunteered to be the coordinator for the class, setting up the time and location for the study groups to meet, along with communicating to everyone in the class.

In those days we didn't have email or cell phones, and we had to rely on the house phone. Soon three of my classmates called my grandparents' house for information. After each call Grandmother would ask me, "Who was on the phone?"

I told her, "A male friend from school. We are meeting up at school tomorrow."

After the third person called, she became concerned and said, "Why are these male friends calling you?" I repeated that we were all meeting tomorrow at the school to study together.

At the time I didn't realize the depth of her concern. When I went home that weekend, my parents sat me down to have "a talk" about these male friends I was meeting all at the same time. Mom said to me sternly, "We got a disturbing phone call from your grandmother regarding you."

Dad said," Your job is to study and not meet with boys."

Mom got to the heart of Grandmother's concern. "What kind of game are you playing? Meeting up with multiple boys? We don't object you having a boyfriend, but having three boys at the same time?"

I was outraged. "Grandmother is so wrong. They are not my boyfriends. They are students in my class. The teacher asked the class to form a study group and work together in preparation for the final exam."

My parents were relieved after hearing my explanation. Mom told me, "You should tell your grandmother that they are your classmates, not male friends."

I used this opportunity to complain to my parents about my unhappy situation with Grandmother and how she scrutinized my every move. She made it impossible for me to continue to live with her.

Dad promised that they would clear up the misunderstanding with Grandmother.

He must have said something else too because my grandmother did loosen her grip.

By this time Hong had graduated from UCLA and started working in Canoga Park. I carpooled with Hong on Monday mornings, as he dropped me off at school before going to work. I was so miserable living with my grandparents that instead of waiting for Hong to pick me up after work on Fridays, I chose to take the bus from Northridge to Alhambra. That entailed taking three bus lines and two transfers. The journey took close to three hours. The first bus was from Northridge to Van Nuys; at Van Nuys, I took a bus to downtown Los Angeles and then from downtown I took the third bus to Alhambra. Every Friday I would look forward to heading home and away from Grandmother's madness.

The weekend went by too quickly. My sadness and anxiety started on Sunday afternoon as I prepared for the week. I would tear up at the thought of enduring the five trying days ahead.

Struggling with the culture shock of living with my grandparents was only part of my challenges. Academically, I was at least a few years behind in the math I needed for college. By the time I graduated high school, I had completed only Algebra II. Since I had come to the United States only a year before high school, a female guidance counselor had signed me up for pre-algebra for high school freshmen year over my objections. I felt she was stereotyping me as a female. I knew that I could handle algebra since both my brothers, Xi and Num, had taken it in their freshmen year. The guidance counselor insisted that I could use summer school to catch up. In subsequent years, I asked to go to summer school to catch up in math, but my parents didn't have money.

Although I didn't take pre-calculus in high school, I decided to take calculus in my freshman year of college. I was shocked, however, by the fast pace of college courses as compared to high school. My professor didn't seem to care about the students. Often, he didn't even remember our names. It took me longer than other students to understand the class material. I couldn't ask Hong or Xi because I didn't live with them, and phone calls cost a lot of money in those days.

My academic struggles were matched by my lack of a social life. In high school, I had many friends and kept busy with many activities. Now in college, I was depressed, missing my family and friends. I became withdrawn, not socializing with others. Part of the problem was that every day Grandmother asked me when I would be home. Spending time at school late was not acceptable. I had to be home by dinnertime. Great Uncle #9's daughter, Aunty Cuc, was a student at CSUN, and she introduced me to her friends. Some of them would ask me to join them for a gathering or dinner, but my usual response was, "Sorry, I can't. Thanks for the invite!" They got so annoyed with me that they stopped asking altogether.

As I struggled, I thought, failure is not an option. I must find ways to overcome my limitations.

To start, I asked one of Aunty Cuc's friends, Vei, to tutor me in calculus. In return, I offered to cut his hair for free. Vei would tutor me an hour a week. To repay him, I would cut his hair every six weeks. I also sought help from the school counseling program in dealing with the culture differences with Grandmother.

In the meantime, my boyfriend Quoc was still a senior in high school, hanging out with the same friends. I, on the other hand, had dramatically changed from my high school days. When I spent time with Quoc and his friends, I would carry my school work with me to study whenever we had down time. One of his friends told me, "College is making you boring. You can only think about studying and nothing else. Life is more than school."

That was a pivotal moment for me. Quoc and most of his friends had decided not to go on to college. Most of them were going to a two-year trade school to become a mechanic or construction contractor. After Quoc graduated high school, he started learning construction at Pasadena College. The gap between us grew bigger. We just didn't have much to talk about. He was not interested in the new things I was learning in school, and I was not interested in talking about construction and cars. I also started working at Supercuts during my second year of college on Friday nights, Saturday, and Sunday. I tried to spend time with

Quoc and his friends, but my time was very limited.

After a few months, I got word from a friend that she had seen Quoc hanging out with one of the girls we knew from Alhambra High School. I asked Quoc if he was seeing someone else the next time I saw him, and he responded, "No. You are crazy." Inevitably, I caught him kissing her. Trying to surprise him by coming back early from Northridge one Friday afternoon, I was waiting at his house when it happened.

I was devastated after witnessing them kissing because Quoc was my first boyfriend. This was the first time in my life that I had to deal with heartbreak. I confronted Quoc when he walked into the house. Quoc finally acknowledged the fact that they had been seeing each other for a few weeks. As a nineteen-year-old male, he needed a girlfriend who was available to him.

Looking back, it was a blessing that our relationship ended. Although I was sad at losing Quoc, I knew that I couldn't manage trying to fit into his lifestyle and focus on school as well.

Up to this point I had not picked a major yet. Northridge allowed students to remain undecided until the end of their sophomore year. I had thought about being a science teacher, but teaching didn't excite me. I wanted to accomplish more than just teaching. Kien thought I should major in accounting or finance, like most Asian females. When I told my family that I wanted to be an engineer, my siblings dragged out the old stereotype that engineering was for men. Kien said, "Engineering is mostly males. It is a male world. You can't compete with the guys in America. You are a five-foot-tall Asia girl."

I replied, "Engineering is not like a physical fight that depends on a person's physical strength. It is a field of study."

Xi was majoring in electrical engineering, and I asked him, "Do you think I can be an engineer?"

"It is up to you. If you like math and science, you will enjoy engineering."

Mom was worried after hearing Kien's comments. She pleaded with me, "Why don't you pick something easier than engineering?"

"Mom, I like designing and making things. Engineering is making things better for people."

Dad reassured me that I was making the right decision. "Nam Moi, you will be a great engineer. Someday, I predict, you will even manage some of smartest engineers. You are as good as your brothers or even better. I support your desire to be an engineer."

That was what I needed to hear: Dad's approval of my decision. With his support, I had the confidence that I could overcome the struggles that I was bound to encounter. One by one, I would conquer each challenge as it came along.

Within our family, we had a trickle-down economic effect. My older siblings were starting to do well. With their assistance, our whole family was doing better. Hong decided to buy a new car and resell his used car, a red Toyota Tercel, to me at a 50% discount. After years of working as a hairdresser part-time, I had saved enough money to buy his car along with financing the monthly insurance payment. Kien made the same offer to Buu when she purchased a new car. She sold her used car to Buu at half the resale value. Although Buu and I had had our driver licenses since we turned sixteen, we didn't drive regularly until we owned a car. Xi did even better. He gave Kau his old car for free with insurance paid for while Kau was still in high school. When Kau complained, saying he wanted a new car instead of Xi's used Honda CRX, we were outraged on how spoiled our younger sibling had become. Buu and I reminded Kau that we had to take a bus everywhere even in college.

With a car I no longer needed to take the three-hour bus ride from Northridge to Alhambra. I had more flexibility to meet up with friends. In my last year of college, I pleaded with my parents for approval to move out of my grandparents' house and live with a girlfriend. Since I was doing well in balancing my school work, my part-time job and personal time, they agreed to my request. Dad said that I had earned enough credit to be trustworthy. With more freedom I finally was able to experience being a college student like everyone else. I met new friends at school while still maintaining contacts from high school, meeting them every month for dinner or dancing at various nightclubs.

In May 1990, I graduated from California State University, Northridge, with a bachelor's degree in electrical engineering. It was a significant milestone at that point of my life. My siblings and I constantly sought our parents' attention. Making them proud of us was our motivation to do well. The sense of duty and responsibility was ingrained in us, the desire to make our parents and ancestors proud.

Dad made it clear, early on, that he would only attend college graduations, not those for elementary or high school. For my college commencement, Dad said he would come with Mom to attend the ceremony. We had so many people at the graduation. I was not able to locate my parents after it was over. I started to wonder if Dad had honored his word. I started crying like a little girl when I did not see my parents among the crowd. After all, my degree was not only my accomplishment but theirs too for all the sacrifices they had made. I wanted them to be proud of me. In America, I had the opportunity to be an engineer, something that would not be possible if we had stayed in Vietnam.

Figure 15-8: Nam Moi and Dad (Ly Sang) at CSUN graduation, 1990.

241

My parents finally found me in the engineering section. I was so relieved; I rushed over and hugged them.

As the eldest son, Hong was under more pressure from our parents than any of the other siblings. My parents often said that he had to be a role model for us. He accepted the responsibility. He never gave my parents any problems while he was growing up. Ever since we arrived in the United States, Hong was always focused on school, staying on a path to earn a college degree. He was a dedicated student and spent all his free time studying. Dad said to the family, "Once Hong earns a bachelor's degree and is able to get a good job, we are going to buy a house." My parents put all their hopes on Hong to lead us out of poverty.

Hong had attended Pasadena City College after high school for two years before transferring to UCLA, where he majored in computer science. He graduated with honors.

Hong was able to get a job shortly after graduation, working as a computer programmer for a small company in the San Fernando Valley. With his good credit rating from his steady job, our family

Figure 15-9: Dad (Ly Sang) and Hong at UCLA graduation, 1985.

was able to buy a small two-bedroom house in the summer of 1986. By that fall, my grandparents Ung emigrated from Vietnam and came to live with my parents. We had twelve people living in that tiny house with beds everywhere—patio, laundry room, garage, as well as a pull-out sofa in the living room. My parents slept in one of the bedrooms and my grandparents slept in the other bedroom. I slept on the sofa on the weekends.

One of my dad's strengths was his ability to envision a desired outcome in the far future, five to ten years in advance. The house was a strategic purchase for my parents. The house was small, with less than 800 square feet of living space, but the lot was large enough to add a separate house in the back. The location was within walking distance to a supermarket and nearby restaurants, which was important to my parents. Although they had many children, Dad never planned to rely on us for their daily needs as they aged. Being able to walk to places for food was important, especially for Mom since she couldn't drive. Dad wanted to make sure she had a way to take care of herself without requiring his services.

In 1988, Dad worked closely with a contractor, managing the construction of our new house in back. The stages of building it reminded me of the construction of our house in Vietnam. Every weekend when I came home from college, I looked forward to seeing how much progress they had made. Dad would share his plans and steps gained during the construction each night at the family dinner. The new house was more than three times the size of the original house, with five bedrooms and two baths, including a large common area that combined the living and dining rooms.

Within ten years since we had immigrated to the United States, the Ung family were proud home owners. Our American dream was being realized.

Chapter 16

End of an Era

My parents had always been a big influence in our lives as we were growing up. Family dinner conversations were an important time in our family. It was one of my parents' ways to set the tone and vision for our future and to pass along their knowledge. Those conversations often included lessons learned from events happening to our family and relatives. We had many discussions on the importance of family, education, creating business opportunities, and investing our money wisely in real estate, both residential and commercial.

In 1988, Kien and Xi saw an opportunity in the computer industry, providing personal computers for individual homes. Kien had already completed her business administrative degree from California State University, Los Angeles, and she was working for the Transamerica Insurance Group in the accounting department. With Dad's support, Xi made the decision to delay finishing his senior project, part of his engineering program at CSULA, and Kien quit her job. For the capital needed to start the new business, they drafted a business plan and presented it to a bank for a loan. Hong was a silent partner, and Tritech, a computer store, was born.

After three years the company was restructured with a new name and a new business model, Quality Computers Incorporated. The computer store was a family business, with everyone behind it. Dad worked as an expeditor responsible for all the pickups and deliveries. He also advised Kien and Xi on their business dealings. Buu and Num worked as computer assembly technicians. Uncle Luong, Dad's youngest brother, had emigrated from Canada after my grandparents arrived to United States from Vietnam. He had earned an engineering degree in Canada, but now he worked as the technical support lead, responsible for all the issues related to technical support for customers. Xi was responsible for sales and Kien was in charge of procurement and financial transactions. They hired several people to support sales.

Hong and I pitched in at computer shows on weekends. The family traveled as a unit to the shows. Mom's job was to make sure we had a good breakfast before heading out. From the beginning Quality Computer developed a good reputation as an honest and reliable store. Dad said in business dealings, honesty and reliability are the foundations of building a good customer base. Many of the new customers were referrals from friends who had bought from us before.

The experience I gained from selling computers gave me an advantage in landing my first job as an engineer at Rockwell International in Seal Beach. I listed in my resume my job experience as a computer salesperson and a technician along with my hair cutting experience. As part of the lunch conversation during my interview, the hiring manager asked me how I would go about determining the right computer for him. I asked him a few questions to understand his needs and came up with my recommendation. I later learned that he was very impressed with my response, which set me apart from other candidates.

My siblings were very surprised that I got the job. Xi and Kien had said that I could work for them at the computer store if I couldn't find a job as engineer. In fact, they even had a desk set up for me. I told Kien that she had too little faith in my ability. In response, she pointed out that several smart friends of hers, with engineering degrees from UCLA and Berkeley, couldn't find a job after graduation. She just didn't want me to be disappointed.

Dad was happy and Mom was relieved when I told them that I got a job offer before graduation. I was grateful to be given the opportunity to work as an engineer and realize my dream.

Although Dad was content with his children's accomplishments, he had to accept his role as merely an expeditor for his children's business. His chance of becoming a prominent businessman again, as he was in Vietnam, was harder to imagine as he got older. Kien and Xi thought Dad didn't need to work so hard when the computer business got better. Kien started to have Num work along with Dad and also hired new technicians to perform the assembly of the computers. Soon Dad was working only a few hours each day for the computer store, and the rest of the time he was free to do whatever he wanted. This was not a lifestyle that was fulfilling for him, however, and he started to become depressed with so much time on his hands. He began to drink too much beer and chain smoke when he was not working.

In 1991, at the age of 55, Dad started to exhibit forgetfulness and disorientation. In August he was diagnosed with a brain tumor. His years of working in an unhealthy environment in Vietnam had caught up with him. Within two months Dad had an operation on his brain, and the biopsy of the tumor indicated cancer. The doctor predicted that Dad had about a year to live.

My family was devastated by this news. I told myself that I needed to be strong for my dad. But when I saw him after hearing the news, I broke down and cried uncontrollably as I hugged him tightly. I told him, "Baba, you can't die on us. We need you and your guidance."

Figure 16-1: Tracy, Mom (Kieu), Nam Moi, and Dad (Ly Sang), August 1991.

He responded calmly, "Don't be silly, my child. Baba is fine."

Dad didn't want us to feel sorry for him; he asked us to carry on with our lives as normal. After the operation he underwent chemotherapy and radiation treatments. My siblings took turns driving him to and from his doctor appointments with Mom always at his side.

My siblings and I spent many hours with my parents during those months. In the back of my mind I knew Dad's condition was serious, and his life was slowly being taken by the cancer. I would spend many hours whenever I could just sitting around or helping Mom with meals. To keep myself busy, I started learning how to cross-stitch a design from a kit purchased at a craft store. This kept my hands occupied and mind calm with a repetitive task. After cross-stitching for many hours, I wanted to work on a bigger project with more variety and decided to make a sampler hand quilt.

While I was working on my quilt project, I asked Dad about his years growing up in North Vietnam and the reasons he chose to study in the French military school. My parents had a wealth of stories to tell about their past as a young couple starting out, their struggles living under the communist government and our journey on the *Tung An*. As I was making the quilt pieces and listening to their stories, I realized that the sampler quilt might symbolize stories of our lives. I decided to design and select unique fabric for each of the square-foot quilt blocks to symbolize a distinct story. My siblings and I were the connections to all those stories like the lattices and borders that made up a quilt. I wanted to savor the moments of Dad's last days in a positive and productive way and be reminded of my time with my parents in a beautiful quilt long after they were gone. I thought of passing it along to my children someday.

Today, the sampler quilt is spread on top of my bed. The quilt gives me a warm feeling and reminds me of my time with my parents.

Dad had always enjoyed a big family and he loved children. He was looking forward to having more grandchildren around. One of his wishes was seeing his children married. At this point in time, Zenh and Xi were the only siblings that had married. Zenh had married Hy, her grade school classmate from Vietnam in 1982, and they lived in Little Rock, Arkansas. They had met in Los Angeles and had one daughter, Tracy.

Xi had married Ta, a foreign student from Thailand of both Thai and Chinese descent, whom he met in college. They got married at a chapel in Las Vegas with only a couple of close friends. My older siblings, Hong, Kien, and Num, were not dating, nor did they have any interest in getting married. I was dating Branson, an American. To my family and relatives at the time, I was pushing the boundaries of our culture, being both a female engineer and dating someone foreign to our culture.

My parents never expressed any disapproval for my choice of boyfriend. However, they were uncomfortable that he came from a divorced family. My parents feared that he wouldn't have a strong sense of commitment to a marriage due to his parents' divorce, and they worried that he would divorce me someday. During one of the emergencies when Dad was rushed to the hospital, he requested that I stand by his bedside. Dad held my hands and said, "Nam Moi, you have my approval to marry whomever you choose regardless of his family background. I wish you a life of happiness. It is important for me to tell you in case I don't make it." I was touched by Dad's expression of love and his wish of a life of happiness. However, at the same time I was burdened with his desire to see me married before he died.

Mom backed up what he said. "Your dad wants to see you get married. It would give him peace of mind knowing you have a husband by your side."

I told Mom that I did not love Branson enough to commit to marrying him yet. Mom said that it was better that Branson love me more than I love him. According to *Hakka* wisdom, love would grow over time after we built a family together. I felt obligated to fulfill my parents' wishes for me.

In November 1991, I accepted Branson's proposal for marriage, and a few months later, in January, we were married in Waikiki, Oahu, with Branson's family and relatives. We had a Chinese wedding ceremony in Los Angeles. My parents requested that only his birth parents attend the wedding ceremony in Los Angeles. Mom was very superstitious and felt it was important to have a perfect wedding day for the newlyweds. Dad was uncomfortable, not knowing how to converse with the stepfather at the wedding. We had over 250 guests with less than twenty people from the groom's side. The majority of the guests were our relatives from both sides of my parents and some of Dad's close friends.

Figure 16-2: Mom (Kieu), Nam Moi, Tam, and Dad (Ly Sang) on Nam Moi's wedding day, 1992.

My wedding was the last time Dad would interact with many of those friends and relatives. His condition became very grave shortly after my wedding.

By the summer of 1992, Dad's speech and physical movements were severely impaired. He was confused and disoriented. He had flashbacks of his days in Vietnam and the slipper factory. He would ask the people around him, "Where am I?" The only thing he was not confused about was the names of his children and Mom.

In the summer of 1992, Dad had a second operation on his brain. Once he recovered from the surgery, his cognitive and mobility abilities returned to normal. The doctor warned us, however, that in a few months the cancer's growth would start pressing against his brain again. I used the opportunity to share my thoughts with Dad. I didn't want to regret not saying what I needed to say to him.

In Chinese culture, parents and family members do not show affection or say "I love you" to each other. Mom would often say that parents should love the children in their hearts and not express affection or love verbally. The belief was that children would become spoiled if they heard those words often by the parents or adult relatives. Despite that, I often told Dad that I loved him, and when I said good-bye, I would give him a hug, which was unusual for a Chinese family.

Today, I often tell my Mom and siblings that I love them, whether on the phone or in person. I hug my sisters and even some of my brothers. I insisted that my children give hugs to Mom and my siblings as part of greeting them and again when they said good-bye. Other younger cousins do the same.

I assured Dad that my job as an engineer was going well. He said that I might need to get a master's degree in order to get ahead at work. I showed him my award certificates from work and a picture of the team and me in the Rockwell corporate newspaper. He told me that he had known all along that I would do well in engineering. Even as a child, I had always been so curious to discover how things work.

Dad reminded me of my fascination with his Omega watch as a young girl. He had owned an expensive watch while I was growing up in the early 70s. I thought it was amazing that after he dunked it in a glass of beer, the watch continued to function. I asked Dad over and over to demonstrate that trick to all my friends in the neighborhood. I studied his watch for hours, amazed with its design and mechanisms. A typical watch in Vietnam would break if you merely splashed water on it.

By Christmas 1992, Dad was confined to a wheelchair, unable to move freely. For the next several months he spent most of the day on a recliner. Although he was unable to speak, he was able to watch us and turn his head. Mom had to feed him. We took turns massaging his back, legs, and arms to help with his body circulation. Mom needed my brothers' help to move Dad around.

By the next summer, Dad was unable to eat solid food. The doctor instructed us to move Dad into a senior care home with a tube installed to feed liquid into his stomach with oxygen to support his breathing. Mom's new daily routine was to sit by his side from seven in the morning till seven at night, seven days a week regardless of holidays or weekends. She packed her lunch each day as though she was going to work. She made sure the senior home staff gave Dad the care he needed.

We wanted her to take a break, suggesting that one of us could go instead. Yet as a *Hakka* wife, Mom felt that her duty was to take care of her husband. She didn't complain or feel burdened by it. She refused our requests every single time. My siblings and I accommodated her by picking her up earlier than seven for dinner or spending more time at the senior home with her and Dad. I visited Dad both days on the weekends in order to keep Mom company. During the week I would visit Dad two to three times after work and had dinner with Mom before going home. Our priorities changed dramatically, revolving around his needs.

On Friday, March 18, 1994, Dad's doctor told Mom to gather the family in preparation of his passing within the next day or two. I got a call from Kien at work, and I left early to see Dad and spent the night with my mother. By this time Kau was a second-year student at the University of California, Berkeley, and he drove home late that night from school. Hong had moved to Huntsville, Alabama, with his company the previous year, and he took a flight home that night. I picked up Hong at the airport close to one in the morning and took him to see Dad directly from the airport because I feared that Dad wouldn't last until the morning.

The entire family did not sleep well that night. I woke up early the next morning while all my siblings and grandparents in the house were still sleeping. Mom was preparing breakfast in the kitchen, and she and I ate together. Afterward, we went to see Dad. For more than three hours, I watched Dad struggle to take his next breath. After Aunty Duc and Uncle Han arrived, Mom asked me to go home and bring my siblings to Dad's side as soon as possible. It was considered bad fortune in Chinese culture if a person died without any children witnessing the passing.

It was pouring rain outside. The weather mirrored my mood, with tears running down my face after seeing Dad struggle for his life. Mom was worried about me catching a cold from the rain, and she told me to drive carefully and use an umbrella.

I didn't make it back in time. Dad must have heard Mom telling him not to worry. The doctor had instructed us not to say comforting words to Dad until everyone was present because those words would allow the sick patient to go peacefully.

When I walked into my parents' house, my siblings and Grandmother were crying like someone has just died. Grandfather was in shock. I asked Buu, "What happened?"

Buu responded sadly, "Uncle Han called and said Dad just passed away."

A few minutes earlier, Dad had still been alive. Now he was gone and I hadn't seen him pass. I could hear Mom's voice in my head. "Your poor dad, he has nine children and none of them were by his side when he died."

March 19, 1994, the day Dad passed away, was a few days before my twenty-seventh birthday. As a result my birthday every year after that became the day I remembered my father's passing. It was a Chinese tradition to remember the day a loved one died. I stopped celebrating my birthday for many years after his death.

Only much later did I realize that if he were alive, he would want me to be happy.

All my siblings except for Zenh drove to meet with Mom, Aunty Duc, and Uncle Han at the senior home. Everyone stood around with tears running down our faces in the tiny room with Dad's lifeless body lying on the bed. Mom, feeling the need to counter the traditional belief, said to Dad, "Old man, your children are here now to see you. You can go in peace and bless your family with good fortune."

I felt guilty after hearing Mom's words. I wished that I had left earlier to get my siblings. At the same time, I wished that I hadn't left at all. At least he would have had one child by his side.

It was hard for me to accept that Dad was no longer around. We had gone through so many hardships together and conquered them all. I felt helpless that I was unable to do anything to change the outcome. I would have sacrificed all I had or would have if it could keep my dad alive.

I couldn't change what happened, though. I was left with the pain of my father's death and the regret of not being able to pay him back for all his sacrifices. Dad's life was cut short at age fifty-seven. He was unable to fulfill his dreams of visiting the Ungs around the world and to go back to Vietnam to see his former house and factory. After my graduation, Dad had predicted that in a few years Vietnam would allow visitors. He had planned to go back in 1993. I started saving up enough money to go back with him.

During the ups and downs of Dad's illness, I had prepared myself mentally for the day he passed away. Yet when the day came, I was not prepared at all. I realized that I could have never been prepared for seeing a parent pass away. The little girl inside me would always want to have my parents around, regardless of my chronological age. Seeing Dad's lifeless body lying there was such a final statement. He was now forever parted from us, at least in physical form.

Honoring Dad's Life

Dad was the first person close to us to pass away. Our grandparents on both sides were still alive. After being in the United States for close to fifteen years, spending most of our teenage years in Los Angeles, my siblings and I had become Americanized. As each of us turned eighteen, becoming a U.S. citizen, we had taken on an American name and a new identity.

That meant we were disconnected from our *Hakka* cultural roots in respect to handling the death of a loved one. We didn't know what to expect at the wake rituals sending Dad to the afterlife in accordance with the Buddhist religion and the funeral memorial service before the burial. We knew Mom would do everything in her power to have the most respectful service to honor Dad's life. My siblings and I were prepared to handle the physical stress, the emotional strain of whatever we were about to experience as our duty as sons and daughters. We asked several of Kien's close friends to take photographs and even some videos of the three-day service to pass along to our children someday. I put the photographs in two albums shortly after they were taken and had not opened the albums in over twenty years until I was recalling the events in writing this book.

As part of *Hakka* tradition, the children of the deceased were not allowed to sleep on a bed or have any comforts until the dead body was buried. My siblings and I slept on the floor for many nights following Dad's passing when we were at Mom's home. We were also not allowed to wear the color red for a hundred days. We were not allowed to joke, smile, or laugh because it would be disrespectful to our family, especially to our grandparents for losing their son.

Mom hired Buddhist monks to conduct a three-day and two-night wake at the family home. The wake started at seven in the morning and went till eleven at night for the first two days. On the third day was the burial service, which ended earlier.

According to Chinese tradition, we had to wear white cotton clothing (shirt, pants, hat) specially made for each one of us and not wear any shoes. We started the wake by receiving the white uniform from the monks.

The shirts for the sons, daughters and the one daughter-in-law had a brown patch stitched on the back of the shirt. The sons wore white caps with a brown patch and a handmade head frame on the outside of the cap. Daughters and the daughters-in-law wore a cone-shaped hat with a brown patch made with a strip of fabric sewn together with one side longer than the other. We could use the longer side of the fabric as a handkerchief to wipe away tears. Each of the children of the deceased had to carry a bamboo stick to symbolize the responsibility we carried as the deceased's children. Mom had to wear the uniform but without a brown patch. Other male relatives wore caps while the women wore cone hats. The relatives did not wear special clothing.

Figure 16-3: Nam Moi and siblings receive wake ceremony uniform, 1994.

Figure 16-4: Nam Moi at the wake ceremony, 1994.

My siblings and I remained on our knees most of the time. As the guests came to pay their respects to Dad, by placing incense in a ceramic cup filled with raw rice in front of Dad's picture, they would bow to us and we would bow back on our knees. We went through various rituals intended to help Dad reach the afterlife.

One of them required that all of us to remain under a blanket for close to ten minutes.

We paraded through the neighborhood in our uniforms, accompanied by the chanting monks. We even jumped over a wok filled with fire. We kneeled, bowed, prayed, and called out Dad's names at various times. We visited the temple to pray to the gods and goddesses. We set free several doves and released goldfish into the nearby lake. The monk released a homemade candle in a bowl on a lake and hoped it flowed within the reach of the daughter-in-law, Ta, to signify blessing her with many sons to keep the Ung candle burning. If my parents had had several daughters-in-law, the candle would go with whomever it reached. One of Kien's friends said that the rituals we were observing dated back five hundred years. He remembered seeing it in movies from Hong Kong depicting old Chinese traditions.

On the second day of the wake, we had to fast for hours. With all the physical demands and the emotional drain from crying, we had a difficult time. Zenh and I were on the verge of passing out after so many hours of bowing and kneeling during various rituals. When we were able to eat, we could only eat food in its raw form, without being processed or cooked. I remembered thinking that all these rituals were part of mourning for the loss of Dad's life. I never cried so much in one day of my life. At the end of the second day, we were exhausted physically, mentally, and emotionally.

Mom was not obligated to participate with us at all the rituals. These tasks were the responsibilities of the children. Nonetheless, Mom sat alongside all her children, supporting us silently.

On the third day was Dad's burial. We started the day in the funeral home with the monks chanting next to his coffin. Each of us lit a stick of incense and planted it in the ceramic cup filled with rice.

Many of Dad's friends and relatives came to pay their respects by bowing with lighted incense in front of Dad's picture. Shortly after Great Uncle #9 entered the room, Mom headed toward him and kneeled down by his feet as a sign of gratitude for being Dad's uncle, and we followed behind her kneeling, like a mother duck with her ducklings. We then walked around behind Mom in order to kneel in front of Great Uncle #7, Great Uncle San, and Great

Figure 16-5: Dad (Ly Sang)'s wake ceremony, 1994 .

Figure 16-6: Hong to walk over a wok of fire at wake ceremony, 1994.

Figure 16-7: Under a blanket at the wake ceremony, 1994.

Figure 16-8: Nam Moi and siblings kneeling in the Buddhist Temple, 1994.

Figure 16-9: Released goldfish into the lake at the wake ceremony, 1994.

Figure 16-10: Ta catching the candle in a lake at Lincoln Heights, 1994.

Uncle Khau. As Mom kneeled down by the feet of each great uncle, she said, "Thank you for the guidance and care you provided to Ly Sang! My sons and daughters are grateful."

At the final viewing, Mom asked all the children to stand around Dad's coffin, and she gave a short speech. She told us that we are different from other people. We were now children without a father.

Figure 16-11: Nam Moi and siblings kneeling by Dad (Ly Sang)'s coffin, 1994.

Figure 16-12: Nam Moi and siblings kneeling in front of Great Uncle #9, 1994.

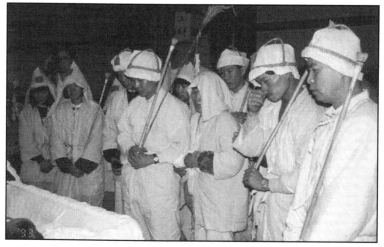

Figure 16-13: Mom (Kieu), Nam Moi, and siblings standing in front of Dad (Ly Sang)'s coffin.

She said that she was an illiterate woman and didn't have my dad's strengths. She asked all the older siblings to watch out for the younger ones. Mom said we were very fortunate that our father had brought us to the United States, but now we would have to rely on ourselves. She asked Dad to bless each of his children.

Chinese tradition, especially the *Hakka*, held that the eldest son took on the role of the man in the house once the father had passed, putting more pressure on Hong.

After Mom's speech, she told us to say our good-byes and ask for forgiveness. It was important not to carry regrets with us. Each of us took turn to say good-bye to Dad in front of his coffin. Some of my siblings said their good-byes out loud; others said theirs silently.

Kien said, "Dad, I am sorry for being impatient with you. Please forgive me. You can rest in peace. We will take care of Mom."

Tam said, "I am sorry for being a rebellious teen and causing you heartache."

I said, "Don't worry about Mom, we will take care of her. I love you, Dad."

As part of the *Hakka* tradition, the sons of the deceased made a bridge with their bodies for the coffin to pass over on its way to the vehicle carrying the coffin to the burial site. This ritual signified the sons carrying the father's body for the burial. There were six pallbearers that helped carry Dad's coffin, and they had to be careful not to step on my five brothers lying on the ground, lying alternately head to toe.

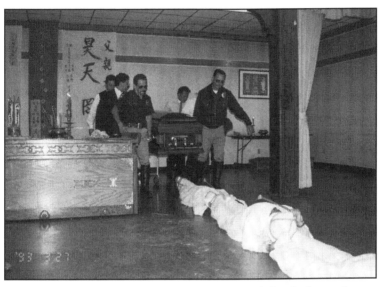

Figure 16-14: Sons of Ung Ly Sang making a bridge with their bodies on the ground for the coffin to travel on top.

Once we arrived at the burial site, the monks continued with their chanting and burial rituals. I have little recollection of the final stage at the cemetery, because I was crying hysterically as they lowered Dad's coffin into the ground. When I was instructed to throw a handful of dirt on top of the coffin, to symbolize helping with burying my father, it was too much for me to handle. I screamed repeatedly, "Baba! Baba! Baba!…" and bowed my head to the ground. I had to be dragged away from the opening and into a car to be taken home.

Figure 16-15: Dad (Ly Sang)'s burial, 1994.

Several hours after the morning burial service, the immediate
family came back to the burial site for a private visit. The stitching
of the females' cone hat was removed and the hat became a strip
of fabric after Dad's burial. The atmosphere was different than
before. We were relieved now that Dad's body was in its final
resting place. We even posed for pictures.

As the sons and daughters of the deceased, we had to continue
with our mourning ritual for seven weeks on the day of the week
Dad passed away. That involved lighting incenses and candles
from Dad's altar to the street. We prayed with food offerings and
called on Dad's spirit to return home as we burned *yi chi*.

In late June 1994, we invited the monks back on the hundredth
day of Dad's passing to finalize the mourning process. Relatives
from Canada and Denmark came to participate in the closing
ceremony. Aunty Tchat came with her three sons, Tuong, Quy,
and Sam. Uncle Chin came with his two daughters, Filipina Moi
and Lan. Phung had already been visiting for six months, and had
participated in the wake and funeral several months before.

Figure 16-16: Family picture taken in front of Dad (Ly Sang)'s grave, 1994.

As part of the final ritual, all the uniforms and items from the wake were burned to signify the ending of the mourning process. At the one year anniversary, the ceramic cup with raw rice and incense was combined with the Ung ancestors' altar and no longer stood by itself.

Each year on Chin Ming, in late March or early April, my siblings, Uncle Luong, his wife, and I visit Dad's gravesite, along with our grandparents, buried next to Dad. We also visit the gravesites in early October. Most Chinese visit the grave of their love ones only once a year on Chin Ming, but Mom said if we loved our father, we should go twice a year. We have been going twice a year for the last twenty years, with food offerings such as roasted pig, boiled chicken, pork, and various desserts. We light incense and candles. The incense is also planted in front of the neighbors' tombstones as an invitation to join the celebration of Dad and the grandparents. We have burned *yi chi* and paper models of shoes, cars, clothing, gold blocks, money, watches, and various things Mom has brought for us to burn over the years.

Visiting Dad and the grandparents' gravesites twice yearly is a very important part of our *Hakka* identity, like so many Ungs before us. It is also our way of respecting Mom. She can rest assured that when she passes, her children will honor her as we do for Dad. When our children are older, we hope to have them participate in the same ritual as a way to pay respect to our ancestors for bringing us here and to remember their sacrifices for the betterment of the next generation.

Figure 16-17: Dad (Ly Sang)'s resting place.

The Legacy Lives On

We have redeemed Dad's sacrifice by executing his vision for us. All of my parents' nine children are doing well. Most of us own property and have a good job or business. Five out of nine children earned a bachelor's degree and three continued on to earn a master's degree. Xi never went back to finish his senior project for a degree in engineering, but he is doing well with his real estate investments. Today, all nine children have families of their own. Mom was finally able to stop worrying about her children not having families.

With Dad gone, our family dynamic changed. Several members got even closer. Although Mom was only in her early fifties when Dad passed away, the thought of getting remarried was unthinkable for her. She follows the *Hakka* tradition for women in which marriage is for life. She was married to Dad in this lifetime, and someday she will rejoin him. Mom continues to be dedicated to her family, even after all the children have married and started a family. Her job is to take care of the ancestors' altar, lighting incense every morning and night, with fruit and food offerings on special occasions. At the beginning of the Chinese New Year she prays for blessings for each of her children and grandchildren at the temple, and she returns to the temple with fruit and flower offerings at the end of the year to thank the gods and goddesses for blessing her family.

My siblings and I have had to step up with helping Mom with matters related to the family. Mom consults with her children as a way to bounce ideas around, getting input before she takes any step affecting the family. Any invitations from our relatives are addressed to Hong as the eldest son, according to Chinese tradition. She also relies on her sons to help with arranging the ancestors' altar for New Year celebrations or representing our family in various occasions. She has twenty grandchildren, with ages ranging from a few months to thirty something years, and she enjoys surrounding herself with them. During the Chinese New Year celebration, her house is full of her children and grandchildren. She had told us that as parents we are responsible for her grandchildren's success. She did her job raising nine children. Mom is a beloved grandmother, and her grandchildren will argue at times about who loves her more.

My siblings and I feel fortunate that Mom is still with us. It gives us a chance to pay back to her when we couldn't with Dad. Our families continue to revolve our lives around Mom, like planets around the sun. Except for Kien, we all live in the Los Angeles area, ranging from a three- to forty-minute drive from Mom's house. Kien and her two boys visit California almost every summer and spend four or five weeks. Kien communicates on the phone regularly with Mom. My siblings and I spend time with Mom almost every weekend, having a casual lunch or dinner or just driving her around town. On Mom's seventieth birthday, Xi suggested celebrating at a restaurant. Normally, she prefers not to have a party for her birthday. Instead we have a casual family lunch or dinner. For the first time, though, she agreed to have her birthday celebrated at a restaurant—with the condition that we would invite only our immediate family, Uncle Luong's family, cousin Lan visiting from Denmark and Xi's mother in-law visiting from Thailand. Even with that restriction we had close to forty people.

Mom went with Xi and Kien to cousin Phung's wedding in Denmark. She also visits many countries throughout Europe and Asia with her sons and daughters. She continues to live out Dad's dream of traveling around the world.

Since we arrived in the United States, I was focused on getting an education and building a career, saving money and had not viewed fun or vacation as a priority. I even worked at the Quality Computer store, helping out my siblings during the two weeks off after graduation before starting my new job. After Dad's passing, I realized that life is a gift, and I had to strike a balance between living for today and building a stronger financial future for tomorrow. Up to this point, I had only talked about taking a vacation or other things someday but hadn't acted on it.

In May 1994, I boldly switched to a new job at Hughes Space and Communication in El Segundo. I ended my four-year employment at Rockwell working as power system engineer and took an engineering position in the solar array department. I spent over nine years working at Hughes and then Boeing after Boeing acquired Hughes in 2000.

During my transition period between jobs, I took three months off and set off on a trip with Branson, Kau, Xi, and Ta, visiting countries in Asia, Hong Kong, Thailand, and Beijing for three weeks. I met up with Branson in Hong Kong after his business trip back from a China rocket launch site supporting the final integration of one of Hughes Communication Satellite's launch campaigns.

In the fall of 1994, I purchased a house within fifteen minutes' walk of Mom's house. For the next three years I supported Branson through law school at University of Southern California.

With him busy with school, I became Mom's driver and companion. After Branson completed law school and our oldest daughter turned two years old, I decided to go back for my master's degree at Loyola Marymount University, a few blocks from work. At this point in my life with a child, I had many obligations; it was not easy to pursue a master's degree since I lived far from work. However, the degree was important to me, acting upon a conversation with Dad about needing it to advance at work. In the fall of 2000, I worked close to full time and attended school in the evening. I registered for two classes each semester, including summer sessions. In the spring semester of 2001, I took a leave from work and a break from school to give birth to my second daughter. In 2002, I graduated with a master's degree in engineering production management. I wouldn't have been able to do it all without Mom's help in taking care of my two girls. For many years I filled the void of companionship in her life, and in turn she helped by baby-sitting my two daughters, until they were pre-school age.

My parents were always a big influence in the lives of their children, both in Vietnam and in the United States. During our family dinner discussions our parents helped shape our views on the importance of family, duty and responsibility, education, creating business opportunities, and investing money wisely.

Dad was more like the captain of a ship in charge of setting a course for the family to travel. Mom was the collaborator and the implementer. Her job was to make sure the family worked together to get to the intended destination. Her strengths were her hard work, dedication, and commitment to her family. Mom never resented her parents for her illiteracy and not attending school as a young girl. She was a good supporting partner for Dad and a caring mother to my siblings and me. She taught us the importance of working hard, being frugal, and spending within one's means. Mom passed on to us the wisdom her grandmother had imparted to her as a young girl: "It takes three days to get used to being lazy, but it takes many years of training to get used to working hard." She often has reminded us that however hard we feel we have been working, we are still learning what takes to be a hard worker. For many years I worked hard on being a loving mother to my two daughters, a good wife to my husband, an accommodating daughter-in-law, and most important, a perfect daughter to honor my parents and ancestors.

Culturally, *Hakka* women have been expected to be hardworking, competent, and subservient to males. *Hakka* have strong family values and marriage has less to do with love than creating a partnership in life to build a strong family to honor parents and ancestors. Four generations after my *Hakka* family migrated from China to Vietnam, I can see what remains of my *Hakka* heritage in me, and also the things that have changed, both because of Dad's influence and our growing up in the United States.

Mom continued to set high expectations for me as a *Hakka* woman in terms of duty and responsibility in my roles as wife, mother, sister, daughter-in-law, and daughter. I was eager to please and wanted her to be proud of me. However, after struggling with my marriage for seventeen years, I made one of the hardest decisions in my life, to get divorced, despite Mom's objections and my *Hakka* cultural heritage. Mom took it hard knowing her daughter was the one initiating the divorce. Somehow, she perceived it as failing to teach me the value of marriage and my duty as a *Hakka* woman. She begged me to stay married and even asked my siblings to convince me not to get divorced. One by one, each of my siblings called or visited in person to deliver mom's message.

In December 2008, as I held firm to my decision, she took the last desperate measure by kneeling in front of me, crying. I responded by kneeling along with her and said, "I have been trying very hard all these years. Please understand that I don't take divorce lightly. I need to do this for me and my two daughters, or I will go insane." I apologized for dishonoring her and our family for getting a divorce.

It took her many years before she could accept my decision to divorce. Over time, she was able to see that I am capable of taking care of myself and my two daughters without needing the financial support from a man, and it was okay for her daughter to live a life that was different from hers. I am still the same hardworking, strong, independent *Hakka* woman dedicated to her family. I have instilled strong family values in my two daughters. Someday when the timing is right, I hope to get a second chance at an equal marriage filled with love, partnership, and helping each other to become our better selves.

In the summer of 2004, with my girls starting daycare and elementary school, I obtained a job at NASA's Jet Propulsion Laboratory (JPL) in Pasadena to be closer to home. I needed a better balance between work and family. Working closer to home, I would not be spending most of my time on Los Angeles freeways but at home. At JPL I took on various roles, including Responsible Engineer for power electronics, Lead Power System Engineer for advanced conceptual studies (like a think tank), and the Responsible Engineer for JPL's Power Distribution Unit for Aquarius/SAC-D satellite. The Aquarius/SAC-D mission is a collaboration between NASA's JPL and Argentina space agency, Comision Nacional de Actividades Espaciales (CONAE), designed to fly over, detect, and measure the salinity of Earth's oceans. From 2009 to 2011, I took several trips to support the Aquarius/SAC-D project on-site in Argentina and Brazil.

From 2009 to 2013, I led a team that designed, built, and delivered the Command and Data Handling (CDH) electronics hardware for NASA's Soil Moisture Active Passive (SMAP) mission, designed to fly over the Earth's land areas, and provide global measurements of soil moisture.

Today in my current role as Section Manager at JPL, I manage a section of six distinct groups with a total of seven managers and several senior staff who directly report to me. My section, with over 120 employees, is responsible for the design, manufacturing engineering, and fabrication of electronic assemblies and critical harnesses for all JPL missions. These missions include the Curiosity Rover, Spirit Rover and Opportunity Rover on Mars, Aquarius and SMAP Earth Science missions and the Cassini mission to Saturn. The section also provides services in facility management, inventory management, and test equipment calibration and rental throughout the JPL campus. I am fortunate to be working as an engineering manager at one of the top aerospace companies in the country.

As I look back on my life and the history of the Ungs, I am amazed at how many times we have faced setbacks and challenges that have required us to start over again with nothing. We have continued to adapt to new homelands. *Hakka* is known as "guest people or visitors coming from afar." Throughout the history of the *Hakka* they have been resilient in adapting to the new lands and challenges. I believe that overcoming these hardships and becoming successful in work and life have happened through good fortune and these important traits of my *Hakka* family.

> **Entrepreneurial mindset:** After Dad retired from the military, his father offered him a job working in his factory, but he took the risk to go into business for himself in order to provide a better life for his family. He approached it as an entrepreneur, creating his own opportunities by fulfilling the needs of small town customers. In United States, Kien and Xi saw the opportunity in business to provide personal computers to individuals.

> **Resilience and persistence:** It hasn't mattered how many times the Ungs have experienced setbacks and had to start over. They continue to demonstrate resilience and persistence, working hard and overcoming adversities in a new land. We started our lives in the United States in poverty, as did our ancestors who migrated from China to Vietnam. Today, my siblings and I have earned bachelor's and even master's degrees, have good jobs and own properties in the United

States. My cousins in Denmark, Switzerland, and Canada are also adapting well in their new lands with college educations and good-paying jobs.

Parents' willingness to sacrifice for a better future for their children: It is part of the Ung *Hakka* identity. A parent's sacrifice for their children was not a foreign concept but an innate part of them. Our Ung ancestors left China to Vietnam in the hopes of a better life. Then my great-grandfather was willing to sacrifice his wealth as a rice plantation owner to migrate from North to South Vietnam in hope of freedom and a better future for the next generation. My parents sacrificed their home, factory, and all their wealth in South Vietnam for a chance of a better future for their children in America.

The experience on the *Tung An* as a young girl had a lasting impact on me, but I didn't know the extent until I took a cruise thirty-four years later. In the summer of 2014, after years of refusing to ever step foot on a ship again, I was invited by my two daughters and several nephews to vacation with them on a cruise ship to Alaska. The experience brought back so many vivid memories. Consciously, I knew I was an adult with two teenagers. Subconsciously, the little girl in me with harrowing memories of hardship on the *Tung An* was frozen in time. Just being on a ship sharply reminded me of our daily hardship as refugees barely hanging on to life.

My daughters told me that the minute I stepped foot on the ship, I was a different person, prone to irrational fear and anxiety. Having many Filipino workers on the ship didn't help my anxiety. Of course, the cruise ship was nothing like the *Tung An*. We had plentiful food and excellent service as paying guests. Yet I experienced anxiety as though it was happening all over again. For seven days on the ship, I was not able to remain in crowded areas; even four teenagers in my cabin blocking the doorways gave me discomfort. My daughters reassured me, "Mom, you are not a refugee here but a guest." Except for meeting with my family for dinner, I spent most of my free time in the spa, where I had a view of the bow and calm waves in front of me. When my anxiety got the better of me and I experienced shortness of breath, I had to take deep breaths and meditate to overcome my anxiety.

One of my motivations for writing this book is to share the Ung family history of overcoming hardships with my daughters and future generations. Telling the stories in this book is my way to pay back my parents and to honor the Ung family. My daughters will also face struggles in their lifetime. Although they may be different from mine, many of the ways in which I have overcome my struggles will be the same for them. I want them to be strong, like *Hakka* women, but able to find success in life even if that means going against the old ways.

I shed many tears in the process of writing this book. It has taken twenty years since Dad's passing to get to this point of being able to revisit and write these stories down. I couldn't have done it without the support of my daughters, Mom, siblings, cousins, great uncles, aunts, and uncles from Denmark and Switzerland.

I had always planned to write my family stories someday when I retired. When my daughters discovered that I was a member of the "boat people" from Vietnam, they requested that I document these stories as soon as possible and not when I retired. Most of the great uncles and great aunties would be gone, including Mom, and the information would be lost forever. I know my girls were right that I needed to do it for them and the next generation of Ungs. As a dedication to my daughters and honoring my parents, I had to find the courage and inner strength to face my pain and sadness of my past that I had been carrying for many decades. I made a promise to my two daughters that I would pursue writing a book. As part of the plan, I took two months off to visit my relatives in Denmark and Switzerland. Dad may no longer be with us but Uncle Chin, Dad's younger brother, reminded me of so many of Dad's wonderful traits. Fortunately, Uncles Hai and Chin were on the *Tung An* with us, and they had a wealth of information. In the safe environments of my uncle and aunties' home in Aarhus, Denmark, and Switzerland, I started writing and recalling our experiences from the *Tung An*. Uncle Chin told me about his time in Song Mao and how Grandfather and Dad started the slipper business.

Looking back on the past challenges, Uncle Chin and Aunty Gin never wished to relive the hardship they had faced. This meant that before the writing of this book, their children's knowledge of their family background was very limited. It was just too painful to bring back the old memories when being reminded of the close family life they knew in Vietnam. This was the price they paid when they decided to go to Denmark, knowing that their children would grow up aware of, but not knowing, their own grandparents, uncles, aunts, and cousins as they would if they lived close by.

Today Uncle Chin and Aunty Gin are in their mid and late sixties, and they are still appreciated in their current workplace. They will retire by the end of March 2015, and since they no longer have any children living in Aarhus, they plan on selling the house and moving closer to their children and their families in order to spend more time with them. They are looking forward to spending the retirement years surrounded by their children and grandchildren. All the children have obtained a good education and are doing well as young professionals. Uncle Chin says he has no regrets and keeps looking forward.

In Contone, Switzerland, I spent over three weeks with Lac, Liam, Uncle Hai, and Aunty Binh. In their home, I spent every night writing down the discussions we had during the day. Aunty Binh said, "Nam Moi, I still have nightmares recalling our many failed attempts to escape the communist government in Vietnam and the hardships we endured on *Tung An*. You are brave for having the willpower to capture these stories in a book. My children growing up in the Western world have no idea where their parents and ancestors came from." She was grateful that I have committed my energy to writing this book.

Coming back to the United States, I continued making progress on nights, weekends, and holidays when my girls were with their father. For close to two years, I took as many week-long vacations as I could in order to make progress on the book.

At times I have wanted to give up or write only the happy memories and not the heartbreaking ones. Recalling the vivid details was painful, and it was even harder to express them in writing. When I found myself feeling defeated and unable to write, I tried to focus on the bigger goal of sharing the Ung family's struggles and my parents' sacrifices with my daughters, nephews, and nieces. I found the inner strength and the gift my parents gave me to be who I am. I wiped away my tears and continued moving forward with one story at a time. In the process of writing *Nam Moi*, I rediscovered who I am. I know in my heart and soul that my dad is proud of his little girl, Nam Moi.

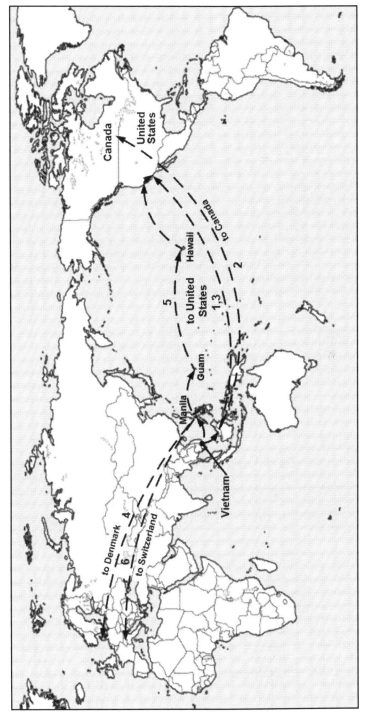

Figure 16-18: Ung migration from Vietnam to United States, Canada, Denmark, and Switzerland.

EPILOGUE

My Siblings in the United States

In his earlier years, Zenh's husband had developed a love for the American South. Hy eventually persuaded Zenh to move to Arkansas with him. They settled in Little Rock, where they stayed for more than twenty-five years. With the help of their daughter Tracy, they ran their Chinese restaurant Eggroll King. The family made many friends in the community through their years of working daily at the restaurant.

2006 was a turbulent year for the Tran family. Hy was diagnosed with Stage IV lung cancer, and died mere months after the diagnosis. That same month Tracy graduated from Yale University, and moved home to help settle affairs. A year later, both Zenh and Tracy moved to California. Zenh moved back to Los Angeles to be closer to family, while Tracy moved to San Francisco to start her adult life. While the years have brought many changes, Zenh is back to running a business again. Her new restaurant is located within walking distance from Mom's house.

Hong went back to school and earned a master's degree in computer science at California Polytechnic University of Pomona. He got married in 1995 after dating his girlfriend from Taiwan for six years. They met on a tour to Thailand. In 1998, Hong moved back to Los Angeles from Huntsville, Alabama. He got a job at Boeing as a software engineer. He, his wife, and two sons live five minutes' drive from Mom's house. Hong visits Mom almost every week for lunch, dinner, or just to stop by to say hello.

Kien got married in 1996 to a foreign student from mainland China studying in England. Her husband was introduced to her by a mutual friend. Her family moved to New Jersey in 1998, and she continued with her computer business. She sold computer cooling fans imported from Taiwan as an extension of Quality Computer. After the downturn of the personal computer business, with Dell and HP being the main personal computer brands, she is now selling iPhone accessories on the internet with several partners. She and her two sons visit California almost yearly during summer vacation.

For many years Xi brought Mom traveling along with his family. Las Vegas has been a common destination for a getaway of a couple of days. After the computer business, Xi became interested in restaurants. His wife, Ta, had been in the restaurant business since 1990, and she owned a Thai restaurant in San Fernando Valley, partnering with a friend. Xi spent two years in culinary school in Pasadena. In 2004, he purchased a Chinese restaurant in Toluca Lake. He sold the restaurant after many years of managing it. Xi has decided to take a break from work and just manages his real estate investments. Xi and Ta have two sons and a daughter. They live in the San Fernando Valley. At least every other week Xi takes Mom to lunch.

Num is now married with three children, two daughters, and a son. He met his wife while visiting Vietnam. His wife lived a few minutes from where we once lived in Vietnam. He helped Xi with managing the restaurant for many years. After Xi sold the restaurant, Num continued working there for the new owner.

Buu married Mom's third cousin's daughter, and they have two sons and a daughter. Buu's wife is probably the only daughter in-law who is familiar with our cultural and religious practices. Buu completed his associate administrative degree at Pasadena City College and transferred to California Polytechnic of Pomona. Given his demanding work schedule at the computer store and helping out with taking Dad to his treatments, Buu had to take a break from college. He never went back to complete his four-year degree in the field of business operation and continued working at Quality Computer. After his years of experience working at the computer store, Buu now works in the IT department for a local company.

Tam graduated from California Polytechnic University of Pomona with a degree in nutrition. She is married with two daughters and a son. Tam's children and my two daughters are more like siblings than cousins, since their dads are brothers and moms are sisters. Tam and her husband met at my wedding and had a six-year long-distance relationship, between Oahu and Los Angeles. After they both finished college, they decided to get married and her husband moved to Los Angeles. He is currently working for Boeing as well. Tam works as the quality control manager for an herb and spice company that has offices in cities all over the country.

After graduating from college and graduate school, Kau has pursued a career in real estate. He currently lives in the Los Angeles area with his wife and daughter.

Ung in Denmark

After high school graduation, Phung was unsure of her choice of career. Therefore, she decided to move to the United States with the purpose of learning to speak Cantonese Chinese and gaining some life experience in addition to getting to know the extended family once again. Later on she trained to become an industrial laboratory technician but was not satisfied with this choice and therefore subsequently studied at Aarhus University to become a dental hygienist. Phung moved to Copenhagen and met Vy. They married in 2005 and have two daughters.

Thu became the first of the Ungs in Denmark to go to college. In 1995 she was accepted to the Royal Danish School of Pharmacy, located in Copenhagen, the capital of Denmark. She obtained her master's degree in pharmacy in the summer of 2001 and worked in a private pharmacy for many years. Since starting a family, she has worked at Rigshospitalet, the largest hospital in Denmark. She met her husband Anders at a party at the dormitory where she resided while attending school. They have two daughters.

One year later, Lan followed in the footsteps of her older sister Thu and moved to Copenhagen in the late summer of 1996 to attend pharmacy school. She successfully completed the pharmacy program and graduated from the same school on the same day as Thu. Following a short period of working in regulatory affairs at Leo Pharma, a large Danish pharmaceutical company, she has made a career as quality assessor at the Danish Health and Medicines Authority.

Filipina Moi studied at Aarhus University and became a dentist in 2005. Shortly after graduating she moved to the northern part of the country in order to work and gain more experience in different dental clinics. While studying in Aarhus, she met Thomas, whom she married in 2010. They now live in Aalborg with their son, Jakob.

Sinh chose a career in engineering and continued to live in Aarhus, where he studied for his bachelor's degree in Architectural Engineering. In 2009, he relocated to Aalborg to complete his master's degree in Management in the Building Industry. While attending college he trained with MOE, a large Copenhagen-based consulting engineering company, where he was offered a job as construction manager shortly after graduation in 2011.

Since the majority of the children now live three hours away in Copenhagen, the whole family mainly gets together on the major holidays, like Christmas and Easter break, when all the children with their families come home for a few days and stay at Uncle Chin and Aunty Gin's house. Also, in the summertime the siblings rent a big summerhouse somewhere in Denmark and everybody meets to vacation together. Man, living only about an hour away, visits Aunty and Uncle more frequently throughout the year. Phung, Thu, Lan, and Sinh all live within a five- to ten-minutes' drive from each other and meet regularly. In their busy daily life, the siblings and their parents stay in touch through phone calls, texting, and emails.

Ung-Ho in Winnipeg, Canada

In 1983, their family saved enough to purchase a modest two-bedroom town house. A few years later, Uncle Minh sponsored his parents from Vietnam, and they joined the rest of the family in Winnipeg. With Minh's parents here to watch the children, Aunty Tchat was able to find work as a seamstress to help the family financially. It was a tight fit in the less than 900 square-foot town-house, but the family made it work and was very happy. Eventually, Uncle Luong emigrated to the U.S. With Uncle Minh's parents settled in, he was comfortable there would be enough people to help raise the three children and so he moved to California to be closer to the rest of the family

Tragedy struck the family when Uncle Minh was diagnosed with cancer in November 1989. He lost his battle in April 1990 when the children were ages of nine to thirteen. In spite of this tragedy, the family persevered on the strength of Aunty Tchat and the help of Minh's parents. Tuong, Quy, and Sam all finished high school with honors at the top of their classes and all immediately went on to college.

Tuong graduated from the University of Manitoba with a degree in Business. He was recruited by a U.S. insurance company upon graduation and has been living in the U.S. ever since. Today Tuong continues to work in finance in New York City and resides in New Jersey with his wife and three children.

Quy graduated from the University of Toronto in 2000 with a Computer Science degree. After graduating, he moved to San Jose, California, to take a position with Sun Microsystems. In 2001, he met his wife and they got married three years later. Quy currently works at Yahoo as a senior software engineer. Quy, his wife, and three children live in Danville, California.

Sam graduated from the University of Manitoba in 2002 with a degree in Mechanical Engineering. In his final year of study, Sam was awarded a full scholarship to pursue his master's degree at the University of Toronto. In 2004, he completed his master's studies in Structural Engineering and decided to return to Winnipeg to stay close to his mother. He was offered a position with a local architectural and engineering firm. After nine years of working at this position, Sam ventured out with two partners to start a mechanical and electrical engineering firm of his own. Today, Sam lives with his longtime girlfriend in a house next door to Aunty Tchat.

Sam regularly has meals next door with his mother and, of course, shovels the snow for her in the cold winter months. Although physically far apart, Tuong and Quy remain very close to the family. Despite their busy schedules, the family communicates regularly and tries to get together at least once a year. Aunty Tchat still works as seamstress but just to occupy her time. With three successful sons, the financial hardships she once endured are a distant memory.

Ung in Switzerland

For thirty years Uncle Hai continued to work at the milling machine company until his retirement in 2013. Aunty Binh retired from her job at the clothing store after working there many years. Over the years, they lived frugally and saved enough money to buy a three-level house in Contone, in the sunny south of Switzerland, less than an hour drive to Italy. They are enjoying their retirement with close friends that became their adopted family over the years.

Liam after middle school took advantage of Switzerland's unique education system to enter a company of high-tech cutting machinery, the same as his father, pursuing an apprenticeship. He was attending a vocational school at the same time, and gaining work experience while learning theory at school allowed him to get an electronics technician diploma. Developing a passion for creating and inventing, he continued his studies and majored in electrical engineering at the University of Southern Switzerland of Applied Science. During and after college he participated in the mandatory military service, where he was trained as a radar operator.

In 2010, after Liam graduated, he took the opportunity to broaden his horizons and leave the mountains behind, moving to San Francisco for the purpose of improving his English and interning in a U.S. company related to his field of studies. After a year he moved back to Europe and stayed in Germany to refresh his German, since it is the most widely spoken language in Switzerland, followed by French and Italian, all part of Swiss official languages, in order to get a better job. He finally concluded his military duty by finishing his days left of mandatory service in a nonprofit foundation as an engineer. He now works as a research and development (R&D) engineer in an electronics manufacturing firm close to his family in Canton Ticino, South Switzerland.

Mann graduated from high school in Switzerland in 2006. Soon after he was admitted to the Ecole Politechnique de Lausanne to study civil engineering, but he decided to study in the United States after only a few months. He was unhappy with his life in Lausanne despite having many of his high school classmates attending the same university. His parents encouraged him to perhaps consider studying abroad. Mann entered Pasadena City College in 2010 with the support of his family in Los Angeles. It was much easier for Mann to adapt to his new lifestyle. After a few years, he transferred to the University of Southern California in 2011. He graduated with a Master's of Science in Civil Engineering in 2013, and he's currently employed by a construction firm in Los Angeles.

TIMELINE

Year	Event
1898	Ung migration from Fang Cheng, Quang Xi China to Ha Coi, Vietnam.
1925	Grandparents Chenh Tac and Sao Lin engaged at ages 8 and 7.
1935	Grandparent Chenh Tac and Sao Lin got married.
1936	Dad (Ly Sang) was born.
1949	Dad (Ly Sang) started French Military School.
6/1954	Dad (Ly Sang) graduated from French Military School.
7/20/1954	Geneva Accords signed to partition Vietnam at the 17th parallel.
11/1954	Ung family moved from North to South Vietnam.
1955	Great-Great-Grandmother Le Sy passed away in Song Mao.
1956	Great Grandmother Nan Sy passed away in Song Mao.
1956	Nam Moi's parents (Ly Sang and Kieu) got married in Song Mao.
1961	Deployment of soldiers in Song Mao to countryside.
1963	Paternal grandparents moved to Saigon and started slipper business.
1966	Family moved from Ben Keo to Saigon.
1966	Dad (Ly Sang) retired from the French military.
1967	Nam Moi was born.
1/30/1968	Tet Offensive; Uncle Bao passed away.
1970	Great Grandfather Tai Hong passed away in Saigon.
4/30/1975	Fall of Saigon; North and South Vietnam reunited.
10/1976	Uncle Tac and Uncle Kan escaped from Vietnam to Thailand.
4/1977	Uncles Tac and Kan immigrated to San Francisco, California.
4/1978	Zenh, Hong, Kien, and Xi left home and Dad (Ly Sang)'s arrest.
5/1978	Government changing money—Liberated dong changed to new dong.
8/1978	Journey on *Southern Cross*.
11/1978	Boarding the *Tung An*.

Year	Event
12/1978	Aunty Tchat and Uncle Ho Minh's family moved to Winnipeg, Canada.
2/1979	Zenh, Hong, Kien, and Xi immigrated to Los Angeles.
3/18/1979	Uncle Chin family moved to Denmark.
3/6/1979	Uncle Hai's family left *Tung An.*
8/8/1979	Transport *Tung An* refugees to Tara Island.
11/1979	Family moved to Fabella refugee camp.
2/24/1980	Family immigrated to Los Angeles.
3/6/1980	Ung Hai's family immigrated to Switzerland.
3/20/1980	Nam Moi moved to first home in Alhambra.
4/1980	Great Uncle #11 immigrated to Los Angeles.
7/1980	Maternal grandparents' family immigrated to United States.
6/1981	Nam Moi graduated 8th grade from Northrop Elementary School.
9/1981	Nam Moi attended Alhambra High School.
4/1982	Zenh married Hy.
9/1983	Nam Moi started John Regel Beauty School in Temple City.
6/1985	Nam Moi graduated from Alhambra High School.
6/1985	Hong graduated from UCLA as a software engineer.
1987	Established Tritek computer store.
1990	Established Quality Computer Incorporated.
5/1990	Nam Moi graduated from CSUN as an electrical engineer.
6/10/1990	Nam Moi started working at Rockwell Seal Beach.
8/1991	Dad (Ly Sang) diagnosed with brain cancer.
1/1992	Nam Moi married in Oahu and in Los Angeles.
3/19/1994	Dad (Ly Sang) passed away.

ACKNOWLEDGMENTS

I would like to say *"thank you"* to all the people who supported me in the making of this book. It would not have been possible without them. *Thank you! Thank you! Thank you!*

To friends who have supported me in making my dream of writing this book a reality. Rick for helping me with making this book possible.

To friends at the Jet Propulsion Laboratory who told me that I have to share my stories, and friends at Boeing (formally Hughes Space and Communication) and Rockwell International for encouraging me to share these stories.

To friends at Life Academy in Los Angeles who believed in me and my ability to realize the dream of writing this book.

To friends from CONAE in Argentina who told me that I had to write this book to share my family's stories with the world.

To my Great Uncles/Uncles: Sao San, Chenh Ninh, Chin, and Hai; Aunties: Binh and Gin. To my cousins: Hanh, Man, Jhunliam, and David for supporting me in writing this book. Diana: for designing this book.

To my younger siblings for being my willing followers as kids and allowing me to lead them, and my older siblings for protecting, guiding, and mentoring me.

To my mother for the courage to share her stories, sometimes sad and heartbroken ones, and for shaping me into the person I am today, and to my daughters for emphasizing the importance of writing this book not only as a legacy for the family but to inspire the younger generation of boys and girls.

ABOUT THE AUTHOR

Today, few people know CHARLENE LIN UNG as Nam Moi. She has made a new life for herself and her two children in Los Angeles. In the United States since 1980, she has overcome many obstacles— learning a new language and culture, earning a bachelor's and master's degree in engineering, and working for one of the top aerospace companies in the country. She is currently a successful engineering manager at NASA's Jet Propulsion Laboratory in Pasadena, California. Many years after her escape from the communist Vietnam, she is still on a journey, but now it's one of discovery to advance our knowledge about the solar system.

SELECTED REFERENCES

1. *Guest People: Hakka Identity in China and Abroad*, Nicole Constable, ed. 1996
2. The Nung Ethnic & Autonomous Territory of Hai Ninh, Vietnam, 2013
3. Wikipedia: Fall of Saigon
4. Wikipedia: History of Dong (Vietnamese Money)
5. *Legitimising Rejection: International Refugee Law in Southeast Asia*, Sara E. Davies, 2008
6. *Becoming American*, Tracia Knoll, 1982
7. *Vietnamese in America*, Lori Coleman, 2004
8. *Vietnam: A History*, Stanley Karnow, 1983
9. Manuel Silva. "Turned Away Elsewhere, Viet Refugees Sail to Manila." *Philippine Daily Express*, 28 December 1978
10. Manuel Silva. "Escape, Voyage Recalled." *Philippine Daily Express*, 29 December 1978
11. Manuel Silva. "RP Sends Food to Viet Refugees." *Philippine Daily Express*, 29 December 1978
12. "*Tung An* Skipper Bares Threats to His Life." *Times Journal*, 22 May 1979
13. "*Tung An* Refugees: A Life of Boredom." *Times Journal*, 23 June 1979
14. Joe Lad Santos. "The Philippines: Filipino People Extended Their Hands in Caring for the Aulacese Refugees." 1978
15. Andy Hernandez. "Photographer Slips onto the Refugee Boat." *Milwaukee Sentinel*, 29 December 1978
16. 200 Refugees Die Boarding Ship." *The Blade*, 1979 December 27
17. "Refugee Problems Mount in Philippines, Hong Kong." *The Spokesman-Review*, 28 December 1978
18. "Conditions Grim on Refugee Ship." *Lakeland Ledger*, 2 January 1979
19. "Nations to Admit Vietnam Refugees." *The Bulletin*, 12 February 1979
20. "Saga of the Boat People (Cont')." *The Evening Independent*, 8 August 1979
21. "Refugees Arrive on Tiny Primitive Island." *The Bryan Times*, 9 August 1979
22. "Refugees Put on Tiny Island." *The Telegraph-Herald*, 9 August 1979
23. "Refugees Sample Water on Solid Land." *The Blade*, 11 August 1979
24. "Boat People Fear Island Refuge." *The Hour*, 30 August 1979
25. "Refugees Fear Island a Ticket to Nowhere." *Reading Eagle*, 13 September 1979

Printed in the USA
CPSIA information can be obtained
at www.ICGtesting.com
LVHW060809140124
768916LV00040B/1586